D1123354

MAFIA

INSIDE AMERICA'S MOST VIOLENT CRIME FAMILY
AND THE BLOODY FALL OF *LA COSA NOSTRA*

PRINCE

BY PHILIP LEONETTI

with Scott Burnstein and Christopher Graziano

RUNNING PRESS
PHILADELPHIA · LONDON

Published by Running Press,
A Member of the Perseus Books Group

Books published by Running Press are available at special discounts for bulk purchases
in the United States by corporations, institutions, and other organizations. For more
information, please contact the Special Markets Department at the Perseus Books Group,
2300 Chestnut Street, Suite 200, Philadelphia, PA 19103, or call (800) 810-4145, ext. 5000,
or e-mail special.markets@perseusbooks.com.

ISBN 978-0-7624-4583-7
Library of Congress Control Number: 2012938752

E-book ISBN 978-0-7624-4687-2

9   8   7   6   5   4   3   2   1
Digit on the right indicates the number of this printing

All photos courtesy of Philip Leonetti
Cover design by Whitney Cook
Edited by Greg Jones
Typography: Garage Gothic, Sentinel, and Forza

Running Press Book Publishers
2300 Chestnut Street
Philadelphia, PA 19103-4371

Visit us on the web!
www.runningpress.com

CONTENTS

ACT TWO

ACT THREE

FOREWORD

THEY WOULD MEET IN THE EDEN ROC HOTEL IN MIAMI, IN THE RESTAURANT THAT LOOKED OUT ON THE SWIMMING POOL.

Meyer Lansky, the aging underworld genius, would be sitting at a table in the corner. And here would come Nicky Scarfo, the Atlantic City gangster who was soon to be the most violent Mafia boss in America, and Philip Leonetti, Scarfo's young nephew and future crime family underboss.

Three generations of American mobsters sitting around talking. Lansky, white-haired and thin, in his 70s at the time and fighting heart and stomach problems, would dominate the conversation with stories about the old days. Scarfo, in his late 40s, his brown hair combed straight back, his eyes darting around the room, would nod and occasionally offer an opinion. And Leonetti, trim and movie-star handsome, in his early 20s, would sit quietly.

Listening.

Learning.

Now one of the most important Mafia informants in history, Leonetti never said much during those meetings down in Miami. He was just happy to be there. He looked at Lansky the way others would look at DiMaggio, Caruso, or Hemingway. One of a kind. A man who defined the world in which he operated.

Lansky was there at the beginning, when it all started, when *Cosa Nostra* was formed. Leonetti, who rode to power with his uncle and who for a time controlled the mob's rackets in Philadelphia and Atlantic City, is a man who helped bring it all to an end.

"This was back in the 1970s," Leonetti said several years ago as he recounted those trips to Florida. "Any time we went, my uncle would call and we'd go over and see Meyer. He'd be sitting there in the restaurant. Him, Nig Rosen. Mickey Weissberg. They used to get together there every day. It was, like, Meyer's hangout. They'd go there and play cards. Meyer liked us. He liked my uncle. So we'd sit around and he'd tell stories about the old days, about Benny and Charlie and how it used to be."

Benny was Benjamin "Bugsy" Siegel. Charlie was Charles "Lucky" Luciano. Siegel, of course, brought the mob to Las Vegas. He built the

Flamingo Hotel Casino in 1947 and that turned the desert into a money machine for the mob. Then he forgot who his partners were. And so he was killed.

Years later, Lansky still talked about it.

"Meyer told us about how upset he was when Benny got killed," Leonetti said. "He really loved Benny. But he said Benny was robbing them guys and he wouldn't lilsten. He said Benny never liked to listen to the Italians. And that he thought the casino was his, which it wasn't. It was theirs. Benny would only listen to Meyer and Meyer said he kept him under control the best he could, but when they decided to whack him, there was nothing he could do. It broke his heart when they killed him, but he couldn't stop it. It was business.

"Then he looked at my uncle and he said, 'Benny was a stone killer, Nick. But you know, there's a lot of killers [in the Mafia].' My uncle just nodded."

Leonetti would eventually become one himself. That's part of his story. How he became a hitman for his uncle, how he turned on the man who raised him, and how he eventually ended up on the witness stand are all part of what this book is about.

There has never been a Mafia witness like Leonetti. Not Joe Valachi. Not Vinnie Teresa. Not Salvatore "Sammy the Bull" Gravano.

Leonetti is the essence of what the America Mafia was in the 1980s and what it has become in the years since. His life was shaped, twisted, and nearly destroyed by it. His decision to cooperate has turned it upside down.

Call it a story of family values gone awry.

A bloody story of murder that ends with personal redemption.

Murder, extortion, loan sharking, and gambling, Leonetti did it all. Then, faced with the prospect of spending the rest of his life in prison and looking at the possibility that his own teenaged son might be heading down the same road, he broke with his uncle, with the mob, and with the life.

From the witness stand he helped bring down high-ranking mob figures in Manhattan, Brooklyn, Boston, Pittsburgh, Hartford, and Philadelphia. Leaders of the Genovese, Gambino, Colombo, Patriarca, and Lucchese crime families are behind bars as a result.

He was, without question, the reason Gravano agreed to testify and, consequently, the reason John Gotti was finally convicted.

Leonetti's story is the saga of the American Mafia. It stretches from Lansky to Gotti, from Los Angeles to Palermo. It's a tale of money, murder, and treachery that puts the lie to the so-called "men of honor." It's the view of a man sucked deep inside the underworld by the pull of a distorted sense of family, honor, and dignity. And it is a lesson in human redemption and second chances orchestrated by someone who had the intelligence, the strength, and the courage to break the chains that had bound him to "the life."

For months after his defection, Leonetti had been trying to explain to the FBI and federal prosecutors what it meant to be part of that life. He wanted them to understand the twisted sense of values he had grown up with, about the Svengali-like influence his uncle—a surrogage father, in fact—had held over him.

"It was like walking with the devil," he said as agents and government lawyers nodded and jotted down notes on the yellow legal pads they always brought to his debriefing sessions. Then they'd go on to the next question, the next topic, and the next chapter in the saga of the rise and fall of the Scarfo crime family. It was clear to Leonetti then that they really didn't understand what *Cosa Nostra* does to a person, how it corrupts your soul.

But Leonetti wanted them to understand. After 20 years, he didn't want to be part of it anymore. He was tired of the murders, worn out by the treachery, and sickened by the deceit. But unless he could explain, unless he could show them, he knew he'd never be able to put it behind him.

Finally, there was one moment when it all came together, when it all made sense.

He was on the stand in federal court in Philadelphia making his debut as a witness. This was in January of 1990, six months after he had broken with the mob and started talking with the feds. He was testifying against four of his former associates, detailing the operations of the crime family he and Scarfo had once controlled, and implicating the four mobsters sitting at the defense table in the organization's activities.

Dressed in a blue blazer and gray slacks with a dark crewneck sweater over a white shirt and tie, he looked more like an accountant than a hitman. But his testimony was proving to be as deadly in court as his actions had been in the underworld.

Leonetti would admit his own involvement in 10 gangland murders as he testified about the secret organization, the code of silence, the extortions, the loan sharking, and the gambling.

On cross-examination, one of the defense attorneys set out to unnerve him, asking sarcastically if he knew "what it means to be ruthless."

Leonetti paused briefly to think about the question.

That's when it all came together. That's when he was able to make them see. That's when, in its own perverse way, it made sense.

"I know what it means to be ruthless," he said in that quiet, firm voice that had the jurors hanging on every word. "But I don't remember ever doing anything, as a matter of fact I know for sure, I never did nothing ruthless besides, well, I would kill people. But that's our life. That's what we do."

In that life, there was no moral dilemma.

No debate over what it meant to murder another human being.

No question of right or wrong.

It was, simply, *Cosa Nostra*.

Phil Leonetti had finally made them all understand.

He has left that life far behind him.

This is the story of where he is and how he got there.

—George Anastasia, Crime Reporter, *Philadelphia Inquirer*

PREFACE

Somewhere Near the Atlantic Ocean, Spring 2011

H E WAS TAN AND FIT, AND WEARING A DARK WINDBREAKER-TYPE JACKET OVER NEATLY PRESSED DRESS SLACKS, WITH HIGHLY POLISHED BLACK ITALIAN LOAFERS. HIS GRAY HAIR WAS NEATLY STYLED, COMBED STRAIGHT BACK. HE WAS WEARING A PAIR OF BLACK DESIGNER SUNGLASSES.

The man seated inside an upscale hotel lobby bar looked like a country club golf pro and not a psychopathic Mafia killer worthy of the moniker "Crazy Phil." Soft-spoken and polite, he was understated and handsome, and carried himself with an air of confidence.

After exchanging pleasantries, he removed his sunglasses and said, "You have to understand, I come from a very different world than you guys." His tone was soft as he spoke, his eyes focused. "We live by a very different set of rules. In *La Cosa Nostra*, if you break the rules, you get *this*," he said, shaping his hand like a gun and pointing it toward the ground. "And I broke the biggest rule of them all, I betrayed my oath."

Philip Leonetti was right there in plain sight more than two decades removed from his life as the underboss of the Philadelphia–Atlantic City mob. Although he had once been a shark, a great white, swimming in a sea of other deadly and bloodthirsty sharks, he now appeared simply as a man—a man with a story to tell.

Over the next three days inside a plush suite high above the sandy beaches overlooking the Atlantic Ocean, Philip Leonetti would provide chapter and verse of his life, both inside the mob and out, to this book's coauthors.

This was our first time meeting Leonetti face to face, but it wouldn't be the last. Over the next year we would meet several times in major cities all over the United States, with our final meeting taking place in winter 2012 back in Atlantic City, just steps away from the Georgia Avenue compound where it had all started.

This is the definitive inside story of the bloody rise and treacherous fall of one of the most ruthless Mafia empires in American history.

At the epicenter are two men: Philip Leonetti and his uncle Nicodemo Scarfo.

Crazy Phil and Little Nicky.

What you are about to read is their story, told, in part, by the coauthors based on extensive research and personal interviews, and also by Philip in his own voice. Different typefaces are used throughout to distinguish the two.

It is part *Godfather* and part *Goodfellas*, with shades of *Casino*, *Donnie Brasco*, and *The Sopranos* spliced throughout.

But this isn't a Hollywood movie or television show; this is the real thing.

ACT ONE

Little Nicky & Crazy Phil

DECEMBER 16, 1979

I T WAS A COLD WINTER AFTERNOON, THE TYPE OF DAY WHERE THE FRIGID AIR COULD LITERALLY TAKE A MAN'S BREATH AWAY. BUT ON THIS DAY IT WOULDN'T BE MOTHER NATURE PERFORMING THIS DAUNTING TASK; IT WOULD BE A 26-YEAR-OLD MOB KILLER WITH ICE IN HIS VEINS AND ORDERS TO KILL NAMED PHILIP LEONETTI, WHOSE NICKNAME, CRAZY PHIL, SAID IT ALL.

As the unmistakable sounds of the powerful and unforgiving white-capped waves pounding the shoreline a few feet away punctuated the crisp air on this dreary day, there was no force more powerful and unforgiving, more omnipresent in Philip Leonetti's life than that of his 50-year-old uncle, Nicodemo Scarfo, the man who had raised him like a son after his own father had abandoned him as a child, and had turned him into a heartless stone-cold killer.

Scarfo, who was nicknamed Little Nicky, stood 5′5″ and weighed a mere 135 pounds. While he may have been small in stature, Scarfo had earned a reputation for committing acts of unspeakable violence that had made him a giant in the criminal underworld.

By 1979, he was the Philadelphia mob's fastest rising star and had become the de facto boss of the boardwalk in Atlantic City, which, with the advent of casino gambling a year before, had become a boomtown for the mob.

His beloved nephew Philip Leonetti had become his right-hand man, his most trusted aide, and his most able killer. During the late 1970s, in the burgeoning Atlantic City underworld the ground shook when and where Little Nicky and Crazy Phil walked.

It was common knowledge to those doing business in Atlantic City that the equally feared and respected Scarfo and Leonetti were not to be fucked with.

So when a young mob associate named Vincent Falcone drew the ire of the extremely volatile Scarfo, Little Nicky decided that the penalty would be death and that Philip "Crazy Phil" Leonetti would be the executioner.

Phil Leonetti spoke to Vincent Falcone as the two men stood in the kitchen of a friend's beachfront home in Margate, an upscale New Jersey beach community a few short miles south of Atlantic City.

Come on Vince, let's make some drinks.

Inside the living room, just a few feet away, sat Nicky Scarfo, his reading glasses perched low on his nose and his Italian leather shoes resting comfortably on a coffee table as he perused the Sunday edition of the *Atlantic City Press* while watching the Philadelphia Eagles battle the Houston Oilers, who were led by future Hall of Fame running back Earl Campbell.

"Vince, bring me a Cutty and some water," said Scarfo in his trademark high-pitched voice, as Falcone set out two glasses for the boss, one to be filled with Cutty Sark, the blended scotch whiskey favored by Scarfo, and the other to be filled with water that Little Nicky used to dilute his drink.

Joining the trio of Scarfo, Leonetti, and Falcone on this fateful afternoon were two aspiring mobsters, young wannabe wise guys who, like Leonetti and Falcone, were members of Nicky Scarfo's Atlantic City crew. The five men had gathered to have a preholiday celebration. Christmas, after all, was just nine days away.

But there was nothing festive about what would happen next.

After placing the bottle of scotch that his uncle had requested on the kitchen table, the 26-year-old Leonetti nodded toward Falcone.

Vince, get some ice.

The unsuspecting Falcone nodded in agreement and walked toward the refrigerator, turning his back to Leonetti and the others as he did.

Leonetti immediately reached into his black leather jacket and pulled out a small .32 caliber handgun that had been tucked in his waistband. Without hesitation, he moved swiftly behind Falcone and pressed the handgun to the back of his head, directly behind his right ear, and squeezed the trigger.

Boom!

Propelled by the blast, Falcone flew forward and collided with the refrigerator, awkwardly landing on his back as a pool of blood began to turn the cheap linoleum floor a dark shade of crimson.

Nicky Scarfo, apparently no longer interested in the Eagles game, got up from the couch and, without saying a word, walked into the kitchen and kneeled down next to Falcone's mortally wounded body, pressing his ear to Falcone's chest to listen for a heartbeat.

"He's still alive," Scarfo said to Leonetti, who was standing over Falcone's body, the gun still firmly gripped in his right hand, "Give him another one," said Scarfo, who added, "Right here," as he pointed to Falcone's heart.

As Little Nicky knelt beside the fallen Vincent Falcone, Crazy Phil pumped another shot into his heart at point-blank range—*Boom!*—causing Falcone's body to violently jerk as the bullet ripped through his chest and immediately ended his life.

"The big shot's dead," said a jubilant Nicky Scarfo, rising to his feet, belittling the dead man as a "piece of shit cocksucker" as he did.

Philip Leonetti, still holding the pistol, turned to one of the other men in the kitchen, a close friend of Falcone's, fixed an icy stare on him and said:

> *He was a no-good motherfucker. I wish I could bring him back to life so I could kill him again.*

It wasn't the first time that Scarfo and Leonetti had killed together, and it wouldn't be the last. Over the next decade, they orchestrated or personally carried out 20 more killings. Another half dozen, or so, that predated the Falcone murder would help define their reign as two of the most notorious gangsters of the 20th century.

Three things figured prominently in many of the murders: money, power, and Atlantic City. Eventually, Little Nicky and Crazy Phil had them all—all the money, all the power, and absolute control over Atlantic City.

They had ascended from a lowly mob street crew, loaning money to cash-strapped gamblers and shaking down two-bit wise guys, and risen to the pantheon of organized crime. They were the boss and underboss of the Philadelphia–Atlantic City mob, the CEO and COO of the nation's bloodiest and most ruthless Mafia empire.

Ten years after the Falcone murder, the life of crime, power, and big money was over for Little Nicky and Crazy Phil. But in many ways, life was just beginning for Philip Leonetti.

In Plain Sight

O N MAY 1, 2011, THE WORLD WAS TRANSFIXED BY THE NEWS THAT OSAMA BIN LADEN, THE EVIL MASTERMIND OF THE 9/11 TERRORIST ATTACKS AND UNDOUBTEDLY THE MOST HATED MAN ON THE PLANET, HAD BEEN HUNTED DOWN AND KILLED BY MEMBERS OF THE UNITED STATES MILITARY'S ULTRAELITE NAVY SEAL TEAM SIX.

For most of the decade leading up to Bin Laden's long-overdue execution, it was widely believed that the world's most notorious terrorist was living inside a network of hidden mountain caves in the Afghan region of Tora Bora under the protection of the terror-friendly warlords who control the area.

But when Seal Team Six made its now infamous "trip to Atlantic City" (that is what they called the hit on Bin Laden), they did not find him inside a dusty mountain cave, but rather on the third floor of a carefully built million-dollar high-security compound in Abbottabad, Pakistan, less than 800 yards from a prestigious Pakistani military academy, the country's equivalent to West Point.

Despite a $25 million bounty on his head, the 6'4" Bin Laden was hiding in plain sight. Within hours of his bullet-ridden corpse being ceremoniously dumped into the Indian Ocean, the FBI removed him from atop its Ten Most Wanted List, replacing him with the notorious South Boston Irish mob boss and former FBI informant James "Whitey" Bulger.

Suspected in more than 20 killings, the ruthless and cunning Bulger had vanished without a trace in December 1994 after being tipped off by a corrupt FBI agent that the feds were preparing to wipe out his gang with a massive indictment under the RICO (Racketeering Influenced and Corrupt Organizations) Act.

As the international FBI manhunt for Bulger intensified, credible sightings were reported in South Florida, New York City, London, and Chicago from tipsters looking to cash in on a $2 million reward. Additional confirmed sightings in nondescript, Podunk towns—like Grand Isle, Louisiana; Sloan, Iowa; Sheridan, Wyoming; and Fountain Valley, California—affirmed the belief that Bulger was traveling with ease, always managing to stay one step ahead of the egg-faced FBI agents who remained hot on his trial.

It appeared that Whitey Bulger was everywhere, yet nowhere, at the same time.

That would all change during the early evening hours of June 22, 2011, when FBI agents and US Marshals acting on a tip, found the 81-year-old fugitive gangster holed up in a posh seaside condominium in Santa Monica, California, that was located three blocks from the Pacific Ocean and the scenic open-air Third Street Promenade that houses dozens of boutique-type shops and trendy restaurants.

Like Bin Laden in Pakistan, the elusive Whitey Bulger was hiding in plain sight. As we watched the television coverage and read the newspaper accounts surrounding their respective captures, we wondered where in the world was Philip Leonetti hiding?

Leonetti, the onetime underboss of the Philadelphia–Atlantic City mob, nicknamed "Crazy Phil," was the crowned prince of the Mafia during the mob's long-lost 1980s heyday in the Northeast United States. A stone-cold killer, he was the nephew and second-in-command of Nicodemo "Little Nicky" Scarfo, one of the most bloodthirsty and ruthless crime bosses in the history of organized crime.

If Leonetti was the prince, Scarfo was undoubtedly the king of the Atlantic City–Philadelphia mob, and together they ran their Mafia empire from their headquarters on Georgia Avenue in the Ducktown neighborhood of Atlantic City, less than three blocks from the world-famous boardwalk and the glitz and glamour of the city's neon-lit casinos, all of which they controlled with an iron fist.

A former associate turned government witness once described Scarfo by saying, "If Nicky had as much power as Hitler, he woulda outdid him," and also said that "Leonetti was 100-percent Scarfo; he was just as ruthless and deadly as his uncle."

Murder, mayhem, and wanton violence became the benchmark of the mob under Little Nicky and Crazy Phil, with more than two-dozen mob killings punctuating what would become one of the most volatile and tumultuous periods in the long and celebrated US history of the Mafia, or its more proper name, *La Cosa Nostra*, which is Italian for "this thing of ours."

Leonetti himself was convicted of participating in 10 gangland killings.

Millions of dollars in cash poured in from traditional mob rackets like gambling, loan sharking, and extortion, while millions more came in from Scarfo's very lucrative underworld street tax and a seemingly limitless skim from Local 54, Atlantic City's largest casino union, which Scarfo and Leonetti treated like their own petty cash fund.

Scarfo and Leonetti worked closely with New York crime bosses, including: Vincent "The Chin" Gigante, the leader of the powerful Genovese crime family who stymied law enforcement for decades by pretending to be crazy—walking around his Greenwich Village neighborhood in a bathrobe, mumbling to himself; and "the Dapper Don" John Gotti, the ambitious Gambino crime family boss known for his $2,000 suits.

Scarfo and Leonetti were recognized as elite *mafiosi*, highly regarded and equally feared in mob circles throughout the United States.

In other words, they were untouchable.

Or so it seemed.

As Scarfo and Leonetti grew in power, so did the efforts of the FBI and the US Department of Justice to stop them. They had become Public Enemy No. 1 and Public Enemy No. 2.

When it was over, the Scarfo organization would be decimated and Little Nicky, its supreme leader and Lord High Executioner would be sentenced to life in prison, narrowly escaping the death penalty, following a series of convictions in both state and federal courts in the late 1980s that rocked the foundation of the Philadelphia–Atlantic City mob. The trials featured testimony from several mob turncoats who had betrayed their sacred oath of *omerta* and agreed to cooperate with the government by testifying against Scarfo, Leonetti, and 15 of their men.

Scarfo, now 83, remains behind bars as this book is published, currently housed at the high-security US Penitentiary in Atlanta, after spending the last 25 years in various maximum-security federal penitentiaries all over the United States.

Leonetti would receive 45 years in prison for his life of crime, which included convictions for murder and racketeering. But Crazy Phil would only serve five years, five months, and five days behind bars after agreeing to cooperate with the federal government in 1989, betraying his uncle Nicky Scarfo and his blood oath to *La Cosa Nostra*, to which he'd sworn his undying allegiance less than a decade earlier.

At the age of 36, Philip Leonetti, who had become the youngest underboss in the history of *La Cosa Nostra* gained the more dubious distinction of being the highest-ranking member of the nationwide crime syndicate to flip and cooperate with the government.

The impact on the underworld was akin to that of a plane flying into the World Trade Center *before* 9/11.

It was unfathomable; but it happened, and the Philadelphia–Atlantic City mob would be left in tatters, its infrastructure so badly damaged that more than two decades later it has yet to fully recover.

Leonetti the government witness proved to be just as deadly as Leonetti the mob killer. Dozens of mobsters and associates were convicted as a direct result of Leonetti's testimony, and he would figure prominently in the demise of New York mob bosses Vincent "The Chin" Gigante and John Gotti and more importantly, *La Cosa Nostra* itself.

When he was done testifying, Leonetti would settle into a life inside the confines of a top-secret world: the witness security wing of a remote federal prison tucked away in a dusty Arizona desert.

Joining him would be Salvatore "Sammy the Bull" Gravano, the former underboss of New York's Gambino crime family, who followed Leonetti's lead and also defected from *La Cosa Nostra*.

Ironically, as Leonetti and Gravano enjoyed life together in the Arizona sun, reminiscing about their glory days in the mob, Nicky Scarfo and John Gotti, the bosses they betrayed, were rotting, locked down for all but a half hour of each day inside eight-by-ten-foot concrete cells in one of the nation's toughest federal prisons, located in Marion, Illinois.

By the early 1990s, the US *La Cosa Nostra* was still a deadly nationwide criminal organization, but it had become a shell of its former self.

Leonetti, the man who brought the mob to its knees, was released from prison and disappeared into the Witness Protection Program with a new identity and a new lease on life. Not yet 40 years old, Philip Leonetti had to start over and completely reinvent himself, and he couldn't have been happier to do so.

While Gigante and Gotti would go on to die inside the federal prisons that became their homes, Leonetti's uncle, Nicodemo "Little Nicky" Scarfo, would remain alive and well in his.

Scarfo has vowed revenge and has openly plotted to kill his once-beloved nephew and his entire family. The evil and vindictive Scarfo would place a $500,000 bounty on his nephew's head, a bounty, which according to the FBI, still stands today.

A letter written in the mid-1990s by a deranged Scarfo to his own mother, Leonetti's grandmother, paints a chilling picture, as the jailed mob boss makes a not-so-veiled series of threats against Leonetti and his mother, Nancy, who is Scarfo's own sister:

"I will never forget them animals and what they did to this family, but you still love them, which makes me know you lost your mind. I want you to live forever, but I want you to have your senses so you could see what is going to happen to those wild animals. If you love that witch, you better say all your prayers for her and her crazy son, because I don't need no prayers and beside all of that, FUCK GOD, too."

In another letter, this one intercepted by the Bureau of Prisons, a tamer Scarfo wrote the following to one of his lawyers:

"I maintain myself to see these people suffer one day, this is what keeps me going."

What keeps Philip Leonetti going is the new life that he started with his family, far away from Atlantic City and the mob, and for the last decade or so, away from the watchful eye of the FBI and the US Marshals who run the Witness Protection Program.

Hiding from both the mob and the government, Philip Leonetti—we would come to learn—was, like Osama bin Laden and Whitey Bulger, hiding in plain sight.

La Cosa Nostra (This Thing of Ours)

WHAT WE KNOW AS THE MAFIA IN THE UNITED STATES IS ACTUALLY AN OFFSHOOT OF SEVERAL DIFFERENT SECRET SOCIETIES IN EUROPE THAT DATE BACK CENTURIES. THE MOST PROMINENT OF THESE SECTS WERE THE SICILIAN MAFIA—THE *'NDRANGHETA*—AND THE *CAMORRA*, WHICH ORIGINATED IN NAPLES.

Originally, the intent of such organizations was not criminal. They existed to protect the common citizens of these regions from a corrupt and oppressive government that did little to nothing to look out for the interests of the regular working man. Over time, as these groups evolved, they became sophisticated criminal organizations.

As Italian and Sicilian immigrants flooded the streets of major American cities in the late 19th and early 20th centuries, a number of loosely organized incarnations of these secret societies began to take form, making their presence felt in ethnic neighborhoods across the country.

Street gangs with ties to the Old Country set up shop and operated a vast array of rackets. The onset of Prohibition in the 1920s made many early mob leaders incredibly wealthy, as their street gangs spearheaded an underworld movement supplying illegal liquor to a thirsty public, while causing heaps of newspaper headlines and bloodshed as they battled over turf.

Nowhere was this more evident than in Chicago, where Al Capone, the most celebrated gangster of his era, became the face of organized crime in the United States.

At first, there was little to no connection between the various burgeoning crime conglomerates operating throughout the United States. A move toward consolidation slowly began to take form as the bosses began to recognize that true power and strength could only be accomplished by establishing a nationwide crime syndicate.

This American organized crime syndicate would come to be known as *La Cosa Nostra*, which in Italian means "this thing of ours."

The inaugural summit of this newly organized syndicate would feature the nation's top gangland bosses, nearly 50 men operating street rackets in US cities from coast to coast. The meeting took place in the spring of 1929 at the legendary Ritz Hotel on the world-famous Atlantic City Boardwalk. Atlantic City, known as the World's Playground, was riddled with vice and became the original Sin City long before modern-day Las Vegas was even contemplated.

Backroom casinos, showgirls looking for a quick buck, and a nonstop flow of booze during Prohibition made Atlantic City the perfect choice for such a gathering.

Two years later in 1931, the modern American Mafia was created in the aftermath of a carnage-filled mob war in New York City that pitted a group of old-school underworld leaders, known as Mustache Petes, against a group of young and hungry underworld visionaries led by a man born Salvatore Lucania, who would come to be known as Charles "Lucky" Luciano. With Luciano's group emerging victorious, the ambitious new "Godfather" called a meeting of fellow mob leaders in Chicago and laid out his vision for what would become *La Cosa Nostra*.

Luciano proposed a nationwide crime syndicate made up of regional mob factions, called Families, which would be overseen and governed by a board of directors known as the Commission. The Commission would be comprised of only the most powerful and respected mob dons—men like Luciano and Capone.

The syndicate and its rules would be paramilitary in structure. Each family would be headed by a boss, an underboss, and a consigliere, or counselor. The hierarchy of the family would also include a cadre of capos, or captains, who would each be responsible for a crew of family soldiers and associates.

Attendees of Luciano's underworld conference, held at the Blackstone Hotel in the heart of the Windy City's famous Miracle Mile on Michigan Avenue, unanimously agreed to the proposal and unanimously pledged their allegiance to the newly established *La Cosa Nostra*.

Following the meeting of the nation's top criminal minds in Chicago, 26 American mob Families were formed. There was one for almost every major city in the country, with the New York and Chicago mobs being the most prominent.

In the city of Philadelphia, John Avena, a longtime lieutenant under Prohibition-era crime lord Salvatore Sabella was named the city's first modern-day mob boss. Sabella had sided against Luciano in his war with the Mustache Petes, and as a result was told to step down and turn over the reins to Avena. From the moment he assumed power, Avena butted heads with a former ally and onetime Sabella lieutenant named Joseph Dovi. Feeling slighted by Avena's promotion, Dovi immediately challenged his authority. The two men and their respective factions battled for control on the streets for nearly five years, a war that culminated with Avena, the boss, being killed in 1936.

Dovi took control of the Philadelphia Mafia for the next decade, expanding the crime family's territorial reach into parts of neighboring states New Jersey and Delaware. When Dovi died from natural causes in 1946, Joe Ida, another former Sabella disciple, was named the city's new don. Ida ruled unfettered for over a decade, but his reign would end following his arrest at the infamous Appalachian mob summit in 1957, which ultimately led to his deportation.

Like the Atlantic City conference in 1929, the Appalachian summit was designed to bring together the top gangland leaders in the nation. But many of these men were arrested as they converged on the upstate New York hunting cottage where the conference was to take place. Law enforcement had been tipped off and was lying in wait as the unsuspecting mobsters converged on the location.

For a brief period of time following Ida's deportation, Antonio "Mr. Miggs" Pollina was named his successor. But Pollina quickly fell out of favor with those within the organization by plotting the murder of a popular mob captain born Angelo Annaloro, who would come to be known as Angelo Bruno. Getting wind of Pollina's plan to murder him, Bruno, a cunning and even-tempered gentleman gangster, turned the tables on Mr. Miggs.

Using his many connections to the New York underworld, which included a deep personal relationship with the powerful Carlo Gambino, Bruno got the Commission to depose Pollina and Bruno was anointed his successor.

Showing a level of mercy not often displayed by men in his position, Bruno spared Pollina's life. Instead of killing him for his indiscretion, he banished the defeated former boss into retirement.

The controversial move earned Bruno the nickname, the Docile Don.

What the future would hold for Bruno and those operating in and around the Philadelphia mob, which now included rackets in neighboring Atlantic City, would be anything but docile, especially once Nicky Scarfo and his nephew Philip Leonetti gained control.

Young Philip

My name is Philip Michael Leonetti, and I was born on March 27, 1953, in Philadelphia. My father's name was Pasquale Leonetti and my mother's name was Annunziata Scarfo, but everyone called her Nancy. I was born into this life, the Mafia, La Cosa Nostra. It was inevitable for me. It was literally in my blood.

Both sides of my family, the Leonettis and Scarfos, had immigrated to the United States from Naples and Calabria, and both families had strong ties to the Mafia in Italy before I was born.

My grandfather Christopher Leonetti was a mob-connected hood who ran with a crew of guys in Manhattan's Little Italy. In the '20s, he got killed after his crew tried to shake down a couple of guys they thought were low-level greaseballs, siggys, but turned out to be high-ranking Sicilian gangsters. They ended up whackin' him and leavin' him in the street.

Growing up, my Uncle Nick would tell me, "The Sicilians, the siggys, they are not like us, they can't be trusted." It's something I would never forget.

My father, Pasquale Leonetti, was a well-respected gambler who was picked by Angelo Bruno to oversee many of the mob-controlled card and dice games that operated in and around South Philadelphia in the late '50s and early '60s. Angelo Bruno was the boss of the Philadelphia mob; he was the Don.

Back then the mob had games in the back rooms of almost every restaurant, neighborhood bar, corner store, and social club in South Philly. Knock-around street guys from the neighborhood would come and gamble, drink booze, smoke cigars, and escape from their wives or girlfriends for a few hours in these joints, and the mob was making money catering to them.

First of all, the mob ran the games, which means they won more than they lost. The house always wins. Second, they were selling booze to the gamblers, which means they were making money on the booze and the gamblers would get drunk and end up gambling more than they should. That's when one of the mob guys who was workin' in that joint would pull the gambler aside and loan him *money at a high-interest rate so that he could keep drinking and gambling, or use the money to pay the rent or the electric bill.*

If a guy borrowed $10,000 and the loan shark charged him two points, he would have to pay $200 a week in interest—which was known as the vig or the juice—every week, and he still owed the $10,000. So let's say it took him 10 weeks to pay the money back; he'd pay $2,000 in juice money and the $10,000 in principal, so he'd end up paying $12,000 on a $10,000 loan. If it took him a year to pay back, he'd pay over $10,000 in interest and still owe the $10,000 in principal. This is primarily how the mob makes its money even today—illegal gambling and loan sharking.

Now my father had a reputation as a serious gambler, not only in South Philadelphia, but in Jersey and even New York. He was so well known and respected that Walter Winchell, the famous journalist, wrote a piece on him. This is why Ange picked my father to run those games. He was that good. But when it came to being a father, he was no good; he was a bum.

After his luck took a turn for the worse, Pasquale went from running the mob's top card games to owing the mob the money he lost and couldn't pay back when he gambled himself. Pasquale Leonetti had crapped out.

When Philip was just a baby, Pasquale left Philadelphia and headed south to Florida, leaving Nancy and young Philip to fend for themselves. Angelo Bruno had taken Pasquale's exterminating business as a way of clearing his debts. Philip and his mother were left with nothing.

By this time Nancy's parents, Philip and Catherine Scarfo, had also left South Philadelphia, moving 60 miles east to Atlantic City. The once booming seaside resort known as the World's Playground had fallen on hard times and was considered down and out by the early '60s. It had literally gone from boom to bust.

The Scarfos purchased two connecting apartment buildings at 26-28 North Georgia Avenue in the city's Italian enclave known as Ducktown. Each building stood four stories tall and was two and a half blocks from the world famous Atlantic City Boardwalk and the sandy beaches leading to the Atlantic Ocean, and was surrounded by other similarly structured row homes.

Nancy's father, Philip Scarfo, was a laborer who worked at Atlantic City's prestigious Chalfonte-Haddon Hall Hotel.

My grandfather, Philip Scarfo, was a wonderful man. I was named after him. When I was little and we lived in South Philadelphia, he had a job where he had a horse with a wagon and he used to give me rides around the neighborhood. He'd also take me crabbing when I was a little boy. He was a hard worker his whole life and was never involved in the mob or anything illegal. He was 100-percent legit.

Nancy's mother, Catherine Scarfo, was a homemaker and a devout Catholic who faithfully attended Mass every morning at St. Michael's Church, which was located less than 50 yards from the Scarfo family home.

My grandmother was the typical old-school Italian matriarch. All of her grandchildren called her Mom-Mom. She went to church every morning, not just Sundays, and her cooking, my God, nobody cooked like her. She was a real character, one of a kind. She was well liked in the neighborhood; if someone had a problem or needed advice, they'd come and see Mom-Mom.

Her three brothers, Nick, Joe, and Mike Piccolo, were all well-respected soldiers in the Bruno crime family, which was based in Philadelphia but maintained a strong presence in New Jersey, particularly in the cities of Trenton, Newark, and Atlantic City. Each had been adorned with the same nickname; they were known respectively as Nicky Buck, Joe Buck, and Mikey Buck, and owned and operated Piccolo's 500, a notorious mob hangout that grew into a popular restaurant and club in South Philadelphia. Michael "Mikey Buck" Piccolo was Philip Leonetti's godfather.

My great-uncle Mike used to take me fishing when I was a little boy with my cousin Ronald. He was a nice man, a gentleman.
My great-uncle Nick Piccolo, Nicky Buck, who was on my mother's side, was married to my grandfather's sister, my aunt Mary, on my father's side.

This marriage strengthened the Scarfo–Leonetti bond.
Then there was Philip's Uncle Nick.

Uncle Nick

NICODEMO DOMENIC SCARFO WAS BORN ON MARCH 8, 1929, TO PHILIP AND CATHERINE SCARFO IN BROOKLYN, NEW YORK. IN 1941, WHEN NICK WAS 12 YEARS OLD, THE SCARFO FAMILY, WHICH NOW INCLUDED YOUNGER SISTER ANNUNZIATA (NANCY), LEFT NEW YORK AND SETTLED IN SOUTH PHILADELPHIA, WHICH WAS BY THEN HEAVILY POPULATED BY SECOND-GENERATION ITALIAN FAMILIES.

As a young boy, Scarfo spent his summers working in the sprawling blueberry fields in Hammonton, New Jersey. Known as the Blueberry Capital of the World, Hammonton is a small town located 30 miles east of Philadelphia and 30 miles west of Atlantic City. It sits smack dab in the middle of the 60-mile corridor that connects the two cities with the Atlantic City Expressway. Scarfo had learned first-hand about the tireless life of a laborer, a life that he wanted no part of as an adult. His big dreams didn't involve picking blueberries for a living. To him, people who worked for a living were "jerk offs," and Nicky Scarfo didn't fancy himself a "jerk off."

Scarfo, who would come to be known as Little Nicky for his diminutive size, stood a mere 5'5". He was voted most talkative by his classmates at Benjamin Franklin High School, which he graduated from in 1947, and his senior yearbook declared the same year that he was out to "lick the world." What Scarfo lacked in height, he made up for in fearlessness. Despite his size, he began to box in his late teens under the name Nick Scarfo and amassed an impressive record in small clubs fights on the Philadelphia boxing circuit. But as the 1950s came, the bantamweight Scarfo decided that he was better suited for life outside the ring.

Nicky Scarfo wanted to be a gangster, just like the movie-star mobsters he grew up admiring in the shoot-'em-up flicks he would sneak into the theater to see as a kid. Guys like Paul Muni in the 1932 gangster classic *Scarface,* not the top baseball players of the late 1940s like Stan Musial and Ted Williams, were Nicky Scarfo's idols. Like the working stiff, athletes were also "jerk offs" to Little Nicky.

> *It's sad to say, but my uncle looked down on his own father because he was a hardworking guy and not a gangster. He was never outwardly disrespectful to his father, but they weren't very close. My uncle's only ambition in life was to be a gangster, even from the time he was young.*

In the late 1940s and early '50s, Scarfo began his mob apprenticeship, working as a bartender and a bookmaker at Piccolo's 500, where his schooling in the ways of *La Cosa Nostra* began under the direction of his uncles, the Buck brothers. While Nicholas "Nicky Buck" Piccolo was teaching his nephew about the ins and outs of mob business life—like how to be a bookmaker and run numbers—Felix "Skinny Razor" DiTullio, one of the mob's most feared hit men, was teaching him how to be a killer.

> *My uncle's first hit, he did it with Skinny Razor. There was a guy in South Philly who had a fruit stand; they called him the Huckster. The Huckster's brother had a problem with Skinny Razor and Skinny Razor got the okay to kill him. So him and my uncle went to the guy's store in South Philadelphia. It was during a real bad snowstorm and the guy let them into the store and they killed him. They stabbed him to death. When they were done, they cut his balls off and put them in the guy's mouth. That's how my uncle learned about killing, from being around Skinny Razor.*

Felix "Skinny Razor" DiTullio took an early liking to the young Scarfo, and Little Nicky was an eager student. Bonding in bloodlust, Skinny Razor taught Scarfo the art of the mob hit. It was a skill he would cherish, continue to hone, and eventually master.

By 1954, at the age of 25, Nicodemo "Little Nicky" Scarfo had acquired the reputation in the underworld that he had sought: he was known as a mad-dog killer, thanks in large part to the teachings of his mob mentor, Skinny Razor DiTullio. Scarfo was proposed for membership in *La Cosa Nostra* by DiTullio and his uncle Nicholas "Nicky Buck" Piccolo, and as a result was formally inducted into the mob by then-Philadelphia mob boss Joseph Ida at an official making ceremony held at a restaurant and lounge named Sans Souci in Cherry Hill, New Jersey, just over the bridge from Center City Philadelphia.

Two of Scarfo's uncles, Tony and Mike Piccolo—the younger brothers of Nicholas "Nicky Buck" Piccolo—were also inducted into *La Cosa Nostra* at the same ceremony.

Nicky Scarfo had achieved his dream: he was a bona fide wise guy, a made man.

The blueberry farms of Hammonton were ancient history. He would never again be a working stiff, a civilian, a "jerk off."

> *Back then it was almost unheard of to be made at such a young age in Philadelphia. My uncle was only 25. His uncles, Tony and Mike Buck, who were made at the same time, were twice his age— they were close to 50 at the time.*

Even then, Nicky Scarfo was on the fast track in *La Cosa Nostra*.

> *Because he was with Skinny Razor, my uncle got to meet a lot of gangsters in North Jersey and New York and they respected him because Skinny Razor had a reputation of being a stone-cold killer and everyone knew it. He was both feared and respected on the streets, and my uncle looked up to him. He wanted to be just like him.*

In 1957, with Pasquale out of the picture, Nancy and four-year-old Philip would leave Philadelphia and settle into the Scarfo family compound in Atlantic City, which at the time was more than a decade past its prime.

Nancy would take a job in Atlantic City working for the Bureau of Children Services, which functioned like an adoption agency and provided care for underprivileged children. With his father out of the picture, Philip gravitated towards Nancy's older brother, his Uncle Nick, as a father figure.

> *At that time, it was just my mother, my grandparents, and myself living on Georgia Avenue. My father was gone. I was just a little boy, maybe five or six years old. My uncle was still living in South Philadelphia, but he used to come down a lot to see us or to do business with Skinny Razor.*

In the 1950s and '60s, Felix "Skinny Razor" DiTullio was a mob captain, a *caporegime*, and the Philadelphia mob's top guy at the Jersey Shore. And Nicky Scarfo was quickly becoming his No. 1 protégé.

When Philip was seven years old, his great-grandmother, Catherine Scarfo's mother, died and the wake and funeral remain etched in Philip's memory more than five decades later.

Back then, the Italian wakes lasted three days. I remember my grandmother and her brothers, the Piccolo brothers—Joe, Mike, and Nick—were standing next to the coffin, and all of these people were coming in to pay their respects. I was standing in the audience with my Uncle Nick and in walked a man with several guys around him. Everybody was going over to pay their respects to him and shake his hand or kiss him on the cheek. I remember this man looked very important, like the president. So I said to my uncle, "Who's that guy?" And he said, "That's Angelo Bruno, he's the boss of the family." And even though I was only seven years old, I understood what he was talking about.

As I got older I started spending more time with my uncle. He was like my father because my real father was gone. When we were alone he would talk to me about what La Cosa Nostra *was all about, how we were different from everyone else, and how we had certain rules that we had to follow. This is how I was raised, from the time I was a little boy.*

When Philip was eight years old, his Uncle Nick was given an order by his mentor, Felix "Skinny Razor" DiTullio. A wayward mob associate named Dominick "Reds" Caruso had disrespected Joseph "Joe the Boss" Rugnetta, the consigliere, or counselor, to the family's boss, Angelo Bruno. And Bruno had handpicked Skinny Razor's up-and-coming protégé, Nicky Scarfo, to oversee Caruso's murder. Scarfo was happy to oblige and show Bruno and DiTullio that he was an able killer, a real gangster.

To kill Reds Caruso, Salvatore "Chuckie" Merlino, one of Scarfo's oldest friends, would go to Caruso's home in South Philadelphia and tell him that Scarfo wanted to see him. Like a scene out of the very type of movie he loved so much as a young boy, Scarfo lulled Caruso into a state of relaxation, taking him to a bar in Vineland, New Jersey, that was owned by an associate of the Bruno crime family.

Two more Bruno associates, Santo "Little Santo" Romeo and Anthony Casella, were inside the bar, with Romeo working as a bartender.

Shortly after arriving at the bar, Scarfo wasted little time in carrying out the hit. Little Nicky pulled out a handgun and shot Caruso six times at point-blank range. But Reds Caruso was still alive.

> *My uncle told me the guy was lying there after he shot him and he said, "You got me, Nick," and my uncle grabbed an ice pick from the bar and he stabbed him over and over again in the back until he died. He told me he stabbed him so hard that the ice pick got stuck in his back and part of it broke off when he tried to pull it out.*

But killing Caruso wasn't enough; the Sicilian-born Bruno had wanted him killed in a certain way to send a message. And while he wanted Scarfo to oversee the murder, he wanted another up-and-coming mobster to actually commit it.

> *Ange had ordered that this Reds Caruso be strangled to death, not shot, because he had talked fresh to Joe the Boss, and he wanted Santo Idone to strangle him and send a message that his mouth had gotten him killed. These siggys were big into sending messages.*
>
> *But what happened is, Santo Idone was late getting to the bar and by the time he got there, my uncle had already killed the guy. Now when the boss says he wants a guy killed and he wants it done a certain way, that's the way you gotta do it. So when Santo got there, my uncle had him choke the corpse with some rope and leave marks around the neck so just in case they found the body, Ange would know that he had been strangled like he ordered.*

Scarfo would also now have a lifelong ally in Santo Idone, who was born in Calabria, the same part of Italy where Scarfo's family came from.

> *My uncle told me that Santo told him, "Thanks for covering for me, Nick. I won't forget it," and my uncle said, "You and me are Calabrese; we gotta stick together around all these siggys."*

The hit team led by Scarfo would leave Caruso's dead body inside the bar as another team removed the body and moved it to another location, where a third team was supposed to dig a hole and bury the body, which was doused in lime to accelerate its decomposition.

But what they did was they got a fourth group to dig up the body and move it somewhere else, so that way the guys who did the killing and the guys who moved the body and the group that buried the body the first time had no idea where the body was, in case someone flipped and ratted them out.

As Caruso's bullet-ridden corpse, still with part of an ice pick lodged in his back, lay buried in a makeshift grave somewhere in South Jersey, Scarfo still had work to do.

Skinny Razor wanted my uncle to take the truck that had been used to transport the body back to Philadelphia so it could be destroyed—so no one could trace any evidence from the killing. My uncle decided to take me along because he thinks that he would look less suspicious driving this truck if he was with a little boy. I was eight years old at the time. As we were driving he told me that he had killed a very bad man the night before and he needed my help in getting rid of the truck they used to transport the body. Here I was, an eight-year-old kid, and these guys that I looked up to, they needed my help. I felt like I was doing what was right, because my uncle said the man they killed was a very bad man who had broken the rules, and when you break the rules, this is what happens. This was what La Cosa Nostra *was all about—the rules. I understood this from a very early age. My uncle was always talking about the rules and how you can't break them. I remember my uncle describing how he killed the guy, how he shot him and stabbed him with an ice pick, and what they guy said to him. Looking back, I didn't think there was anything wrong with it.*

In Philip's young world, everyday life and organized crime were interchangeable.

My uncle taught me about our life, the mob, La Cosa Nostra, *from an early age. It was natural, almost instinctive for me. I remember just knowing what it meant without someone having to spell it all out for me. I understood what it was.*

All of the men I looked up to were part of this world, so naturally I wanted to be a part of it, too. When I was ten, my uncle taught me how to shoot. He used to take me hunting and we would shoot .22s. He said it was important for me to know how to use a gun in our life. Even though I was this young kid, my Uncle Nick always talked to me like I was an adult. He didn't treat me like I was ten or eleven. Everything he did, I wanted to do. I wanted to be just like him. In my mind, he was a man of honor and respect.

Obviously, my uncle wasn't your average uncle. I mean, he wasn't out in the yard playing catch with me or coaching my Little League baseball team. He was teaching me how to shoot guns and how to commit a murder, and then how to successfully cover your tracks. That's the kind of stuff I grew up around. And it seemed completely normal to me. I felt like Marilyn on that old TV show, The Munsters, *the one human member of the family who lived amongst all of these strange characters, but I didn't think twice about it. It's scary to think how natural it all was.*

As Philip got ready for junior high school at St. Michaels in Atlantic City, his uncle had to deal with his first serious brush with the law.

In May of 1963, my uncle and Chuckie Merlino were in the Oregon Diner in South Philadelphia. My uncle gets into an argument with this longshoreman, this big Irish guy. And my uncle's little; he's only 5'5" and weighs like 135 pounds. So he and the longshoreman get into an argument over a booth and the guy grabs my uncle by the throat and starts choking him. As he's choking him, he pushes my uncle up against the counter. My uncle is getting ready to pass out and he reaches on the counter behind him and grabs a butter knife and stabs the guy in the chest. The knife went right into his heart and the guy died. My uncle used to love to tell this story about how he gutted this big Irish guy. The way he would tell the story, you'd think he was talking about hitting a home run to win the World Series. He would act it out. He'd take his hands and simulate what the guy had done by putting his hands around his neck, showing how they guy had choked him, then he'd show how he grabbed the knife and thrusted it right into the guy's heart. He was so proud of himself that he killed this guy, who was bigger than him, with a butter knife.

Nicky Scarfo would plead guilty to manslaughter for the killing of William Dugan, the Irish guy in the diner. His sentence was a mere 23 months in prison. He was out in less than a year and would join the rest of his family in Atlantic City, leaving Philadelphia behind . . . for now.

Ducktown

IN THE MID-1960S, DUCKTOWN WAS A SMALL, CLOSE-KNIT ATLANTIC CITY NEIGHBORHOOD POPULATED BY PROMINENT WORKING-CLASS ITALIAN FAMILIES WITH NAMES LIKE RANDO, FORMICA, DIGIACINTO, MATTEO, BASILE, SACCO, AND MANCUSO.

And now it would be home to the Scarfos and Leonettis.

Spanning a few short blocks, Ducktown covered the area of Texas, Florida, Georgia, Mississippi, and Missouri Avenues, from Atlantic Avenue, to Fairmount Avenue, and to the bay. The neighborhood was named Ducktown for the duck houses that were built along the bay front. Poultry and waterfowl were raised there, and then slaughtered and later resold in neighborhood markets.

Ducktown was Atlantic City's Little Italy. Within two blocks of where we lived on Georgia Avenue, you had the White House, which is the best sub shop in the world. Everyone has been there—the Beatles, Muhammad Ali, Frank Sinatra, you name it—they've all eaten at the White House.

You have Angelo's and Angeloni's, two of the city's best Italian restaurants two blocks away. Before Angeloni's became Angeloni's it was called the Madrid. There was Dock's Oyster House right around the corner, which had the best seafood in Atlantic City.

Barbera's Fish Market and the city's top Italian bakeries—Rando's, Formica's, and Panarelli's—were all a block or two away.

There was a coffee shop called Tommy Howe's, right next to Angeloni's on Arctic Avenue. The older men used to go in there and play the number, and there was always a card game going. When I was a little boy, my grandfather used to take me down there when he would go. Joe DiMaggio used to go in there every time he was in Atlantic City, and I'd see him hanging out with the guys from the neighborhood, playing cards and drinking espresso. This was not even 50 yards from where we lived.

On Missouri and Atlantic, you had Skinny D'Amato's 500 Club, which at the time was the biggest nightclub around. People would come from Philadelphia and New York to go there. The lines would be around the block every night. Frank Sinatra, Dean Martin, Sammy Davis Jr.—they all used to perform there. Skinny was a friend of my uncle, so we always got the best seats in the house.

I remember this guy we used to call Blah Blah Buckets. He was older and the neighborhood kids would tease him because he was slow. I think he worked at the 500 Club. He was nuts. He'd always be chasing someone up the street, cursing and threatening to kill them. He was out there every day, and the kids never stopped breaking his balls. Like clockwork, if you stayed on the street long enough, you'd see a group of kids running and Blah Blah chasing after them, threatening to kill them.

I had a lot of fun growing up there; this was my home.

Philip's weekly regimen at that time included waking up at 6:30 a.m. on Fridays and walking a block and a half to Barbera's Fish Market on Mississippi Avenue, where he would pick up fresh fish, and then deliver it to the nuns who worked and lived at St. Michael's, the neighborhood's Catholic Church and the namesake of the adjacent school that Philip attended. The back of the school was directly across the street from the Scarfo compound.

Everyone in the neighborhood went to St. Mike's. I went to Mass every morning before school and I'd go on Sundays with my grandmother.

After my uncle got out of jail for killing the guy in the Oregon Diner, he left South Philadelphia and he moved in with us on Georgia Avenue. Living there at the time were my grandparents, my mother, myself, my uncle and his wife, Mimi, and right around this time, Nicky Jr. was born. Things were quiet for a while, and a couple years later I was getting ready for high school.

Upon graduating from St. Michael's, Philip would move on to Holy Spirit High School located in Absecon, New Jersey, less than 10 miles from the Scarfo family home in Ducktown.

I was on the basketball team at Holy Spirit with a lot of kids from the neighborhood, and we were a very good team. My uncle used to come to the games and sit in the bleachers and he would take bets on the games right there in the gymnasium. There was even this guy named Hoffman who used to write the betting lines on our games in the local paper. When our team played it was a very big deal.

A fellow Ducktown resident and Holy Spirit teammate named Chris Ford would eventually go on to Villanova University, and then to the NBA, where he played for both the Detroit Pistons and the Boston Celtics. After retiring as a player, Ford coached NBA teams in Boston, Milwaukee, Los Angeles, and Philadelphia.

Chris Ford was a big deal to all of the kids in Ducktown because he was such an amazing athlete and he was one of us. He grew up right there on Missouri Avenue on top of Capone's Bar. His brother Harry eventually moved into one of the apartments in our building and would always tell us who was coming around when we weren't there. He stood all day on the porch above our office—which was on the ground floor of 28 North Georgia Avenue—smoking a cigarette and just watching what was going on in the neighborhood. Who was coming, who was going. He'd also help my mother and grandmother if me or my uncle weren't around. My uncle would always have me give him a few bucks.

While Ducktown may have been energetic and thriving in the mid- to late '60s, the rest of Atlantic City was desolate and 20 years past its prime as the World's Playground. Nicky Scarfo was surviving on traditional mob rackets like bookmaking, extortion, and loan sharking to make ends meet.

> *Skinny Razor died in 1966, so my uncle became the top mob guy in Atlantic City. He basically inherited what Skinny Razor had and Ange gave him the okay to run it how he saw fit. For the most part, he was the only game in town. He was making book and writing small loans, but he was struggling, as there wasn't a whole lot going on down there at the time. Him and a friend of his named Tommy Butch opened a place called the Penguin Club, and he was also involved in a couple of dirty book stores with this guy named Alvin Feldman, who called himself the King of the Jews.*
>
> *He wasn't making a lot of money, but to him at that time, the money wasn't important. He would always say, "The money will come, but this thing is about respect and honor, it's not about money." He was making a name for himself within the Bruno organization and that's what mattered the most to him—his reputation.*

While the nuns at Holy Spirit were teaching Philip the basic curriculum of English, algebra, and history, his Uncle Nick continued to educate him in the ways of the mob.

> *He was constantly talking to me about La Cosa Nostra. It was all the time. He told me: in this life you never rat, you keep your mouth shut, and you mind your own business. He told me, "We don't ever discuss our business with women and we don't discuss our life with outsiders. You don't tell nobody nothing; it's just me and you talking." He would say, "If you want to get involved with me in this thing, just because I'm your uncle, I can't help you." He told me I had to do things on my own and be my own man. At this point, I was ready. I wanted to be like him. I wanted to follow in his footsteps.*

With his uncle ready to begin his second stretch in jail, Philip would have his chance to do just that.

Yardville

I N 1971, AS PHILIP WAS GRADUATING FROM HIGH SCHOOL, NICKY SCARFO WAS CALLED TO TESTIFY BEFORE THE NEW JERSEY STATE COMMISSION OF INVESTIGATION (SCI) THAT WAS INVESTIGATING THE INFILTRATION OF ORGANIZED CRIME INTO VARIOUS LABOR UNIONS.

After refusing to answer any questions, including his name, Scarfo was charged with contempt and sentenced to an indefinite prison term. He was sent to Yardville State Prison just outside of Trenton, New Jersey, with several other powerful mobsters, including the boss of the Philadelphia mob, Angelo Bruno.

Scarfo could have been released at any time had he honored the subpoena and testified before the SCI, but instead he followed the same rule that he had taught his nephew Philip and refused to testify.

Scarfo would spend the next two years behind bars.

Already a proven killer, it was now known that Little Nicky could keep his mouth shut.

Besides Scarfo and Bruno, there was longtime New York mob leader Jerry Catena, Trenton mob captain Nicky Russo, North Jersey mobster Ralph "Blackie" Napoli and Genovese crime family capos Anthony "Little Pussy" Russo, Joseph "Bayonne Joe" Zicarelli, and John "Johnny Coca-Cola" Lardiere, and an up-and-coming Genovese soldier named Louis "Bobby" Manna.

Like Scarfo and Bruno, the others were also jailed for refusing to testify before the State Commission of Investigation. Organized crime investigators and members of the press dubbed them the Yardville 9.

For Scarfo, the two-year prison sentence did wonders for his career. Not only did he get valuable face time with Philadelphia mob boss Angelo Bruno, but he also got close to men deeply entrenched in mob operations in North Jersey and New York and forged bonds that he would exploit to his advantage in the years to come.

For Philip Leonetti, his uncle's prison term would help jump-start his career in the underworld, as he acted as an emissary for both his uncle and for Bruno, and ingratiated himself with the mob heavyweights from New York, whom Philip would interact with when visiting his uncle.

When my uncle was in Yardville it allowed him to get closer to Angelo Bruno, which was a good thing. Back then, my uncle had a lot of respect for Ange, and Ange respected my uncle because he knew my uncle was a killer, a gangster, and that my uncle was 100-percent committed to La Cosa Nostra. Once a week I used to drive my grandmother to see my uncle and I would take Ange's wife to see him. On the way back I would take them both out to lunch. Before long, my uncle and Ange had me taking messages back to their guys on the street in South Philly and Atlantic City. Guys like Phil Testa and Chuckie Merlino. At the end of each visit, me, my uncle and Ange would huddle in a corner and they would tell me who to see and what to say. I did exactly what they told me. I was still a teenager, 18, 19 years old. My uncle also started getting real close to guys like Jerry Catena, Nick Russo, Blackie Napoli, and Bobby Manna.

Gerardo "Jerry" Catena was a powerful captain in the Genovese crime family and had been a prominent underworld figure for more than 50 years, after joining forces with Lucky Luciano and Meyer Lansky in the 1920s during the legendary Castellammarese War.

Catena was the influential boss of the Genovese family's operation in Northern New Jersey and was one of four men who ran the family via a structured ruling panel following the imprisonment of family namesake Vito Genovese in 1959.

Raffaele "Ralph" Napoli, known as Blackie, was a mob solider associated with the Philadelphia mob's North Jersey operation based out of the Down Neck section of Newark.

Napoli's capo and direct superior was the powerful and treacherous Sicilian born Antonio "Tony Bananas" Caponigro, who would become Angelo Bruno's consigliere and the boss of the family's North Jersey crew.

Louis "Bobby" Manna was a rising star in the Genovese family and was a trusted member of the notorious Vincent "The Chin" Gigante's Greenwich Village crew.

My uncle and Bobby Manna became extremely close when they were in Yardville. They were the same age and spent a lot of time together. They would walk the track together and talk about their future plans. They were both considered up and comers in the mob and they were both very committed to La Cosa Nostra. *My uncle used to tell me, "Bobby is gonna be big one day, you watch." He would tap his index finger to his head and say "Bobby has this," meaning he had brains, that he was intelligent. My uncle would always say, "In* La Cosa Nostra, *in this thing, you need this," and he would tap his index finger to his head, "and you need this," and he would shape his finger like a gun and point it to the ground.*

A few years after Scarfo and Manna were released from Yardville, Nicky Scarfo's prediction came true about Bobby Manna when Manna's close friend, Vincent "The Chin" Gigante, became the boss of the Genovese family (and would eventually become the most powerful mob leader in the United States during the 1980s) and immediately named the "intelligent" Bobby Manna his consigliere, or third in command.

The relationship Nicky Scarfo cultivated with Bobby Manna during their "walk-talks" at Yardville State Prison would benefit Little Nicky and by extension Philip and play a profound role in shaping the Philadelphia–Atlantic City mob in the years and decades to come.

Philip had graduated from high school and was now becoming immersed in his uncle's secret world, *La Cosa Nostra*.

During the time my uncle was in Yardville, I flew down to Florida to see my father. I hadn't seen him since he left me and my mother when I was a little boy. He had an Italian restaurant in the Orlando area called Leonetti's. We spent a few days together, but that was basically the extent of my relationship with him. He died a few years later and that was it. From that point on, I was with my uncle every day.

College was out; life in *La Cosa Nostra* was in.

L'inizio [The Beginning]

H IS UNCLE'S PRISON TERM HAD BROUGHT PHILIP INTO THE MOB'S INNER CIRCLE. HE WAS ACTING AS A DRIVER FOR ANGELO BRUNO'S WIFE AND WAS DELIVERING MESSAGES FROM HIS UNCLE AND BRUNO TO THEIR RESPECTIVE CREWS IN SOUTH PHILA-DELPHIA AND ATLANTIC CITY.

He was rubbing shoulders with men like Jerry Catena, Nicky Russo, Blackie Napoli, and Bobby Manna.

He wasn't even 20 years old.

> On the days I didn't drive my grandmother and Ange's wife to Yardville, I'd go by myself to see my uncle or Ange and they would give me messages to take back to Philadelphia. Usually I'd bring the messages to Phil Testa or Chuckie Merlino. My uncle would also give me messages for the Blade, who was in Atlantic City.

Philip "Chicken Man" Testa was a man whose star was on the rise in the Philadelphia mob under Angelo Bruno and would soon be named the family's underboss.

When Scarfo's mentor Felix "Skinny Razor" DiTullio died in 1966, his immediate supervisor or captain became an old-time South Philly mobster named Alfred "Freddie" Iezzi, who was close with Testa. By extension, Scarfo had also become close with Phil Testa. Testa's son Salvatore, who was known on the streets as Salvie, was only a few years younger than Philip.

What Scarfo was doing by way of grooming Philip for life in the mob, Phil Testa was doing for Salvie.

> I had known Phil Testa and Salvie since I was a kid. When I was a baby, Phil Testa would watch me when my mother went shopping on Seventh Street in South Philadelphia. Salvie and I were always very close; he was one of my best friends. We were basically raised the same,

we were both taught about La Cosa Nostra *when we were very young. Me and my Uncle would go see them in Philly, or they would come see us at the Shore. Chuckie was also close with Phil Testa and Salvie.*

Salvatore "Chuckie" Merlino was Nicky Scarfo's closest friend. Merlino, who was 10 years younger than Scarfo, looked up to him like an older brother and Scarfo mentored him in the ways of *La Cosa Nostra*, just like Skinny Razor had done for him. Merlino had assisted Scarfo in the Reds Caruso killing and was by his side when he killed William Dugan in the Oregon Diner.

Now, with Scarfo behind bars, Chuckie Merlino was running Scarfo's operation in South Philadelphia and Atlantic City, carrying out Scarfo's orders in the messages that Philip delivered to him, messages that soon included murders that the imprisoned Scarfo wanted carried out.

Chuckie was a great guy and he loved my uncle. He understood La Cosa Nostra *from being around my uncle. My uncle had mentored Chuckie the same way Skinny Razor had mentored my uncle. Chuckie was a bookmaker and had his own crew in South Philadelphia, and they were all under my uncle, so they treated me with a lot of respect. When I'd go see him, we'd hang out together at the 9M Bar downtown; that was one of Chuckie's main hangouts. He also had a social club at the corner of Shunk and Sartain Streets in South Philadelphia where there were always a handful of neighborhood guys playing cards or we would go to the city's best restaurants like the Saloon or Bookbinders. Chuckie was a lot of fun, and I enjoyed being around him. He was a very classy guy and always dressed real sharp. He looked like the singer Al Martino who was also from South Philadelphia and had played Johnny Fontane in the* Godfather *movies. But most importantly he was fiercely loyal to my uncle. My uncle used to confide in him; he trusted Chuckie.*

Another one of Scarfo's close underworld associates was Nicholas "Nick the Blade" Virgilio, who was two years older than Little Nicky and a boyhood friend of Scarfo going back to their teenage days on Wharton Street in South Philadelphia. He would later join Scarfo in Atlantic City in the mid-1960s, becoming one of his bodyguards and top enforcers.

Like Scarfo and Leonetti, Virgilio and his family had left South Philadelphia and settled in a Ducktown row home right around the corner from the Scarfo compound on Georgia Avenue.

> We called him the Blade because he stabbed a guy eleven times and killed him. The guy was a sailor and him and the Blade got into an argument. It happened in 1952, the year before I was born in South Philadelphia. If someone who didn't know him would ask him, "Why do they call you the Blade?" he'd say, "Because I'm a sharp dresser. Sharp as a blade."

But Virgilio would prove to be versatile in his murderous ways.

While Scarfo was in Yardville, Virgilio had killed a man on an Atlantic City street corner, shooting him right in front of a marked Atlantic City police cruiser and as a result was looking at a long prison stretch.

> The Blade had a girlfriend whose stepfather was abusing her and she'd always cry to him about it. So one night when he was drunk, he sees the stepfather on the street and he shoots him, right in front of the cops. That was the Blade—he didn't give a fuck that the cops were right there. He'd shrug it off and say, "That fuckin' guy had it comin', I don't care who was watchin'."

From jail, Scarfo had arranged for the Blade to get a lenient sentence using a wheeler-dealer Atlantic City lawyer and part-time municipal court judge named Edwin "Eddie" Helfant. Helfant was paid $6,000 to pay off the judge in Virgilio's case in exchange for a reduced sentence. Helfant took the $6,000, and Virgilio got 15 years, not the lenient sentence he or Scarfo had in mind.

> The Blade was like Dr. Jekyll and Mr. Hyde. He was the nicest guy in the world when he was sober, but when he was drunk he was evil. He was like Skinny Razor and my uncle in the sense that was a no-nonsense stone-cold killer. The three of them used to hang together in Atlantic City in the early days, before Skinny Razor died. When my uncle got out of Yardville, the Blade was in prison. Judge Helfant had made a big mistake by crossing the Blade, but an even bigger mistake by crossing my uncle. On

the very day he was released from Yardville, my uncle told me he was going to kill Helfant. The fact that Helfant was a judge meant absolutely nothing to my uncle—my uncle didn't give a fuck. He'd say, "This Jew cocksucker wants to play games with me, we'll see about that."

A few days later he told me we were going to wait until the Blade got out of jail, because the Blade had gotten word to my uncle from jail that he wanted to do it himself. You've heard the phrase, forgive and forget? My uncle would never forgive and he would never forget. Once he got something in his mind, that was it, it was over.

When Scarfo got out of Yardville and returned to Atlantic City in the summer of 1973, his gang was beginning to take shape and things were on the upswing. In addition to Philip, who was now 20 years old and well schooled in the ways of La Cosa Nostra, Scarfo's two childhood friends, Salvatore "Chuckie" Merlino and Nicholas "Nick the Blade" Virgilio, formed the inner circle of Scarfo's gang.

With the Blade in jail and Merlino based in South Philadelphia, Scarfo decided it was time to infuse some new blood into his Atlantic City crew.

Among the new faces was Chuckie Merlino's younger brother Lawrence, who had recently relocated from South Philadelphia and was living in an apartment inside the Scarfo family compound on Georgia Avenue in Atlantic City.

Lawrence was a great guy and, like his brother Chuckie, he was very loyal to my uncle. He and I were closer in age, so we spent a lot of time together.

One time I was at a bar in Atlantic City with Vince Falcone and a few girls and I got into a fight with some kid who was involved in a local motorcycle gang. We were at a place called the Sand Bar and this guy tried to pick up the girl that I was with. So me and him got into it, we got into a fight, and it had gotten broken up and we ended up leaving the bar. So I go home and I grab a ski mask and a pistol and I go back to the bar, I walk right in and the kid was still there with his whole gang, a bunch of wannabe tough guys. I walked right up to him, raised the gun, and shot him in the arm. I wasn't trying to kill him, but I did want to send a message to him and his friends that you don't raise your hands to us. That's something my uncle always taught me. The guys he was with start running out of there. They are going out every exit, every door they could find. I think one of them jumped out the fuckin' window. This kid I shot, this fuckin' punk motherfucker is screaming, he's going nuts, he's crying like a little girl. This is in the early '70s, before the casinos. Later that night, around 1:00 a.m., here comes all these motorcycles down Georgia Avenue, revving up their engines, making all this fuckin' noise. They woke the whole neighborhood up. The leader of the gang is in the middle of the street and he is hollering, "Where's Philip Leonetti?" He started banging on the door and he woke up my grandparents. These guys are looking for me because they knew I shot their friend.

Lucky for him, neither me nor my uncle were home at the time. We woulda killed him right there in the street and left him in the gutter. The next day we hear all about it from my mother and my grandparents. My uncle asks me what happened at the bar and I tell him the whole story about the fight and me shooting the guy in the arm. The whole thing was no big deal to me. Now my uncle is furious. He tells me, "You find out who this big mouth, cocksuckin' jerk off is and where he lives and we're gonna send this mother-fucker and anyone connected to him a message, before they come around here and bother our people again. You understand?" My uncle told me to use Lawrence and he said, "I want everyone down here to get the message loud and clear."

So I tell Lawrence what my uncle said and we find out who the guy was and that he lived on Chelsea Avenue. My uncle takes me and Lawrence down there and we see his house and we work out a route back to Georgia Avenue for after we shoot him. So one night me and Lawrence are watching his place and we see him leaving and Lawrence jumps out with a .22 and he shoots him in the stomach a few times, which is exactly what my uncle had ordered. My uncle had said, "If he dies, he dies. If he doesn't, he doesn't. Him and his friends will get the message either way."

Lucky for the guy, he didn't die, and after that we didn't have any more problems with him or his gang and my uncle was happy. All the other tough guys in Atlantic City had gotten the message. Lawrence proved to my uncle that he would follow orders to a tee and that he wasn't afraid to use a gun. It showed my uncle that Lawrence was a solid guy and that Chuckie had taught him all about La Cosa Nostra.

Two local cement contractors named Alfredo Ferraro and Vincent Falcone, who had befriended both Scarfo and Leonetti and were constantly in their presence, and a business-savvy, street-smart Jewish gangster named Saul Kane, who had relocated to the Jersey Shore from North Philly, rounded out the core of Nicky Scarfo's Atlantic City crew in the mid-1970s.

I used to hang around a lot with Vincent Falcone, me and Lawrence. He was with me that night at the Sand Bar when I had the problems with the motorcycle guys. Vince was a few years older than me and he was married, but he used to go out and drink several nights a week. He always had a lot to say, he was very opinionated and had a bit of an ego. Vince was always complaining about money—who he owed, who owed him, how much he was making, how much other guys were making—just constant complaining. My uncle liked him but would always say, "He's not Cosa Nostra," *meaning he didn't have the right mindset or attitude.*

Alfredo was a bit older, and he and Vince were very close. Their families had come to the United States together from Argentina. They were both Italian, but they were from Argentina. My uncle, he'd say things like, "These two guys, they're not like us," meaning they didn't think like us. Both Alfredo and Vince were cement contractors and Alfredo had taught me the ins and outs of the concrete business.

Now Saul Kane was a character. He loved Meyer Lansky and he was Jewish, so we called him Meyer. Years later my uncle arranged for Saul to meet Meyer Lansky down in Florida. It was like a Catholic priest meeting the Pope. Saul was in heaven. Saul was a great guy and a lot of fun to be with. He owned a bar in Atlantic City, the My Way Lounge, and he worked as a bail bondsman. He used to hang out a lot with me and Lawrence either at the My Way or Teddy's West End Lounge on Trenton Avenue.

My uncle loved Saul and would do like he did with Bobby Manna, tap his index finger to his head, meaning Saul was smart. But he'd say, "He can never get this," and he'd rub his thumb and

index finger together, meaning his button, because he was Jew-
ish and not Italian. In this thing, La Cosa Nostra, *you had to be*
100-percent Italian to be made, that was one of the rules. We could
do business with Saul and he could be with us, but he could never
get straightened out and become a full-fledged member.

As Scarfo continued to build his mob crew, Atlantic City, the down-and-out seaside resort which Scarfo controlled, was about to be brought back to life with legalized casino gambling coming to town as a way to stimulate the once thriving resort.

Overnight, both Scarfo's and Atlantic City's futures began to look much brighter.

The World's Playground

THE CITY ON THE ATLANTIC WAS FOUNDED IN 1854. ITS NAME WAS A TESTAMENT TO ITS LOCATION, WHICH WAS BUTTRESSED BY THE PICTURESQUE SEASCAPE OF THE ATLANTIC OCEAN'S WATERFRONT. THIS NEW CITY WAS UNCHARTED TERRITORY AND QUICKLY BECAME A REAL ESTATE DEVELOPER'S DREAM, RIPE WITH COMMERCIAL OPPORTUNITY AND PROMISE.

From the moment that Atlantic City was incorporated, it was designed to appeal to tourists from all over the world as a premiere resort locale and vacation destination with sandy beaches, fine dining, world-class entertainment and some of the nation's most luxurious and lavish hotels.

The city's crown jewel, the Atlantic City Boardwalk, would be constructed in 1870 and was a seven-mile stretch of oceanfront property that featured a diverse array of decadence and commerce.

In 1878, the Philadelphia to Atlantic City railroad was constructed as a means of bringing tourists to the seaside resort.

In 1880, the city was officially open for business.

Within five years, Atlantic City was one of the top tourist attractions in the world and by the turn of the 20th century the area experienced a massive real estate boom, finding itself on the cutting edge of both hotel architecture and high-society culture.

Extravagant hotels and posh restaurants and nightclubs dotted every inch of the boardwalk and its surrounding area and the city became a playground for the country's rich and famous.

During Prohibition, Enoch "Nucky" Johnson, the colorful Atlantic County treasurer and racketeer ushered in an era that bolstered more corruption and decadence than the notoriously crooked coastal enclave had ever seen.

Controlling the state's extremely powerful Republican political machine with an iron fist, Johnson became the unofficial ambassador for Atlantic City and oversaw a wide array of vice rackets that included bootlegging, illegal gambling, and prostitution. Nucky encouraged racketeers from all over the country to set up shop in Atlantic City and many obliged him, paying him for the opportunity to do so.

The city by the Atlantic was now the World's Playground. With booze and broads by the boatload, it became the mecca of vice, in essence, the original Sin City long before modern Las Vegas was even contemplated.

Nucky Johnson's life would forever be memorialized in HBO's popular television series *Boardwalk Empire*, which chronicled Atlantic City in the 1920s from the perspective of a corrupt political boss named Enoch "Nucky" Thompson, a character played by actor Steve Buscemi and loosely based on Johnson and his political regime.

Nucky Johnson's reign as both Atlantic City's political boss and top vice lord crumbled in 1941 when he was convicted on charges of tax evasion for hiding proceeds from several policy lottery operations he was running throughout the city. He was sent off to federal prison for the next few years.

As World War II came to an end, so did Atlantic City's tenure as the World's Playground.

By the 1950s, Atlantic City had lost its luster. Year-round tropical destinations like Florida, Cuba, and the Bahamas had become cheaper and more popular alternatives with everyday Americans and the rich and famous, also heading west for Las Vegas, the up-and-coming desert oasis that had by then eclipsed Atlantic City as the new mecca of vice.

With the Atlantic City Boardwalk decaying and poverty engulfing the city's economy, most of the grand hotels of yesteryear, like the Breakers, the Shelbourne, the Traymore, the Mayflower, and the Marlborough, were all demolished.

Drugs and crime replaced fun in the sun as the region's most prominent features. Press coverage of the city's plight, stemming from the conditions encountered by the national media when they descended on Atlantic City for the 1964 Democratic Convention sent tourists scurrying.

As the late 1960s became the early 1970s, the once bustling resort town had gone bust.

It was practically a ghost town.

It wouldn't be for long.

And the "boardwalk empire" that Little Nicky was building would make Nucky Johnson wet his tweed trousers.

The Resurrection

THE DATE WAS JUNE 2, 1977, AND EARLY THAT THURSDAY MORNING THERE WAS SOMETHING IN THE AIR—SOMETHING THAT HAD NOT BEEN PRESENT IN THESE PARTS FOR MORE THAN THREE DECADES.

Hope.

Hope that the big announcement, scheduled for noon at Kennedy Plaza, the ceremonious pavilion in front of the mammoth Convention Hall on the Atlantic City Boardwalk would restore the city to prominence.

Hope that the governor's announcement would breathe life into a city rapidly decaying under an increasing influx of crime, poverty, and neglect.

Hope that the second coming of Atlantic City was imminent and that the World's Playground was about to be resurrected.

It was hope that filled the air that Thursday morning, hope mixed with optimism, skepticism, and a palpable sense of excitement that things were about to change.

As the crowd swelled, nearing 1,000, the dignitaries begin to take their seats behind the podium on the makeshift stage. Francis "Hap" Farley, the once powerful state senator who succeeded Nucky Johnson as the boss of the Republican political machine that controlled Atlantic City, was already seated. Once considered the most feared politician in the state, Farley was now a shell of his former self, and on this day he was merely a spectator.

Seated near Farley was the man who dethroned him, Atlantic City's new state senator Dr. Joseph McGahn, the cosponsor of the bill that was about to change Atlantic City forever, the man who was once lauded by the *New York Times* as the "principal architect" that made that change possible.

But the star of the show on this day, the man everyone came to see was New Jersey governor Brendan Byrne. Byrne was here to announce that legalized casino gambling was coming to the Atlantic City Boardwalk.

But Byrne's message of a renaissance for Atlantic City came with a warning—a warning for men like Angelo Bruno, Phil Testa, Nicky Scarfo, Nicholas "Nick the Blade" Virgilio, and Philip Leonetti:

"I have made this pledge before to all law enforcement agencies and I will repeat it again. We will keep the limelight of public opinion focused upon organized crime. I've said it before and I will repeat again to organized crime: keep your filthy hands off of Atlantic City; keep the hell out of our state."

At that very moment, less than four blocks away in a small ground-floor office located at 28 North Georgia Avenue, Nicodemo "Little Nicky" Scarfo and Philip "Crazy Phil" Leonetti—precisely two of the men that Byrne was speaking of—were watching the pomp and circumstance on live television.

"What's this guy talkin' about?" Scarfo said out loud to Leonetti, "Doesn't he know we're already here?"

Leonetti just laughed.

There was nothing funny about what would happen next.

Becoming a Killer

I N FACT, SCARFO HAD BEEN ATLANTIC CITY'S PRIMARY UNDER-
WORLD FIGURE FOR MORE THAN A DECADE, HAVING ASSUMED THE
POSITION LONG BEFORE ANYONE EVEN DREAMED OF LEGALIZED
CASINO GAMBLING AND A REBIRTH FOR ATLANTIC CITY.

*My uncle had built a nice little crew. For the most part it was
me, Chuckie, Lawrence, and the Blade. We were all with my uncle
and my uncle was basically reporting directly to Phil Testa, who by
now had become Ange's underboss. We were the top guys in Atlantic City. Everything down there went through us. Nobody made a
move or thought about making a move without checking with my
uncle first.*

*My uncle had two posters that hung on the wall of our office on
Georgia Avenue, each showing a baseball field with all of the bases and
home plate. My uncle never watched a game of baseball a day in his life
and he thought baseball players, athletes, and anyone who wasn't in
the mob were jerk offs. But these posters weren't about baseball to my
uncle; they symbolized his philosophy of being a gangster.*

*The first poster had the words "This is a Home Run" at the top
and showed the hitter rounding the bases, touching each base and
eventually crossing home plate. The second poster had the words
"This is NOT a Home Run" at the top and showed the hitter rounding the bases, but missing second base. My uncle would show people those posters and say, "Ya see what happened?" and he would
point to the second poster and say, "This motherfucker hit a home
run, but he didn't touch the base, so it didn't count. This thing we're
doin', this ain't baseball and this ain't a game. In this thing, if you
don't touch the base, you get this," and he would make his sign like
the sign of the gun. He wanted to know what everyone was doing at
all times. Touching base with your superiors in the mob was also
one of the rules.*

By this point Scarfo's reputation as a killer had made him the premier force to be reckoned with in Atlantic City, and in 1976 and when a low-level card shark and hustler named Louie DeMarco had run afoul of the Bruno mob and was hiding out in Scarfo's town, Angelo Bruno sent word from Philadelphia down to Nicky Scarfo in Atlantic City that DeMarco was to be killed.

Scarfo was happy to oblige.

This kid Louie DeMarco was robbing Chickie Narducci's crap games in Philadelphia. Chickie Narducci was one of Angelo Bruno's top guys. His crap games brought in a lot of money for the family. So Chickie Narducci goes and sees Phil Testa and Angelo Bruno and makes a beef about what is going on. Bruno and Testa tell Narducci they are gonna find Louie DeMarco and have him killed. Disrespecting a made guy is against the rules and Chickie Narducci was a made guy.

So what happens is, Phil Testa waits a week before calling my uncle and telling him that he wants us to kill Louie DeMarco for robbing Chickie Narducci. Phil Testa and Chickie Narducci had a kind of love/hate relationship. They were always on again, off again, and at the time they were having problems, so Phil Testa was kind of dogging it. My uncle was unhappy because Phil Testa waited a week and didn't tell him right away. My uncle wanted people to know what kind of people we were, that if we were asked to kill someone, we would do it right away, without any hesitation. Our philosophy was Bang! Bang! And that was that. So my uncle assigns the killing to me and Vince Falcone so we can prove to my uncle and guys like Ange and Phil Testa that we were killers and that we were serious men like my uncle.

So we put some feelers out on the street to see if anyone has a line on where this Louie DeMarco might be hiding out at. We hear that he is staying at the Ensign Motel on Pacific Avenue. So I go see a guy I know named Harry the Hat who had a coffee shop on Missouri Avenue. It was like a hangout; everybody would hang there. Harry the Hat was Skinny Razor's brother-in-law, and he knew everybody in Atlantic City. So I ask him if he knows who Louie DeMarco is and Harry the Hat pointed him out to me—he was actually sitting right there in the coffee shop playing cards. So I have Vince Falcone with me and we stay for a little while and when Louie DeMarco leaves, we follow him to the Ensign Motel. He has no idea who we are or that we are following him. There was a local bartender who was with us who had a room at the Ensign, and he gave us the key to his room so that we could wait until DeMarco came out of his room—so that we could get him.

Philip Leonetti, just 23 years old, was about commit his first murder.

I remember my uncle telling me and Vince that Chickie Narducci wanted this guy real bad and that if we killed him it would put me and Vince on the map with Philadelphia, which meant Angelo Bruno and Phil Testa and make my uncle's stature in the family stronger, because everyone would know that his crew was serious and that we were gangsters and killers.

I remember being nervous, but I wasn't scared. I didn't think I was doing anything wrong. Louie DeMarco was robbing Chickie Narducci and Chickie Narducci was in our family. Louie DeMarco had broken the rules and when you break the rules, you get killed. This is what my uncle had always taught me. This is what La Cosa Nostra *was all about. Before the money, before the power, before everything came the rules.*

Louie DeMarco was getting ready to leave his room at the Ensign Motel and he had no idea what was coming.

So we see him walking out and we run up on him. Me and Vince had masks and gloves on. We were behind him; he never saw us coming.

I was the first one to shoot and I blasted him right in the back of his head. After I shot him I thought he was running away, but it was the force of the bullet that made him fly forward and he landed face down. Then me and Vince just emptied our guns into him. I think the first shot killed him. We did it right in the parking lot, right on Pacific Avenue in broad daylight. I remember standing over him and emptying my gun into him. I remember the feeling I had; I felt cold and I didn't feel any remorse.

Louie DeMarco was dead and Philip Leonetti was now a bona fide mob killer, just like his uncle Nicky Scarfo.

My uncle had me and Vince go over an escape route a few days before the killing. We walked that route several times to make sure we knew where we were going. My uncle told us that after we killed him, he wanted us to throw the guns on the roof of a nearby building, which we did. We then followed the route that we had planned and my uncle was waiting there in a car to pick us up. We get in the car and no one says a word, we just drive to the apartment on Georgia Avenue.

Now a few days before the killing, my uncle took me and Vince for a walk-and-talk through the neighborhood. My uncle didn't discuss killings in the house, and he was paranoid about listening devices. He didn't own a phone. Everything with him was face to face. So while we are walking he's telling us that we can't wear any jewelry when we do a hit, in case it came off and could be traced back to us. He told us not to say a word when we got in the car and not to speak about the murder when we got back to Georgia Avenue. He told us we had to immediately take a shower and wash real good under our nails and make sure that we had gotten rid of any possible gunpowder residue. He told us to take all the clothes that we had worn and to put them in a trash bag. After we got cleaned up, we would have to go somewhere outside of Atlantic City and dump the bag with the clothes in it. That's what we did after a killing; that was the routine.

Just like the lessons his uncle had repeatedly taught him about the rules of *La Cosa Nostra* when he was a young boy, Nicodemo Scarfo was still the teacher and Philip was still his student, his most prized pupil.

Only now the lessons had advanced on how to commit murder.

And with the DeMarco killing under his belt, Philip had just graduated into the big leagues.

Chickie Narducci came down to see us, to thank us for what we had done. My uncle was ecstatic. The killing had enhanced not only his reputation within the mob, but mine as well. The guys in Philly knew what we were about, that we were killers, real gangsters. It's what my uncle always wanted, ever since he was around Skinny Razor.

It was a reputation that both Nicky Scarfo and Philip Leonetti would enhance, time and time again.

Sending a Message

SHORTLY AFTER THE DEMARCO KILLING, PHILIP HAD GONE INTO BUSINESS WITH A FRIEND OF HIS FROM THE NEIGHBORHOOD NAMED VINCE BANCHERI.

We needed $12,000 to buy equipment so we could start our own concrete company. I had been working with Alfredo, but I told my uncle I wanted to do my own thing and he agreed, so I went into a business with a friend of mine from the neighborhood. My partner Vince Bancheri burned his house down and we used the insurance money to start our company. So one night, me and Vince go out and we stop by the Flamingo Motel on Pacific Avenue; they had a lounge that a lot of people liked to go to. Judge Helfant, the guy that had double-crossed the Blade, owned it. My uncle still wanted to kill him, but the Blade was still in jail, so we put killing him on the back burner for the time being. My uncle would say, "Let it simmer; let it be until our friend comes home."

So when we go in to the lounge, we see this kid named Pepe Leva who was a bookmaker who hung around Judge Helfant and the Flamingo. Vince had loaned him $3,000, and Pepe Leva was talking bad about Vince, like threatening him to people around Atlantic City saying he wasn't going to pay him back. So Vince tells me about it and I called Pepe Leva over and asked him to step outside, I told him that I wanted to speak with him. So we go outside and I tell him, "You really shouldn't be threatening people." I tell him that Vince is my friend and I said, "You owe him the money; do the right thing and pay him." I'm talking to him like a gentleman, that's how I talked to people. I never came off like a tough guy unless I had to and usually at that point it wasn't me, it was the gun doing the talking.

Well this Pepe Leva starts talking sideways to me and I don't go for that, so I punched him right in the mouth and knocked his tooth out. There was no more talking nice to him. This is in the parking lot right in front of the Flamingo. Judge Helfant comes running out *and he is going nuts, yelling and screaming. He has no idea that we are going to kill him when the Blade gets out of jail. He thinks we don't we know that he kept the $6,000 for himself. He just sees me punch this Pepe Leva and he goes crazy. So me and Vince leave.*

The next day, Judge Helfant makes an appointment to see my uncle. I think they went to the Lido restaurant. Judge Helfant says to my uncle, "Nick, your nephew hit this kid and he wants to press charges." My uncle is placating him, telling him to relax. He says, "Take it easy, we're all friends. Tell the kid to relax and not to press charges, and we will straighten it all out."

On June 28, 1977, two days after his fight with Philip Leonetti, Giuseppe "Pepe" Leva filed a criminal complaint in the Atlantic City Municipal Court charging Philip Leonetti with assault.

So, what we did was, my uncle worked it out through one of his lawyers Harold Garber and Judge Helfant that me and Pepe Leva were going to meet and we were going to shake hands and bury the hatchet between us.

So the next day, Pepe Leva and I meet up at the My Way Lounge, which was Saul Kane's place, and my uncle makes us shake hands. He tells him, "We're all Italian. We need to stick together." My uncle tells him to go to the court and to drop the charges and to come back around the next day. So Pepe Leva comes back around the next day and tells me and my uncle that he dropped the charges and that he doesn't want any problems with us. My uncle put his arm around him and said, "We have no problem with you. You're a friend of Judge Helfant's. We're all friends." So as Pepe Leva is leaving he apologizes again and shakes hands with my uncle, and then he shakes my hand. My uncle says, "See, it's all over; we shake hands like gentlemen and that's the end of it."

Four days later on July 3, 1977, Pepe Leva was found shot to death with the remnants of four .32 caliber slugs in his head. His body was found near a landfill in the Farmington section of Egg Harbor Township, less than ten miles from the Georgia Avenue apartment building where Nicky Scarfo and Philip Leonetti lived.

Right after this Leva kid filed the charges against me, my uncle went to Philadelphia and got the okay from Angelo Bruno and Phil Testa to pop him, to kill him. This guy was going to testify against me and I might go to jail. My uncle wanted him dead even if that wasn't gonna happen because he had dropped the charges.

To my uncle it was a mortal sin that anyone would raise their hands to us or treat us with anything other than respect. That's why he wanted me and Lawrence to shoot the guy from the motorcycle gang and that's why he wanted Pepe Leva dead. He wanted to send a message to everyone that we weren't fuckin around. So he got permission to whack him out. That was another one of the rules—you always had to clear a murder with the boss or you might be the next one to get killed.

I was present when my uncle orderd the hit on Pepe Leva. A guy in our crew asked Pepe for a ride home from the city. On the way home, he said to Pepe, "Pull over, I gotta take a piss."

They got out to take a piss, and that's when he shot Pepe in the head. They had pulled into a trash dump, a landfill. He emptied his gun into Pepe and then finished taking his piss.

He then walked several miles through the woods to his home in the middle of the night. When we saw him a few days later, he was all cut up from the bushes. My uncle said to him, "Jesus Christ, what the fuck happened to you?" When he told my uncle what had happened and how he ran through the woods to get home, my uncle said, "Why didn't you take the fuckin' car; it was right there?" He tried to explain himself, but my uncle just shook his head and walked away. That's how he was. Nothing was ever good enough for him.

Nicky Scarfo's gang had all participated in murders, which ingratiated them to the bloodthirsty Scarfo and to the mob leaders in Philadelphia—men like Angelo Bruno, Philip Testa, and Frank "Chickie" Narducci—and would one day make them eligible for initiation into *La Cosa Nostra*.

Chuckie was with my uncle on the Reds Caruso hit; the Blade was in jail for murder; me and Vince Falcone had killed Louie DeMarco; Lawrence had shot the motorcycle guy; and now Pepe Leva was dead. My uncle loved it; he loved the killings. He used to say, "Do it cowboy style—bang 'em right out in the street in broad daylight." He wanted people to know that we were serious, that we weren't playing games.

The Atlantic County Prosecutors Office knew that Nicky Scarfo and his gang were serious and charged Philip Leonetti with the murder of Pepe Leva.

The detectives knew I didn't kill Pepe Leva because they had me under surveillance the night that he got killed. I was in a bar the whole night and they were in there watching me the whole time, those motherfuckers, but they tried to pin it on me anyway. They got a guy who worked at the trash dump where we did the killing to give a statement and identify me as the shooter. A couple weeks later the owner of the trash dump's wife called Harold Garber, who was one of our lawyers and told him what had happened and that the cops had made the guy say that it was me and that he wanted to set the record straight and tell the truth that it wasn't me. My uncle always hated the police, he called them all "no good dirty cocksuckers."

Now this woman used to hang out at the old Penguin Club that my uncle owned with Tommy Butch. So Harold has her bring the guy to Vince Sausto's insurance office and he takes a statement from him where he says is wasn't me who did the killing, which it wasn't. Now at the time the witness was being watched by two detectives from the prosecutors office who were protecting him from us. They were convinced that me and my uncle were going to kill this guy so he wouldn't be able to testify against me. The cops thought he was going to do some insurance business with Vince, so they waited outside. They had no idea that Harold was inside the office and that the guy was coming to give a statement that would ultimately kill their case against me. The guy turned out to be a stand-up guy and just wanted to tell the truth.

Based on the witness recantation, the murder charges against Philip Leonetti were dropped.

Scarfo and Leonetti's reputations were not only known in Atlantic City and Philadelphia, but in mob circles in North Jersey and New York, where guys like "Tony Bananas" Caponigro and Bobby Manna were updating their crews on what the gangsters in Atlantic City were up to.

What was about to happen next would put them in a whole different stratosphere.

The Payback

ONE OF NICKY SCARFO'S OLDEST FRIENDS AND TOP ASSOCIATES, NICHOLAS "NICK THE BLADE" VIRGILIO, HAD RECEIVED A 12- TO 15-YEAR SENTENCE FOR A 1972 KILLING THAT OCCURRED WHILE NICKY SCARFO WAS LOCKED UP IN YARDVILLE.

From behind bars, Scarfo, through his nephew Philip Leonetti and attorney Harold Garber, had arranged for a $6,000 bribe to be paid to the judge on the Blade's case in exchange for a lenient sentence.

The deal had been brokered using a wheeler-dealer Atlantic City lawyer and shyster named Edwin "Eddie" Helfant, himself a part-time municipal court judge who was facing an indictment for fixing cases in the Somers Point Municipal Court. Helfant owned the Flamingo Hotel in Atlantic City where Philip Leonetti and Pepe Leva had gotten into a fight eight days before he was killed.

Instead of paying off the judge in the Blade's case, Helfant kept the money for himself and split it with a friend—an associate of Nicky Scarfo's named Alvin Feldman. The Blade received a substantial prison sentence.

The double-cross would eventually cost both Eddie Helfant and Alvin Feldman their lives.

Back in 1972, when my uncle was in Yardville and he found out what Judge Helfant and Alvin Feldman did to the Blade, he went nuts. He was furious. I'd never seen him this angry. Adding to that, my uncle believed that Judge Helfant gave testimony to the SCI—the same commission my uncle, Angelo Bruno, Jerry Catena, Bobby Manna, and those guys refused to testify in front of—and that he had talked about my uncle and Ange to the SCI. My uncle also believed that Judge Helfant was talking to the FBI. He would say, "This guy is a double agent. He's no fuckin good."

Scarfo shared the same sentiment about his partner, Alvin Feldman.

This Alvin Feldman was no fuckin' good. He called himself the King of the Jews. He had a couple of dirty book stores with my uncle, and the word going around Atlantic City was that Alvin Feldman was going to kill my uncle by putting a bomb in his car. In addition, my uncle knew that he was ripping him off, skimming money from the businesses. This was going on before my uncle went to prison. My uncle used to say he was a "backstabbing cocksucker" but my uncle couldn't get the okay to kill him because, at the time, Alvin Feldman owed $60,000 to Pappy Ippolito, who was one of Ange's top guys. Ange told my uncle that once Pappy got his money back, my uncle could have him killed. I remember my uncle saying to me, "I wish I had the $60,000. I'd pay the Jew's debt to Pappy myself, that's how bad I want to whack this motherfucker."

So one day my uncle approached Ange in Yardville and told him he wanted to kill three people. He told him he wanted to kill his two partners in Atlantic City—Tommy Butch and Alvin Feldman— and that he wanted to kill Judge Helfant. After my uncle gave his reasoning for each of the killings and told Ange that he knew Pappy Ippolito had gotten his money back from Alvin Feldman, Ange gave him the okay to kill all three.

Thomas "Tommy Butch" Bucci ran the Penguin Club with Nicky Scarfo in the late 1960s and early '70s on Atlantic Avenue, near the corner of Virginia in Atlantic City. The lounge, which featured strippers, was considered a "bust-out" joint where the working girls tried to hustle male customers by enticing them to buy overpriced bottles of champagne.

The Penguin Club was a dump, but my uncle was making money there. My uncle was loaning money and making book out of there, but when my uncle went to jail, Tommy Butch stopped paying off the cops and eventually the place got shut down. This made my uncle furious and this is why he wanted to kill Tommy Butch.

He would say, "If this cheap motherfucker didn't stop paying those no-good greedy cocksuckers, I'd still be making money over there."

Bucci knew that Scarfo would want him dead and within weeks of the Penguin Club closing down, Tommy Butch left Atlantic City and resettled himself in South Philadelphia, working for Funzi and Mark Marconi, two guys that Scarfo knew well. The move would save Bucci's life.

When my uncle was younger, he and Mark Marconi were the best of friends but they had a falling. It was a big mess and it put a strain on their relationship. My uncle told me, "If Tommy Butch starts coming back down to Atlantic City, I want you to tell the Blade to kill him on the spot. If he stays in Philadelphia, I will leave him alone for now." This was before the Blade went to jail, probably 1971.

While Tommy Butch got a pass, the King of the Jews wasn't as lucky.

Joseph Scalleat was a member of our organization who was based in Northeastern Pennsylvania. He was part of Santo Idone's regime. Joseph Scalleat reaches out to Alvin Feldman and tells him that he wants his help in torching a warehouse in Pennsylvania, and Alvin Feldman goes for it, thinking it's a score. This guy never turned down an opportunity to make money. My uncle used to say, "This cocksucker is so greedy, he'd kill his own mother for 200 dollars." So once Scalleat gets Alvin to the warehouse, Santo Idone, Chickie Narducci, and Chickie Ciancaglini run up on him and start roughing him up. Santo Idone grabs him from behind and Chickie Narducci goes to stab him with an ice pick, but Alvin gets away and Chickie ends up stabbing Santo. As Alvin is running away, Ciancaglini grabs him and Ciancaglini is big and is strong as an ox.

The King of the Jews didn't have a chance.

Chickie ended up killing him with the ice pick while Ciancaglini held him, and they dumped his body down some sort of sewer out in the woods. When my uncle heard the details, he loved it.

He said, "I hope the rats in that sewer ate the eyeballs out of his fuckin' head."

Eddie Helfant, the third person Scarfo had gotten permission to whack was living on borrowed time, only he didn't know it.

> My uncle decided to wait for the Blade to get out of jail before they would kill him. He wanted to give the Blade the opportunity to kill him himself. When my uncle got out of jail, Judge Helfant came to see him and had concocted some story about the judge in the Blade's case taking the money and not doing the right thing. My uncle pretended like he bought it, but we knew he was lying. He was no good and my uncle had had enough of him.

But Scarfo decided to lull the unsuspecting Helfant into thinking everyone was okay, that all had been forgotten.

> Judge Helfant was having problems with his own indictment for fixing cases and he came to see my uncle for help. He wanted my uncle and Harold Garber to fly down to Atlanta and talk to one of the witnesses about not testifying. So my uncle flies down to Atlanta with Harold and meets with the witness and low and behold, the guy doesn't want to testify and now Judge Helfant might actually beat his case. So one day I'm having lunch with my uncle at the Madrid, Chuckie and Lawrence were with us, and Lawrence says, "Nick, why would you go all the way to Atlanta to help this guy, after everything he has done." So my uncle says, "I don't want him to go to jail, I want to kill him." That's the extent that he went to to set the trap for this guy. Like Louis DeMarco and Pepe Leva, Judge Helfant never saw it coming.

Loud and boisterous and somewhat tipsy, Helfant was in good spirits as his legal team expected to win a motion to dismiss his indictment in two days, thanks to Nicky Scarfo's recent trip to Atlanta, ending what had been a decade-long fight by prosecutors to put the crooked judge in jail.

Eddie Helfant was sitting on top of the world.

He had less than 30 seconds to enjoy the view.

Judge Helfant, his wife, and another couple were sitting at a table.

The Muhammad Ali–Leon Spinks fight was showing on a closed-circuit television behind them. As the snow fell on this cold February night, no one thought anything of the tall and somewhat lanky man who walked into the Flamingo with a snow shovel in his right hand and wearing a black ski mask. The man placed the snow shovel near the door and moved swiftly toward the judge's table, which had been pinpointed moments earlier by a spotter, who relayed the information to the man with the shovel.

The lounge was packed and dimly lit and no one seemed to pay attention to the man in the ski mask swiftly approaching the judge's table.

That was about to change.

Placing his left hand on the back of the man seated at Judge Helfant's table, the man in the black ski mask raised his right hand carrying a .38 caliber handgun and a six-year-old grudge and fired four shots at his target, one in the head and three in the chest, as his wife shrieked in horror.

The judge was dead before his body crumbled to the floor.

The man in the black mask calmly walked through the lounge toward the door and back out into the Flamingo's parking lot, the same lot where Judge Helfant had broken up the fight between Philip Leonetti and Pepe Leva. Now, less than a year later, both Pepe Leva and Judge Helfant were dead. And the man in the black mask, Nicholas "Nick the Blade" Virgilio, fresh out of jail after serving six years, had gotten his revenge.

As the Blade walked the escape route from the murder scene at the Flamingo, his old friend Nicky Scarfo was parked in a predetermined spot to drive him away just as he had done when Philip Leonetti and Vincent Falcone killed Louis DeMarco less than five blocks away three years earlier.

This was big, big news in Atlantic City and Philadelphia. The fact that a judge got killed—it made all the papers. Everyone was talking about it. The mob guys in South Philly and up in North Jersey knew it was us and a lot of the guys in New York took notice. My uncle loved the attention, especially the fact that other mob guys were talking about how ruthless we were. He would say to me, "We can hold our head high when we are around our friends," meaning other mob guys and other Families, "because everyone knows who we are and what we are, and there ain't too many guys out there like us."

My uncle saw himself as an old-school gangster, even though by this time he wasn't even 50 years old. He looked up to the old-time guys, the Capones and Lucianos and especially the killers, like Skinny Razor. And he was right; there wasn't too many guys like him in La Cosa Nostra. In fact, I don't think there was anyone who enjoyed killing as much as he did except maybe the Blade.

But the Blade wasn't all bad. He had a good side when he wasn't drinking or killing people. There was this kid who was around at that time who we called Bidda-Beep. He was a bookmaker and he was a good kid, he didn't bother anybody. He used to go to Harry the Hat's coffee shop and play cards and some of the older guys in there used to cheat him and take his money because he didn't know how to play all the games. They were hustling him. I guess the Blade had heard about it and one day when Bidda-Beep was playing cards in the coffee shop, who comes walking in but the Blade. Everyone in that shop knew who he was and that he was a serious, no-nonsense guy who was a killer and was around me and my uncle.

The Blade goes over to Bidda-Beep and taps him on the shoulder and says, "Let me play your hand." Bidda-Beep has no idea what's going on, but what's he gonna do, say no to the Blade? So he jumps up and the Blade sits down and tells the guy dealing to deal the cards. The guy deals and the Blade never turns his cards over and looks around the table at every one of the guys who had been robbin' Bidda-Beep and says, "I won; deal another hand." The dealer deals the next hand and the Blade does the same thing, he never looks at his cards and he says, "How 'bout that, I won again, deal another hand." This went on for almost an hour. He took every penny off of those guys, several thousand dollars, and handed it all to Bidda-Beep. No one ever cheated him again.

The Scarfo gang was now thriving in Atlantic City, but things in South Philadelphia were going from bad to worse for Scarfo's boss, Angelo Bruno.

Losing Control

I N 1979, CASINO GAMBLING WAS IN FULL SWING AND ATLANTIC CITY WAS IN THE MIDST OF A COMEBACK. REAL ESTATE DEVELOP-MENT WAS THRIVING AND CONSTRUCTION WAS BOOMING.

So were traditional mob rackets like bookmaking, loan sharking, and extortion. Nicky Scarfo and his crew had positioned themselves to cash in on all of it.

While things were looking up for the Scarfo crew in Atlantic City, longtime Philadelphia mob boss Angelo Bruno was slowly starting to lose control of the crime family he had overseen since 1959.

When Ange became boss, he aligned himself and the Philly mob with the Gambino family in New York. Ange and Carlo Gambino, the boss of the Gambinos, were very close and had worked together as bootleggers when they were younger. Carlo Gambino had used his influence on the Commission to help Ange win the dispute with Mr. Miggs, and that's how Ange became the boss and he remained loyal and indebted to Carlo Gambino. At the time, the Gambinos were the most powerful family in La Cosa Nostra *and Carlo Gambino, who was known as Don Carlo, was the* il capo di tutti capi, *the boss of all bosses, who sat at the head of the Commission.*

But in 1976, the 74-year-old Gambino would die from a heart attack and almost overnight it seemed that Angelo Bruno's power began to wane.

Around this time Angelo Bruno and Phil Testa started having problems with each other. Ange was the boss and Phil Testa was the underboss, but they were at odds about money and how to run the family. Ange was more of a white-collar guy and Phil Testa was a blue-collar guy, a street guy, so they both had different philoso-phies. There's an old saying that Sicilians love their money more than they love their children, and that they really love their chil-dren. With the Sicilians, it always came down to money and both

Ange and Phil Testa were hardheaded Sicilians. We called them siggys, which is slang for Sicilian.

So one day, we're at the office on Georgia Avenue and Ange comes down to see my uncle. It was in the summer and Ange used to have a home in Ventnor. Sometimes when he was down, I would be his driver. Ange knew that my uncle was 100-percent La Cosa Nostra, that he knew all the rules, all the moves, and knew all the angles better than some guys who had been around this thing for 50 years. He knows that there was no bullshitting my uncle. You had to always give it to him straight. He got to know my uncle real well when they were in Yardville together and me as well. We had already done the DeMarco hit for Chickie Narducci and Chickie was one of Ange's top guys, one of his top earners. He, too, was a hardheaded siggy.

At the time Chickie Narducci was also having problems with Phil Testa.

So Ange comes in and says, "Nick, you know that me and Phil Testa are having problems and I just wanted to see what side you were on."

Now here's the boss of the family and coming to see us about a problem he was having with the underboss. That's how far we had come. Angelo Bruno was the guy at my great-grandmother's wake, the guy I thought was the president when I was seven years old, and now he's coming to see us because he needs our help. He told my uncle that if you come with me and be on my side, it will be $1,000 per week for you, and the kids—meaning me, Lawrence, and Vince Falcone—would make $500 per week. Ange was trying to get us lined up against Phil Testa so that they could take him out and make Chickie Narducci the underboss. My uncle listens to all of this and says to Bruno, "What do you mean what side am I on? This is una familia, one family. Let me think it over."

My uncle always told me, "It don't matter what the guys in South Philly say, it matters what the guys in New York say, because only they can make or break a boss." That's something that Skinny Razor had taught him way back in the '50s, and he never forgot it. Now around this time my uncle and I were going to North Jersey quite a bit and spending time around guys like Caponigro and Bobby Manna, and getting their take on things. My uncle was a great listener and had an ability to get people to say more than they should. When we'd come

*back, my uncle would say, "If you wanna know what you're lookin'
at, you gotta look at the whole picture, otherwise what's the fuckin'
point?" What he was saying was that there was more goin' on then we
were aware of with this beef between Ange and Phil Testa, and with my
uncle. He always got to the bottom of things before he made his move.*

Nicky Scarfo, the boss of the family's Atlantic City operation knew
from his one-on-one meetings with Antonio "Tony Bananas" Caponigro,
the boss of the family's North Jersey operation, that Bruno was quickly
losing his grip over the North Jersey faction of the family.

Scarfo also confirmed this in his private meetings with Bobby
Manna, his old pal from Yardville, who told him that Bruno's days as boss
might be numbered.

*My uncle would always check things out, and if there was a way
to double-check, he'd double-check. He always knew what everyone
else's moves were gonna be before he made his move. He'd say, "In
this thing, in La Cosa Nostra, if you go off half cocked, you end up
with this," and he made the sign of the gun.*

Scarfo's separate meetings with Caponigro and Manna, and his belief
that Bruno was a sinking ship—more so than his loyalty to Phil Testa—
were the reasons for Little Nicky to turn down Bruno's request.

*So about a week or so later Ange comes around and him and my
uncle go outside for a walk and talk up Georgia Avenue towards the
Madrid. I'm walking a few feet behind them. I had a pistol on me.
I'm keepin' an eye out for the law and anyone who may have tried to
hit either one of them. I remember things were tense in the family
at this time and everyone was on edge. I hear my uncle say, "Listen,
Ange, this is una familia, I'm not on anyone's side. I know Phil a
long time and I'm friends with him and I know you a long time and
I'm friends with you. I know you guys will eventually work things
out." So basically my uncle told him, no. He turned Ange down and
Ange wasn't happy.*

Scarfo's refusal to side with the boss in his dispute with Phil Testa
did not sit well with Bruno, but Scarfo's decision was carefully measured.

You have to understand our family, the Philadelphia mob, controlled Philadelphia, Trenton, Atlantic City, North Jersey, and all points in between. Bruno was the boss of the family and Testa was the underboss, but they were both in South Philadelphia. My uncle was the boss of Atlantic City and Caponigro was the boss of North Jersey. My uncle and Caponigro were very much alike, in the sense that they were both killers, that they both had strong crews, and that they both had strong connections to New York.

I remember as Ange was driving away, my uncle told me, "I think Lefty's got some trouble coming his way and when it does, he ain't gonna know what the fuck hit him." As he was walking away he said to me, "Always watch out around these siggys; we can't trust 'em, they're not like us. The only things on their brain are greed and treason."

As 1979 was drawing to a close, Angelo Bruno had been the undisputed ruler of the Philadelphia mob for two decades. Nicknamed the Docile Don, Bruno was an underworld diplomat who preferred a conciliatory approach to dispute resolution, a sentiment not shared by his subordinates in Atlantic City, namely Philip Leonetti and Nicodemo Scarfo, and his consigliere, Antonio "Tony Bananas" Caponigro, based out of Newark.

In La Cosa Nostra, *you're either a racketeer or you're a gangster. Ange was a racketeer; we were gangsters. My uncle started sensing things changing with him and Ange after he turned him down on the thing with Phil Testa. My uncle started called Ange, Lefty, because he started throwing curveballs at us. My uncle would come back from a meeting and say, "Lefty threw us another curve," little stuff like that. I know that at the time Chickie Narducci was in Ange's ear, talking subversive about Phil Testa. You see Chickie Narducci was an earner, a multimillionaire. But he wanted power; the money wasn't enough for him. He wanted Ange to make him the underboss so that he could take over the family when Ange retired. It was just like my uncle said with the siggys; it was always greed and treason. They were treacherous people by their own nature, my uncle would say, "It's in their fuckin' blood."*

As if the growing rift between Bruno and his underboss, Philip Testa, wasn't bad enough, Bruno began to have problems with Little Nicky Scarfo in Atlantic City, as Scarfo grew more powerful and ambitious.

When they announced that the casinos were coming to Atlantic City, my uncle went to Philadelphia and had a sit-down with Ange to put it on record that he wanted Frank Gerace to run Local 54, which was the main union that was organizing hotel and restaurant workers in Atlantic City. This was going to the biggest moneymaker yet, better than bookmaking and loan sharking. If we controlled the union, we controlled the union's money, which meant we would have access to millions of dollars at any given time.

Frank Gerace was a bartender, and he was always around. His mother lived in one of the apartments on Georgia Avenue in our building. Now when my uncle went to Philly about the unions, no one else had gone on record about it, which means it should have directly gone to us, without any interference. You have to remember, by this time my uncle had been the only made guy in Atlantic City for more than ten years since Skinny Razor died, so he felt entitled to the unions, and he was right. They should have gone to us, no questions asked.

But what Ange did, he told my uncle, "Nick, let me think about it and I'll get back to you." Now this is what my uncle did to him on the Phil Testa thing and now Ange was kind of giving it back to him. I remember driving back to Atlantic City after the meeting and my uncle wasn't happy, but we never discussed business in the car. When we got back to Atlantic City we went to Scannicchio's for dinner. The owner, Vince Sausto, was a good friend of ours and he always took good care of us. Sometimes I'd go there for lunch and I'd end up eating lunch and dinner, staying for hours, talking and laughing with Vince. He was a great guy and a terrific friend. He was the absolute best. Vince was also an insurance agent and we had used his office to take the statement from the guy in the Pepe Leva case.

But on this night, following his meeting with Angelo Bruno regarding control of the unions in Atlantic City, Nicky Scarfo wasn't in the mood for laughing and joking.

My uncle said, "If this cocksucker, Lefty, tries to throw us a curve with this union business, there's going to be resistance and we ain't backin' down."

Now in all the years that I had been around my uncle, I had never once heard him curse Angelo Bruno. This was the first time. His colors changed, he really went in on him. You have to remember, Ange was the boss and my uncle was all about La Cosa Nostra, *the rules. The boss was the boss, and that's it. You never questioned the boss, you never talked subversive about the boss. If you did, you'd be killed. Those were the rules and my uncle lived by those rules, 24 hours a day, 7 days a week, 365 days a year. That's how committed he was to* La Cosa Nostra. *I remember saying, "Yeah, but what can we do, he's the boss," and my uncle's response was "Not all of our friends are happy with Lefty."*

Nicky Scarfo knew from his conversations with Genovese power broker Bobby Manna that Bruno's consigliere, Antonio "Tony Bananas" Caponigro, the family's North Jersey boss, was starting to question the effectiveness of Bruno's leadership.

Manna didn't learn this from Caponigro himself, as Caponigro—aware of Manna's close relationship with Scarfo—circumvented Manna and spoke directly to another powerful, old-school Genovese mobster named Frank "Funzi" Tieri he thought that he could trust.

Tieri relayed everything that Caponigro was telling him to both Manna and Vincent "The Chin" Gigante, the soon-to-be boss of the Genovese family. Tieri, Manna, and Gigante saw a major opportunity for the Genovese family when Caponigro started putting out feelers regarding a change in leadership should something unfortunate happen to Angelo Bruno.

Ange had aligned the Philly mob with the Gambinos. Ange had been very close to Carlo Gambino and when he died, Ange became close with his successor, Paul Castellano.

Philadelphia occupied a seat on the Commission and under Bruno Philadelphia was essentially a proxy vote for the Gambinos. If Bruno was eliminated and Caponigro succeeded him, Caponigro had assured Tieri that Philadelphia's proxy vote would go to the Genovese, tipping the balance of power on the Commission in favor of the Genovese.

The problem for Caponigro was that Bobby Manna had solicited similar information from Nicky Scarfo regarding the underboss Philip Testa.

Bobby Manna asked us to come see him in Hoboken. It was me, my uncle, Chuckie, and Bobby. We went to Casella's, a restaurant where Bobby did some of his business. While we were eating, Bobby asked my uncle, he said, "Nick, if God forbid something were to happen to Angelo and Phil Testa were to succeed him, I'd like to know where we would stand with your family." My uncle responded to him in Italian and said, "Una familia," which means, one family.

My uncle was basically telling him that should something happen to Ange and Phil Testa was named boss, that Philadelphia would align themselves with the Genovese. I remember Bobby saying, "My friends are going to be very happy to hear that."

The friends Manna referred to were the other members of Vincent "The Chin" Gigante's inner circle who were on the verge of assuming control of not only the Genovese crime family, but had their eye on a much bigger prize: control of the Commission, the governing body of *La Cosa Nostra*.

My uncle said to him, "Tell this guy," and he touched his chin, that's how we referenced Gigante, "that we know who our friends are and that's something we never forget." Bobby nodded and smiled and patted my uncle on the hand.

The ambitious Genovese mobsters, led by Bobby Manna and his boss, Vincent "The Chin" Gigante, were now in a powerful position, having assurances from Bruno's underboss and consigliere that should something happen to Bruno, Philadelphia would become their proxy vote.

Antonio Caponigro's top lieutenant in the North Jersey faction of the Bruno mob was Ralph "Blackie" Napoli, the same Blackie Napoli who used to walk the track at Yardville State prison with Bobby Manna and Nicky Scarfo. Manna knew that should something unfortunate happen to Caponigro, that Blackie Napoli would take over North Jersey and that the Genovese could influence him and, in essence, insert themselves into a position of power over the Bruno family's vast North Jersey operation, which included a thriving multimillion dollar gambling and loan-sharking business that the powerful Caponigro controlled with an iron fist.

This Machiavellian plot of treachery made both Angelo Bruno and Antonio Caponigro expendable to forward-thinking mafiosi like Funzi Tieri, Bobby Manna, and his boss Vincent "The Chin" Gigante. To them, the Brunos, the Caponigros, and the Napolis were pieces on one big *La Cosa Nostra* chessboard.

Now around this time Ange gets back to my uncle on what he wants to do with the unions in Atlantic City and just like my uncle predicted he throws us a curveball. He tells us that he wants to put John McCullough, who is with the roofers union in Philadelphia, and Ralph Natale, who is in the bartenders union out of Camden, in place to organize the hotel, restaurant, and casino workers in Atlantic City, ultimately shutting my uncle out. Chickie Narducci was very close with McCullough and this was another example of what he and Ange were up to. Their greed knew no end. Typical siggy shit. Now what they don't know is that it's easy to control a local, but if you want real power with a union, you have to control or have influence over the national. And when my uncle talked to Ange about the unions in Atlantic City, what he didn't tell him was that he had also talked to Bobby Manna because the Chin and the Genovese family were calling the shots. So there was absolutely no way for my uncle to lose, but Ange and Narducci didn't know this. Ange thought if he put his local in there that was it. But the Genovese were backing my uncle.

By the end of 1979, Angelo Bruno had no idea what was happening around him. While he and Chickie Narducci were trying to box out Phil Testa in South Philadelphia and now Nicky Scarfo in Atlantic City, he had no clue what was in store for him in 1980.

The Big Shot Is Dead

A S 1980 APPROACHED THINGS IN AND AROUND ATLANTIC CITY WERE STARTING TO HEAT UP FOR NICKY SCARFO AND HIS GANG.

After we killed Judge Helfant, there was a lot of heat on us in Atlantic City. Our names and pictures started appearing in the newspaper and everyone knew who we were. My uncle couldn't have been happier. He loved the publicity. There was this local radio talk show host named Mike Sherman who started calling me Crazy Phil. I hated the nickname, but my uncle said, "Are you kidding? Guys would pay money for a name like that."

Around this time Philip Leonetti's partnership with Vince Bancheri ended, and he and his uncle formed their own concrete company and named it Scarf, Inc.

Our office was on the ground floor of our building at 28 North Georgia Avenue in Atlantic City. My cousin Chris, who was my uncle's oldest son, came to work for Scarf, Inc. He was totally legit and never involved in anything connected to La Cosa Nostra. Him and my uncle would constantly argue about everything. They fought like cats and dogs.

Despite all of the heat on Nicky Scarfo and Philip Leonetti, Scarf, Inc. was able to secure site work on four casino projects that were being built in Atlantic City, including the short-lived Playboy Casino and what would eventually become Harrah's in the Marina District.

And Little Nicky and his nephew Crazy Phil weren't the only gangsters moonlighting as contractors. The Merlino brothers, trusted members of Scarfo's inner-circle formed a rebar company called Nat Nat and they too were doing site work on several casino projects.

Chuckie and Lawrence started Nat Nat right around this time and they worked out of the same office we used for Scarf, Inc. Every day it was the same crew hanging around Georgia Avenue waiting to speak to my uncle, or waiting to speak to me so that I would speak to my uncle for them. It would be me and Lawrence, the Blade, Saul Kane, my cousins Chris and Nicky Jr., and a couple of other guys. If Chuckie was down from Philly he'd be there, usually with his son Little Joey and Phil Testa's son Salvie. I always got along with Chuckie, but I never liked his son. He was a fresh kid and I always thought he was no good. Him and Nicky Jr. were the same age and they used to hang together with Lawrence's kids. Me and Salvie were very close. I had known him my whole life. What my uncle was doing with me, teaching me about La Cosa Nostra, Salvie's dad was doing with him.

This included learning not only the rules, but learning how to become a killer as well.

> *Right after we killed Judge Helfant, my uncle went to Phil Testa and Angelo Bruno and told them he wanted to kill a guy in South Philadelphia named Mickey Coco who had sold drugs to the son of Frank Monte, who was a made guy and had been close with my uncle since they were kids. Drugs were against the rules and my uncle detested drug dealers.*
>
> *That ruffled a lot of feathers with the old-timers that my uncle would come up to South Philadelphia and tell the boss and the underboss that they needed to kill a guy in their own backyard, in South Philadelphia. We were killing all of these guys in Atlantic City and everyone in the mob knew it. They knew we weren't playing around, that we were gangsters. But on the Mickey Coco hit, my uncle was basically telling Ange and Phil Testa, "This guy's selling drugs to the son of a member of this family. He's breaking the rules of La Cosa Nostra; he's gotta go. He needs to be killed and you guys shouldn't need me to come up from Atlantic City, 60 miles away and tell you when it's time do a killing." What he was saying, basically, was that this is how gangsters act: pay attention.*

Reports of Scarfo's moxie regarding ordering the hit on Mickey Coco began to circulate in neighborhood bars and social clubs in South Philadelphia, Newark, and on Mulberry Street in New York's Little Italy, just like it had after Scarfo whacked out crooked Judge Eddie Helfant.

There was no doubt about it: Angelo Bruno was a racketeer; Nicky Scarfo was the gangster.

Following Scarfo's lead, the plan to execute Michael "Mickey Coco" Cifelli began to take form and would manifest itself on a cold day in January when Salvatore "Chuckie" Merlino and Salvatore "Salvie" Testa, both wearing ski masks and carrying handguns, entered a neighborhood bar at the corner of Tenth and Wolf in South Philadelphia and shot Cifelli at point-blank range as he sat at the bar, sipping a beer and waiting to meet with Bobby Lumio, a Scarfo associate who was conveniently talking on a pay phone when the masked gunmen entered the bar.

> *My uncle wanted Chuckie to be one of the shooters because he had proposed him for membership into* La Cosa Nostra, *and in order to be made, you had to be 100-percent Italian and you had to have participated in a murder.*
>
> *Philip Testa wanted Salvie to be the other shooter because, like my uncle was doing with Chuckie, Phil Testa was proposing Salvie for membership. My uncle had also proposed Bobby Lumio for membership for his role in setting Mickey Coco up.*

As Nicky Scarfo became more of a force in *La Cosa Nostra*, he started to distance himself from members of his Atlantic City crew that he thought were dead weight.

Two men who fit that description were Alfredo Ferraro and Vincent Falcone, both of whom had been trusted members of Nicky Scarfo's gang since the early '70s.

> *My uncle decided he didn't want either of them around us anymore. He would say things like, "These two guys are useless," or "These two guys are holding us back." He grew to detest both of them.*

What happened next is vintage Nicky Scarfo.

> *Now Alfredo and Vince were the best of friends. They were Italian, but they came to the United States from Argentina and they came over together.*
>
> *They were very close these two. So my uncle decided that he wanted to kill Alfredo and he wanted Vince to be the shooter. Now*

if Vince doesn't kill Alfredo, my uncle will have him killed and then we'd kill Alfredo anyway. It's like killing two birds with one stone. So my uncle gives Vince the order to kill Alfredo and right away Vince is dogging it, making up excuses. Alfredo must have started getting vibes and he just disappears, he stops coming into Atlantic City. We stopped seeing him. But one night Vince is out drinking with Alfredo, and Chuckie and Lawrence bump into them, and they both get drunk and they tell Chuckie and Lawrence that my uncle is crazy and that we shouldn't be in the concrete business.

A few days later, my uncle and Chuckie end up going on vacation together to Italy and while they are there, Chuckie tells my uncle what Vince and Alfredo had said about us. My uncle told Chuckie, "When we get back I'm gonna whack 'em both."

And so begins the plan to kill Vincent Falcone.

My uncle never really liked Vince; he didn't think he was cut out for La Cosa Nostra. *My uncle would say about Vince and Alfredo, "They are not meant for* this thing," *meaning* La Cosa Nostra, *this thing of ours. Now Alfredo had stopped coming around. He even stopped doing business in Atlantic City with his concrete company. And even though my uncle wanted to kill him, it wasn't a top priority at the time. But now with Vince Falcone not following orders and then talking subversive to Chuckie and Lawrence about me and my uncle, my uncle became obsessed with killing him. He used to call Vince, "the Big Shot" when he spoke about killing him. He'd say things like, "We're gonna show the Big Shot who's in charge," and things like that. Vince had been around long enough to know how my uncle was and I think he knew that we were going to kill him, so like Alfredo did, Vince stopped coming around.*

Now at the time, Vince was married, but he was seeing a young girl who lived on Georgia Avenue right across the street from us. The girl's name was Maria, and she and her family had moved from South Philadelphia to Ducktown, just like we had. She was a beautiful young Italian girl with dark hair and a pretty face.

Now when Vince would pick her up or drop her off, he would never drive down Georgia Avenue because he knew we wanted to kill him.

I used to tell her that Vince was no good and that she should stop seeing him, but she was young and she didn't listen to me. There was something special about that girl, even back then I felt it.

But not every murder had to take place right away. Some were business, like the Louie DeMarco and Pepe Leva murders, and some were more personal like the Judge Helfant killing. To Nicky Scarfo, killing the Big Shot, Vincent Falcone, had become personal and just like he did with Judge Helfant, Scarfo set out to lull Falcone into a comfort zone and then kill him when he least expected it.

Now around this time a position opens up in the concrete union and my uncle puts the word out that he wants Vince Falcone to get it. This was a big deal and something that Vince had always wanted. So my uncle sets the trap and Vince goes for it. My uncle is acting like everything is fine, and now Vince starts coming around Georgia Avenue again. We are playing along like nothing ever happened. Me, Chuckie, Lawrence, the Blade—and Vince is doing the same because he really wants to be the boss of the concrete union. Now at this time Alfredo isn't around anymore, and Vince is hanging with a kid from South Philadelphia named Joe Salerno, who was a plumber.

Joe Salerno had borrowed $10,000 from me and my uncle and was paying us two and half points (or $250 per week) in interest on top of the $10,000 he owed us. It was a standard juice loan and at the time we were doing a lot of loan sharking. Every week I'd go out and pick up envelopes or guys would come to the office. Everybody paid because they knew our reputation. These types of loans were our bread and butter.

With the holidays approaching and the promise of a new job waiting for him in the New Year, Vincent Falcone thought he had a lot to look forward to.

He thought wrong.

My uncle organized a little party at a house in Margate nine days before Christmas. He was already there waiting for us to arrive. Lawrence had a Thunderbird at the time and he was driving.

I was sitting in the passenger's seat, and Vincent Falcone and Joe Salerno were in the backseat. It took us about ten minutes to drive from the office on Georgia Avenue to the house in Margate, which was right on the beach. Now my uncle is in the living room of the apartment on the second floor, and to get up there you had to climb a set of wooden steps that were adjacent to the outside of the house. The house was a two-story duplex. It was cold and windy and starting to get dark and you could hear the wind coming off of the ocean. Looking back on it, it was kind of eerie. I was wearing a black leather jacket and it was zipped all the way up and I had a .32 revolver tucked into my waistband. Lawrence and Joe Salerno were ahead of us and talking as they went up the steps. Joe Salerno had no idea what was going to happen, but Lawrence did. Now Vince is a few feet in front of me and I am behind him as we are going up the steps but he's kind of hesitating, like he's uncertain of what's going on.

He said, "Where's everybody at? I thought Chuckie was coming down." I put my hand on his back and said, "He'll be here; let's go inside and have some drinks," and kind of ushered him up the steps. His antenna was definitely up but I had positioned myself behind him so that if he decided not to go up the steps or if he tried to get away somehow, I would have blasted him right there.

When the four men reached the top of the steps, they walked into the apartment, where Little Nicky Scarfo was seated on a couch watching a football game waiting for them.

Little Nicky didn't just want Vincent Falcone to be killed; he wanted to be present when it took place.

This wasn't business; it was personal.

While most powerful mob leaders would seek to insulate themselves from the murders they order, Scarfo wanted to bask in them and personally savior the experience in any way he could.

The Falcone killing also provided Scarfo with the opportunity to commit a murder alongside his nephew, to literally bind the two men together in what was becoming Scarfo's never ending bloodlust.

To Little Nicky, the entire universe seemed to revolve around three things: the mob, murder, and family, specifically in that order. The killing of Vincent Falcone in the manner he foresaw, gave him the chance to combine all three of these at the same time in one giant orgy of death, lineage, and *La Cosa Nostra*.

> *When we walked in, Vince kind of froze and I continued to usher him inside and to break the little bit of tension that was in the room, I said, "Come on, Vince, let's make some drinks." My uncle, who was still in the living room watching TV, said, "Hey, Vince, bring me a Cutty and some water."*
>
> *Now, at the time, Lawrence was in the dining room area talking with Joe Salerno, kind of distracting him. That was all happening within seconds of us walking into the apartment. So we grabbed the bottle of scotch for my uncle and put it on the kitchen table, and then I said, "Vince, get some ice." When Vince started to walk away towards the refrigerator to get the ice, I reached into my jacket and took the gun from my waistband and I walked right behind him and blasted him right behind his right ear. As soon as I shoot him, his body propelled forward just like what happened to Louie DeMarco, and then he crashed into the refrigerator and crumbled to the floor.*
>
> *All the sudden, Joe Salerno starts going nuts. He says to my uncle, "Nick, I didn't do nothing," and then to me, "Philip, I didn't do nothing." He's like hyperventilating. My uncle watched the whole thing, he was watching as I shot him. Now he gets up from the couch and comes in and tries to calm Joe Salerno down. He says, "I know you didn't do nothing, Joe. Relax, everything is gonna be okay."*
>
> *Now Lawrence was standing two feet away from me when I hit him and somehow his eyebrow caught on fire—it got singed from the flame of the gun. So my uncle is trying to calm down Joe Salerno, Vince is on the ground bleeding, and Lawrence starts complaining about his eyebrow being on fire. So I say, "Jesus Christ Lawrence, you knew I was gonna shoot him. Why the fuck were you standing so close to him?"*
>
> *With all of this going on my uncle manages to calm down Joe Salerno.*
>
> *My uncle comes over to where Vince is lying and kneels down next to him and says, "He's still breathing, give him another one right here," and he moves Vince's jacket a bit and points to his heart. So Vince is lying there and there is a pool of blood forming*

underneath of him and he is like gurgling, trying to breath and I stood over him and raised the gun and shot him one more time in the chest. The impact of the second shot caused his body to jerk and then that was it, he was dead.

At this point my uncle was ecstatic. He jumped to his feet and said, "The big shot is dead, look at him," and he kind of mocked him by gesturing to the body and called him a "piece of shit cocksucker." He was actually cursing at the corpse. Now I have the gun in my hand and I turn to Joe Salerno, who is standing right there and I look him dead in the eye and I said, "He was a no good mother-fucker. I wish I could bring him to life so I could him kill again." I was prepared to kill Joe Salerno, too. I didn't give a fuck; I woulda shot him right there on the spot without any hesitation, but he stopped carrying on.

Scarfo then resumed his role as coach and articulated precisely what would happen next; he didn't miss a beat.

He said to Lawrence, "You drive Philip back to the office and bring back Vince's car. Me and Joe will stay here and clean up." Now Lawrence drives me back to Georgia Avenue and I take all of my clothes off, put them in a bag, and I get right into the shower. I'm scrubbing under my nails, the whole bit. Just like I had done after the DeMarco hit. Now I'm dressed and I go downstairs to the office and Chuckie and the Blade were there. We were all waiting for my uncle to get back.

Now I see someone walk by the window and I recognize that it's Maria from across the street. So I go outside to see what she wants, and she tells me that she noticed that Vince's car had been moved and did I know where he was. Now what was I going to tell her: yeah, he's in the trunk of his car. I can't say nothing, so I said, "I don't know where Vince is." After she leaves I go back in the office with Chuckie and the Blade, and while we are waiting for my uncle to get back I call up a friend of mine named Joe Disco who was a DJ at a local radio station. He picks up and he says, "Hey, Philip, do you want to hear a song?" So I tell him, "Yeah, Joe, play that song, 'Do or Die,' " and he plays it. Now Joe Disco was related to Sam Scafidi, who was a captain under Angelo Bruno based out of Vineland, New

Jersey. Sam Scafidi was one of the guys who helped my uncle when they killed Reds Caruso. I'm thinking if I ever get charged, I can bring Joe Disco in as a witness and he would testify that I had called the radio station. Joe Disco never knew the real reason I called.

Joe Salerno would later testify that while he and Nicky Scarfo cleaned the apartment, Scarfo told him, "You're one of us now," and patted him on the back before doling out more instructions.

"Tie him up like a cowboy with his hands and feet tied up behind him."

When Lawrence Merlino arrived back at the home about 30 minutes later, he discovered that Vince Falcone's body had been wrapped up in a blanket and tied up exactly as Scarfo had instructed.

He also discovered something else.

Lawrence told me when he got there that my uncle was fall-down drunk and he couldn't even stand up.

According to Salerno, while he followed Scarfo's instructions on tying up the body and cleaning the kitchen, Little Nicky sat at the kitchen table and drank the entire bottle of scotch that had been used as a ruse to trap Falcone, and was belittling the dead man and waxing philosophical about what the future held, not only for the Scarfo gang, but for the entire Philadelphia mob.

"When Lefty goes, I'm gonna be right next to Phil Testa and you're gonna be one of us," said a slurring Little Nicky to a shell-shocked Joe Salerno.

Following Scarfo's instructions, the men loaded Falcone's corpse into the trunk of the car they had retrieved, and Scarfo continued to celebrate, saying "I love this" as Falcone's body was lowered into the trunk.

Lawrence Merlino then got behind the wheel of Vince Falcone's car with Falcone's dead body in the trunk and abandoned it several blocks away on a desolate street, as another car being driven by Falcone, with Little Nicky in the backseat, pulled up beside him and the three men drove back to Atlantic City.

Margate was a resort town that was full of summer vacationers from Memorial Day to Labor Day, but nine days before Christmas, it was a ghost town—the perfect place to commit a murder and dump a body.

That night, following the killing, Scarfo, Lawrence Merlino, and Joe Salerno would return to the Scarfo compound on Georgia Avenue, where they encountered Philip Leonetti, Salvatore "Chuckie" Merlino, and Nicholas "Nick the Blade" Virgilio.

Merlino greeted them by saying, "Lights out, huh?" and gave celebratory hugs and kisses on the cheek to everyone present.

The five men then settled into Scarfo's dining room and feasted on a large, home-style Italian meal, while an extremely drunk and elated Little Nicky held court and talked in a hushed tone about who his next victims would be.

"I wanna cut this Alfredo's guts out and fry 'em in a pan. He makes me sick. Him and that no good cocksucker Mad Dog DiPasquale; we're gonna do him next."

Philip had never seen his uncle in such a state of delirium.

> *You woulda thought he won the lottery; that's how happy he was that we had killed Vince Falcone. I remember him kissing me on the cheek and telling me that he loved me. That was the first and only time that he did that, and he did it because he was drunk. My uncle never loved anyone or anything in his entire life, except for* La Cosa Nostra. *That's all he lived for. He didn't give a fuck about nothing else, that's how sick he was.*

Nicky Scarfo even planned a holiday of sorts for the men involved in the killing, telling them that they would travel to Philadelphia the next day for a relaxing steam bath in the shvitzing room of a decades-old, Russian-style bathhouse on Camac Street in South Philadelphia, to be followed by a celebratory dinner at one of Scarfo's favorite restaurants, the Saloon.

Scarfo's jubilation would be short-lived.

Within a matter of days the body of Vincent Falcone was found and detectives from the Atlantic County Major Crimes Squad were soon knocking on both Scarfo and Leonetti's doors.

> *So I'm in the office and these guys come around, two detectives. They had pictures of the body tied up in the trunk of the car. They say, "Look, Phil, can you help us out? We're not looking at you guys for this; we know that you and your uncle were friends with Vince. We want to show you what they did to him." I looked at the pictures and pretended I was sad, and I said, "Guys, I don't know nothing. I wish I did, Vince was my friend. I don't know who would do this to him." So after these guys leave, I drive down to Longport and grab*

my uncle. We had bought a house for him down there, but no one except for he and I knew about it. Our code name for the house was "toothpaste," because it was on Colgate Avenue.

He always had a girlfriend on the side, and whoever he was seeing, lived in that house. So I go down and I tell him what had just happened with the detectives. He was happy. He said, "Tell Lawrence and Joe Salerno to lay low for the next coupla weeks; let's let this thing die down." He tells me to pick him up in a couple of hours and that he wants to go to Scannicchio's for dinner, Vince Sausto's place.

When I get back to the office Lawrence was already there, waiting for me, and we went outside and I told him what had happened and what my uncle said about laying low. Lawrence said, "Got it," and told me he was going to go to Philly for a couple of days.

Now me and my uncle are eating dinner at Scannichio's and were both relaxed—we feel good that were not being booked for killing Vince.

All the sudden, who comes in but Joe Salerno, and he looks like he hasn't slept in a week. He's all worked up. He starts saying, "Nick, they're gonna know that that was my gun that killed him because it was a .32." My uncle says, "Calm down, Joe, there's a lot of .32s out there. No one's gonna know nothing. Just keep your mouth shut and everything's gonna be fine." Now a couple weeks before the killing, my uncle asked Joe Salerno, "Hey, Joe, do you have any guns?" Joe told him he had a .32 and my uncle said, "Bring it around, let me take a look at it." So a few days later Joe Salerno brings the gun around and my uncle tells him, "Let me hold on to this for a while." What's Joe Salerno gonna do, say no to my uncle? So we kept the gun and we ended up using it when we killed Vince Falcone.

Now the next day, the same detectives go see Joe Salerno at his house in Brigantine because they knew he hung around Vince. It's the same drill they did with me in the office: "We know he was your friend, we want to know who did it." And Joe Salerno cracks right on the spot. He says, "Philip Leonetti killed him and I was right there." Now these detectives can't believe what they are hearing, because they really didn't think that we were involved, but the more Joe Salerno talks, they realize he's telling the truth and they are ecstatic because they hated me and my uncle with a passion.

I mean, these guys wanted us dead. One time after we had Pepe Leva killed, a couple detectives scooped me up and threw me in a van and drove me out towards NAFAC, which is like a military airport 20 miles away from Atlantic City. They thought that I had threatened one of them, which I didn't, but as we were driving on this deserted road out by the airport, they slide open the door of the van and are hanging me outside like they are going to push me out. The van was going like 60 miles per hour at the time. They are telling me, "If anything happens to one of us, we will kill all of you. Do you understand?" They've got a gun to my head while I'm dangling out of the van. I stopped paying attention to them and started thinking about jumping and how I would land if I did. I remember thinking to myself, "These are the good guys?" But after a few minutes, they pulled me back in the van and took me back to Atlantic City. So I know that when Joe Salerno gives us up, to these guys it was like winning the Super Bowl.

Within a few hours, Joe Salerno was in protective custody giving law enforcement officials a play-by-play account of exactly what had happened to Vince Falcone.

It was clear that Joe Salerno had chosen not to accept Nicky Scarfo's invitation to join the mob.

The next thing you know, me, my uncle, and Lawrence are sitting in the Atlantic County Jail, and guess who's not there with us—Joe Salerno. We found out that the cops from Major Crimes went right to Joe Salerno's house in Brigantine, and he gave us right up. Now my uncle is pacing, like a tiger in a cage. Me, him, and Lawrence are sitting in the holding cell. My uncle is talking out loud to himself, and me and Lawrence are just sitting there. "This isn't good," he said, "This is gonna be bad. We're in trouble with this one." Now I'm sitting there thinking to myself, Jesus Christ, I can't believe how stupid I was to get arrested again for murder. First, the Pepe Leva thing, and now this. I was also angry with myself because I knew I should have shot Joe Salerno the way he was carrying on. I shoulda blasted him right there, and instead of ratting us out to the cops, he'd be in the trunk of the car with Vince. So while we were in the holding cell, my uncle says to me, "Call this cocksucker, Joe Salerno, and see if you can get a read on him."

So I call Joe's house and his wife answers and she puts him on. So I said, "Hey, Joe, what's going on?" And he said, "What's going on with you guys? I saw on TV that you guys got locked up. I know your uncle has to be going nuts in there with his allergies and all the dust in there." He was all worked up; just like he was the night we killed Vince. So I told him, "My uncle is fine, me and Lawrence are fine, we're all doing good." Then I asked him, "Did you go see that job in Brigantine? There was a contracting job that me and him were supposed to go look at it; we were going to work on it together." So Joe says, "I can't do nothing, the cops are everywhere." So I said, "Hey, Joe, why don't you come down and see us. I'd love to see you and I know my uncle and Lawrence would love to see you." And Joe says, "I can't, Philip, I got nine-thousand cops here, asking me questions." So I said, "Joe, we didn't do nothing wrong, did you do something wrong?" He said, "I didn't do nothing wrong, Philip." I said, "Don't worry about this. This is a big misunderstanding." He said, "I know, Philip." I said, "Just tell the truth, Joe. We didn't do anything to Vince. He was our friend." And Joe says, "Okay, Philip." So I hang up and I tell my uncle what he said and he just shakes his head. He sits down on the bench and he tells me and Lawrence, "Look, we got our hands full on this one with this Joe Salerno. But we're gonna make bail and we're gonna fight the case. We're gonna do whatever we gotta do to beat this thing."

Scarfo, Leonetti, and Merlino would spend the Christmas holiday in the Atlantic County Jail as detectives from the Atlantic County Major Crime Squad packed up Joe Salerno and his family, and moved them out of town and into the Witness Protection Program.

Our bails were $150,000 and we had the lawyers working on getting that together.

By New Year's Eve, all three defendants were out of jail and back on Georgia Avenue, awaiting a trial that was several months away.

As the clock struck midnight and the ball dropped in Times Square, the 1970s were over.

It was 1980.

The Ides of March, Part I (1980)

A S NICKY SCARFO, PHILIP LEONETTI, AND LAWRENCE MERLINO SETTLED INTO LIFE OUTSIDE OF THE ATLANTIC COUNTY JAIL, THEY WERE NOT ENTIRELY FREE.

Our bail restricted us from traveling outside of Atlantic County. That meant we weren't able to meet with guys like Caponigro or Bobby Manna to know what was going on in North Jersey or New York. Now remember, a few months before we killed Vince Falcone we had that dinner with Bobby Manna in North Jersey and that got my uncle's antenna up that something was going on, that maybe there was gonna be a move against Ange. Also, we were still going back and forth with Ange over the union dispute.

With our bail, we couldn't go to Philadelphia either. Chuckie and Salvie were coming down from Philly a few times a week to see us and let us know what was going on, but they didn't know anything about Caponigro or Bobby Manna; all they knew was the stuff in South Philly. So at the time, we were basically stuck in Atlantic City and out of the loop of what was really going on. My uncle said, "We're gonna let things play out and see what happens with Lefty," meaning Ange, "And we're gonna lay low for a while and get ready for this trial. If we don't win this trial nothing else matters because we're dead."

At the time, I was busy with Scarf, Inc. and Lawrence was busy with Nat Nat, his rod company. My uncle was meeting a lot with Harold, going over the discovery in the Falcone case with the lawyers.

Meanwhile, up in North Jersey, Antonio "Tony Bananas" Caponigro, the consigliere of the Bruno crime family, was doing everything but lying low; he was planning to assassinate his boss, longtime Philadelphia mob don Angelo Bruno and take over the family.

The Chicago-born Caponigro earned his nickname, Tony Bananas, from his early days in the underworld, when he ran a profitable sports book and juice loan operation out of a produce market in the Down Neck section of Newark.

As 1979 turned to 1980, he was the head of a growing intrafamily movement that opposed the old-school Bruno's strict opposition to allowing mobsters to engage in the extremely lucrative distribution of narcotics and his continued resistance to exploit the family's Atlantic City operation beyond the traditional street rackets, which at the time consisted primarily of gambling, loan sharking, and extortion under the careful watch of Nicodemo "Little Nicky" Scarfo, who ran Atlantic City, much like Caponigro ran North Jersey.

In the months prior to his death, Angelo Bruno had all but lost control of the crime family he had led for the previous two decades.

Bruno and his longtime underboss, Philip "Chicken Man" Testa, were feuding over money and power and not speaking with one another. Bruno was involved in a dispute over control of the Atlantic City casino unions with Nicky Scarfo, whom he had unsuccessfully tried to turn against Testa a few months prior.

And unbeknownst to the boss, the biggest threat came from Antonio "Tony Bananas" Caponigro, his trusted consigliere, who seemed to revel in the backstabbing politics and ruthless violence of mob life that Bruno had shunned for two decades.

The ambitious and treacherous Caponigro had started flirting with the idea of killing Bruno sometime around the summer of 1979 after a series of clandestine mob sit-down's with Frank "Funzi" Tieri, the powerful Genovese gangster who Caponigro thought had given him the green light to kill Bruno by telling him, "Our friends on the Commission said do what you gotta do."

For more than two decades, beginning in 1959, Bruno ran the Philly mob like a business, not like a gangster. He was considered a racketeer, and was dubbed the Docile Don by the local media. While the manner in which he ruled the underworld may have been docile, the manner in which he was about to die was not.

The bespectacled, soft-spoken Bruno was known as Ange to those who knew him well and Mr. Bruno to those who didn't. At around 10:30 p.m. on March 21, 1980, Bruno was sitting in the front passenger seat of a Chevy Caprice being driven by a young Sicilian-born mob associate named John Stanfa.

Bruno's normal driver, his trusted aide Raymond "Long John"

Martorano, had conspicuously made himself unavailable a short time earlier when it was time to drive the don home from a dinner meeting with subordinates at a popular South Philadelphia restaurant named Cous' Little Italy, which was owned by one of Bruno's capos, a siggy named Frank Sindone, and had previously been the site of Piccolo's 500 Club, which had been owned by Nicky Scarfo's uncles, the Piccolo brothers.

Over the last few months, Sindone, who was known as the Barracuda, had become close with Antonio "Tony Bananas" Caponigro. Sindone, who ran a very large gambling and loan sharking operation in South Philadelphia, seemed to share Caponigro's belief that Bruno was no longer the best fit to run the family.

Bruno was not aware of any of this as he accepted a kiss on the cheek from Sindone as he was leaving Cous' Little Italy that night. Some underworld observers believe that Sindone had purposely marked Bruno with the kiss of death.

As the Stanfa-driven Caprice approached Bruno's home, which sat at the corner of Ninth and Snyder in the heart of South Philadelphia, Bruno had no idea he was living the final seconds of his life. Waiting in the shadows with a sawed-off shotgun under his trench coat was Bruno's executioner, Antonio "Tony Bananas" Caponigro, the power-hungry and treacherous North Jersey mob leader who was Bruno's consigliere and had set in motion the palace coup to remove Bruno from power.

It was all about greed and treason, which was the Sicilian calling card, according to Nicky Scarfo.

As Stanfa pulled the car to the curb, he lowered the front passenger window so that Bruno could flick his cigarette into the gutter. As he did, Caponigro emerged from the shadows, removed the sawed-off shotgun from under his trench coat, aimed it square at the back of Bruno's head, and fired from close range.

The blast instantly killed the 69-year-old mob don.

Things would never be the same in the Philadelphia mob.

On the night that Ange got killed, I was at Caesars with the Blade. We had just finished eating dinner and we were downstairs in the lobby getting ready to leave. As we were leaving, we bumped into Sal Avena, who was Ange's longtime lawyer.

So Sal is making small talk with me about the Falcone case when all the sudden some guy he was with comes running up to him and says, "Oh, my God, they killed Ange. It's on TV. They shot him outside his home. He's dead."

Now Sal Avena is going nuts. He's saying, "Oh, my God, oh, my God." Me and the Blade tried to calm him down, but he was very upset. He and Ange were very close.

So me and the Blade leave Caesars and we are walking back to Georgia Avenue, which is a few blocks away. Now, as we are walking home, a black cat runs in front of us and the Blade goes nuts—he's very superstitious. He tells me, "First, Ange gets killed, and now this," meaning the cat. He says, "Come on, Philip, we gotta walk a different way to undo the bad luck from the cat." There was no arguing with him—he was dead serious. Here's this guy who is a stone-cold killer and he's spooked by this stupid black cat.

So we walk a few blocks out of our way until the Blade thinks we have undone the curse and we make it to Georgia Avenue. I go right up to my uncle's apartment and I ask him if he heard the big news. He was sitting on the couch reading a newspaper with his reading glasses on.

He put the paper down, took off his glasses, and motioned for me to follow him outside.

When we got outside he said, "What's the big news? What's going on?" So I tell him, "Ange is dead. He got shot outside his home."

My uncle made a face like he was he was both happy and surprised, and we went into the Scarf, Inc. office and watched what was going on, on TV. It was live on TV, all the Philly stations were carrying it.

A little while later Lawrence comes to the office and says he spoke to Chuckie, who was in South Philadelphia, and that everyone down there is going nuts trying to figure out what happened.

Chuckie also sent word that Phil Testa was sending Salvie down first thing in the morning with a message for my uncle.

Now, at the time, we couldn't leave Atlantic County because of our bail and Phil Testa couldn't come to New Jersey because the same SCI that had sent my uncle to Yardville wanted to give him a subpoena to testify. If he had gotten served he wouldn't have testified and he woulda wound up sitting in jail like my uncle and Ange when they went to Yardville.

So everything was being done through messengers.

The morning after the most sensational gangland killing in the history of the Philadelphia *La Cosa Nostra,* the heinous picture of the slain godfather's corpse, his mouth agape and missing most of his cranium, was splashed across newspaper front pages throughout the world and has since become an iconic image of crime in the 20th century, used in hundreds of print and television gangland retrospectives over the last three decades.

First thing in the morning, like clockwork here comes Salvie. It's like seven-thirty in the morning and he's by himself. Me, him and my uncle take a walk up Georgia Avenue towards Atlantic. There was a little coffee shop there that we used to go to called the Cup and Saucer.

While we're walking, Salvie says to my uncle, "My dad needs you to go to New York and find out what's going on. Nobody knows nothin'. No one knows who did it and no one knows who's in charge. It's chaos out there."

My uncle says, "I'll see what I can do, but we can't leave Atlantic City because of our bail restrictions, and these cocksuckers watch us all day. They don't let up."

As we're eating our breakfast, my uncle pulls me aside and tells me to call Harold Garber and to have him meet us on Georgia Avenue. So I excuse myself and I call Harold and give him the message and he says he'll be there in 20 minutes.

As we're walking back, my uncle says to Salvie, "Tell your father he's in charge, he's the underboss. That's the way it works in this thing, in La Cosa Nostra, *and don't let nobody tell him any different." My uncle says, "You make sure you guys are careful, watch out for this," and he shapes his finger like a gun, "because this plot may not be over." He says, "Give me a few days and I'll find out what is going on from my friends in New York."*

Salvie says good-bye and he drives off as Harold is pulling up.

My uncle says to Harold, "I need to go to North Jersey tomorrow I need you to make it happen." Harold says, "Nick, you can't go to North Jersey; you can't leave Atlantic County—you know that." My uncle cuts him off and says, "Find a way, Harold, work your magic, but I need to be in North Jersey tomorrow."

That morning, Scarfo's lawyer, Harold Garber, filed an emergency motion with the judge in the Falcone case seeking permission for Nicodemo Scarfo to travel from Atlantic City to Newark to meet with a criminal defense attorney he wanted to interview regarding the possibility of adding him to the defense team for the Falcone case.

So later that day Harold calls and he tells my uncle he's all set. He can go to Newark and meet with the lawyer the next day at 1:00 p.m.

Harold had a lawyer friend in Newark and this guy gave Harold the okay to let my uncle use his office for the meeting.

Now my uncle wants to get word to Bobby Manna that he wants to meet him, but my uncle didn't use telephones and neither did Bobby Manna. Normally we'd get word to Bobby using Blackie Napoli, but my uncle didn't want any of the North Jersey guys to know that he was coming up there, and even though my uncle and Blackie were tight, Blackie was Caponigro's right-hand man.

So my uncle has Lawrence call Chuckie and tell him that my uncle needs to see him right away in Atlantic City. An hour later, here comes Chuckie.

My uncle tells him, "I need you to go to New York and get word to Bobby Manna that I need a sit-down with him tomorrow." And he gives Chuckie the address to the lawyer's office in Newark, and on the paper it says 1:00 p.m.

Now Chuckie doesn't know these guys in New York like we do, but Bobby knew Chuckie and that he was with my uncle. So Chuckie leaves Atlantic City and goes to New York, to Greenwich Village, where my uncle told him to go.

I think it was a bakery. Chuckie leaves the message with the guy at the bakery and turns around and drives back to Atlantic City. He never sees Bobby, but this is how it was done.

So me, my uncle, Chuckie and Lawrence go for an early dinner at Angeloni's. This is the day after Ange is killed. All this happens within a few hours—the meeting with Salvie, Chuckie going to New York—and we start hearing bits and pieces about what happened. We knew that John Stanfa was the driver, and my uncle tells us at dinner, "I think the guy in North Jersey," meaning Caponigro, "and the Barracuda," meaning Sindone, "have something to do with this, and if I'm right, they have a few more names on their list," meaning Phil Testa, Chickie Narducci, and maybe even my uncle.

My uncle says, "Tomorrow when I meet with Bobby I'll find out exactly what's going on."

Chuckie says, "Nick, you want me to ride up with you? I mean, Christ, you could be walking into an ambush."

My uncle said, "Nothing's gonna happen to me. Bobby is with us. I'll be fine."

The next day my uncle is up early and he is showered and shaved and he is wearing a suit and heads up to Newark by himself. We had a black Cadillac at the time and that's the car that he drove. The night before I parked it a few blocks away so that he could sneak away on foot and get in the car without being picked up by any surveillance.

Now I'm in the Scarf, Inc. office all day and it seems like everyone and their brother are stopping in. Lawrence was there, the Blade was there, Chuckie and his son came down. Harold came by. Saul Kane was hanging around. Everyone was anxious, worried about my uncle going up there alone and also anxious at what Bobby Manna was going to tell him.

So around 4:00 p.m. the office phone rings; my cousin Chris answers it and hands it to me and says, "It's my dad."

I get on and he's talking to me in code. He says, "I'm gonna lie down and get some rest, call and wake me in about two hours," which meant he would be back in Atlantic City in two hours. Then he said, "I'm starting to feel a lot better, ever since I saw the doctor," which meant everything went well with Bobby Manna. Then he said, "If I'm feeling better, I want to have dinner with my friend tonight. Set it up." I knew by that he meant he wanted to have dinner with Phil Testa. Everything was always in code with my uncle; he constantly talked in circles. Sometimes Chuckie or the Blade would say, "You're losing me, Nick," which always made me laugh, but I was able to follow everything he was saying. I know what he was going to say before he said it, that's how well I knew him.

So I hang up and I clear the office out. I tell Chuckie that we need to get word to Salvie in Philadelphia and tell him that my uncle wants to see him and his father for dinner in Atlantic City. Chuckie says, "No problem."

So around six-thirty, seven, my uncle pulls up and maybe 20 minutes later here comes Salvie. He had already dropped his father off at the restaurant to avoid us all being seen.

We went to Scannicchio's and Vince sat us in the back and made sure that no one was seated around us, where we were was very private, secluded.

It was me, my uncle, Chuckie, Lawrence, Salvie, and Phil Testa.

My uncle starts off by saying, "It was North Jersey, Tony Bananas and his crew. Tony's making a play to take over the family and the Barracuda is with him."

Phil Testa just shook his head, said something in Italian and slammed his fist into the table and then said, "Okay, Nick, so what happens next?"

My uncle said, "Let New York get to the bottom of this plot and figure out what they're gonna do about it, but in the meantime you step up. You were the underboss and you become the acting boss, and we sit back and wait for New York."

Phil Testa proposed a toast to Ange's memory, and we all toasted, and then my uncle proposed a toast to the future, and we all toasted to that as well.

While we were eating, Phil Testa said, "If I get straightened out with this thing," meaning if New York made him the boss, "you guys are all gonna get made," meaning me, Chuckie, Salvie, and Lawrence.

And then we toasted to that.

While Scarfo, Leonetti, the Testas, and the Merlino brothers were busy toasting the past, present, and future at Scannicchio's, Antonio Caponigro and his crew were toasting to a very different future at Caponigro's club in Newark, the 311 Club.

That toast saw Tony Bananas as the new don and the Barracuda, Frank Sindone, as his underboss.

See Caponigro thought that he had the okay to kill Ange. When he went to Funzi Tieri, Tieri told him that he had gotten the okay from the Commission, but Tieri never presented it to the Commission; they would have never sanctioned it.

For one, Ange was close with Paul Castellano, who had the top seat on the Commission, and two, our family was aligned with the

Gambinos. If Funzi Tieri, who is with the Genovese, comes to the Commission and says, "Tony Bananas wants to kill Angelo Bruno," Castellano would have known it was designed to empower the Genovese, and Castellano wasn't stupid.

But apparently Antonio "Tony Bananas" Caponigro was.

So when Caponigro is talking to Funzi Tieri about killing Ange, he thinks he's talking to the boss, because everyone thought that Tieri was the boss, but he wasn't. The Chin was.

So Tieri strokes Caponigro along and all the while, Tieri, the Chin, and Bobby Manna are manipulating the whole thing. They want Ange dead so that my uncle gets the union, which benefits them. They also want Ange dead so that Philadelphia's Commission vote now goes with the Genovese and not the Gambinos, which benefits them, and on top of it, they want Caponigro dead so they can take his gambling and loan sharking operation, which is worth several million, which also benefits them.

A few years before all this, there was a beef between Caponigro and Funzi Tieri over a North Jersey bookmaking operation that Caponigro controlled, but Tieri was trying to move in on.

They took the dispute to the Commission and Ange backed Caponigro and since the Gambinos had the votes and we were with the Gambinos, the Commission voted in favor of Caponigro instead of Tieri.

While the ambitious Caponigro double-crossed Bruno, the ruthless old-school Brooklyn-bred gangster Tieri triple-crossed Caponigro.

Within a few days of Bruno's killing, Caponigro was called to a meeting inside a dingy social club in New York City's Greenwich Village that served as the primary headquarters of the Genovese crime family

Caponigro thought he was being called to the sit-down to be named the new boss of the Philadelphia mob, and, once again, Tony Bananas thought wrong.

Joining the 67-year-old Caponigro on this fateful trip was his 64-year-old brother-in-law Alfred "Freddie" Salerno, who was made to wait at the bar of a nearby Italian restaurant, as Caponigro was ushered into a private meeting with the hierarchy of the Genovese crime family, which included the cigar chomping Anthony "Fat Tony" Salerno, the treacherous Frank "Funzi" Tieri, the underworld power broker Bobby Manna, and the supreme leader of the Genovese crime family himself, Vincent "The Chin" Gigante.

Bobby Manna told me and my uncle what happened next: So Caponigro is called in and he sits down in a chair and faces Fat Tony, Tieri, Bobby Manna, and the Chin, who are seated across from him behind a table. So the Chin says, "We're here to find out who gave you permission to whack out your boss, Angelo Bruno. Can you tell us?" So Caponigro looks at Tieri, and Tieri looks back at him stone-faced. So Caponigro says, "Funzi told me I had the okay, that the Commission approved the hit." So the Chin says, "Frank, what's he talking about?" And Tieri looks at Caponigro and says, "I told you to straighten it out, not to kill him."

Sensing he had been double-crossed, Caponigro began pleading for his life with the men, but was already being beaten by Genovese enforcers, who had suddenly appeared in the room.

At the direction of Vincent "The Chin" Gigante, Caponigro was brutally and unmercifully tortured, sodomized, and murdered, sending a powerful message to the entire United States underworld that the unsanctioned killing of a boss would not be tolerated, certainly not by the likes of Vincent "The Chin" Gigante, who was now in prime position to be the head of the Commission.

As Caponigro's corpse lay dead in the clubhouse basement, several Genovese enforcers walked a few blocks to a nondescript Little Italy café to retrieve Caponigro's brother-in-law, Alfred "Freddie" Salerno, under the ruse that Tony Bananas had asked them to come and get him.

When the men arrived they discovered that Salerno was conversing with a man at the bar that one of them mistakenly believed was Nicky Scarfo and another man, whose identity they did not know. With the knowledge of what had just happened to Caponigro and what was about to happen to Salerno, one of the would-be Genovese hit men told the man they believed to be Scarfo and his companion to wait at the bar for Caponigro and Salerno to return.

The men walked Freddie Salerno into the prearranged death trap. Salerno, like Caponigro, never saw it coming. He too was brutally beaten, tortured, sodomized, and murdered, his corpse left to rot next to Caponigro's.

When the Genovese death squad reported back to Gigante, Manna, and the others that Caponigro and Salerno were dead, one of them mentioned that they believed Nicky Scarfo was sitting at a bar around the corner with another guy they didn't recognize.

Manna immediately ordered the men to go back to the bar and bring the two men to the Genovese clubhouse, as he knew that his men were mistaken.

The man at the bar was not Nicky Scarfo, it was John Stanfa, the young Sicilian-born mob associate who had driven Angelo Bruno home on the night that he was killed, and the man he was with was longtime Bruno mob captain Frank "the Barracuda" Sindone.

When the men returned to the bar moments later, Stanfa and Sindone were gone.

The next day after they killed Caponigro in New York, Blackie Napoli comes down to Atlantic City and tells us, "Tony's dead, his brother-in-law Freddie, too." He then says to my uncle, "Bobby wants to see you and Phil Testa in New York tomorrow."

Now with Caponigro dead, Blackie is the top guy in North Jersey. He was one of the guys in Yardville with my uncle and Bobby Manna. Blackie told me and my uncle that he is the one who gave Caponigro the shotgun that he used to kill Ange.

So my uncle calls for Salvie to come down from Philadelphia and he tells him, "Tell your dad, me and him gotta take a drive tomorrow."

Now me, my uncle, and Lawrence are still restricted, meaning we can't leave Atlantic County because of our bail in the Falcone case.

So my uncle says to me, "Find a way I can sneak out of here tomorrow through one of the back alleys and I will meet Phil Testa and Salvie a couple blocks away." Salvie was gonna drive his dad and my uncle to New York.

My uncle says, "Park the car right in front of the office on Georgia Avenue and I want you to stay outside all day in front of the office."

He's saying this because he wants me to attract the attention of the detectives that would watch us, so that he could sneak away, and then sneak back without getting caught.

The Scarfo compound on Georgia Avenue backed up to a maze of alleys and terraces that went in many different directions.

If you knew your way around back there, you could go a few blocks without anyone seeing you. It was perfect for us when we were trying to avoid the law.

So my uncle and Phil Testa go up to New York and meet the same group that killed Caponigro. It's basically the same setup, except this time the Chin tells Phil Testa that the Commission has decided that he is now the boss of the Philadelphia mob and that the Commission wants him to name my uncle either underboss or consigliere, and that the Commission wants anyone and everyone involved in Ange's death to be identified and killed. He also tells him that Blackie Napoli is to remain as boss of the family's North Jersey operation.

Now what Phil Testa doesn't know, but my uncle does, is that the main reason Ange is dead and now Caponigro, too, are the four guys sitting across from him in this room. They set it all up and now they want everyone who had a hand in it to be killed. That's how treacherous they were. But to them this was all about money and power, it was business and nothing personal.

The bodies of Antonio "Tony Bananas" Caponigro and Alfred "Freddie" Salerno were found stuffed in the trunk of a car on a deserted street in the South Bronx.

Their mutilated bodies had $5 bills stuffed in their mouths and in their anuses, a message from their killers that the men had become greedy.

A few days later Phil Testa called a meeting for the upper brass of the Philadelphia mob in a back room at Virgilio's, the popular Old City restaurant that he owned, which also served as his headquarters.

In attendance were longtime reputed South Philadelphia Bruno mob captains Santo "Big Santo" Idone, Joseph "Joe" Scafidi, Alfred "Freddie" Iezzi, John "Johnny" Cappello, and the newly appointed boss of the family's North Jersey operation, Ralph "Blackie" Napoli.

Nicodemo "Little Nicky" Scarfo, the boss of the family's Atlantic City operation, was also in attendance, having successfully avoided detection as he snuck out of Atlantic City, despite his bail restriction.

Scarfo would arrive at the meeting with his longtime pal, Louis

"Bobby" Manna, the Genovese family consigliere and mob power broker who had played a significant behind-the-scenes role in the deaths of both Bruno and Caponigro.

Manna's attendance was designed to both legitimize Testa as the family's new boss and to solidify the relationship between the new Bruno family leadership and the Genovese crime family, which Manna represented.

At the meeting, Phil Testa announced that Pete Casella would serve as underboss and that Nicky Scarfo would serve as consigliere.

> *Now my uncle doesn't say anything, but he was expecting to be underboss, not consigliere. Pete Casella was an old-time guy who was around Ange who had recently gotten out jail for dealing drugs. My uncle never fooled with drugs; the rules of* La Cosa Nostra *forbid it. Now we have a drug dealer as our underboss. The best way I can describe it is when John McCain picked, what's her name, Sarah Palin, to be his running mate in the 2008 Presidential election. Pete Casella as underboss? It had everybody scratchin' their heads, me and my uncle were stunned, but there was nothing we could do. In* La Cosa Nostra, *the boss is the boss.*

The once-stable Bruno crime family was off to a rocky start with new boss, Philip "Chicken Man" Testa, at the helm.

> *Almost immediately after he becomes the boss, true to his word, Phil Testa sends word to my uncle that he wants to make me, Salvie, Chuckie, and Lawrence—formally induct us into* La Cosa Nostra.
>
> *He knows that we have the Falcone trial coming up in a couple of months and he tells my uncle, "If, God forbid, you don't win, I want these kids"—meaning me and Lawrence—"to be able to go to jail as men," meaning as made members.*

Being initiated into *La Cosa Nostra* was the dream of every knock-around guy, every wannabe wise guy.

For Philip Leonetti, it was about to become a reality.

Blood Oath

PHILIP LEONETTI HAD ALL THE BONA FIDES NECESSARY TO BECOME A MADE MAN, A FULLY INITIATED MEMBER OF *LA COSA NOSTRA*, THE SECRET SOCIETY THAT LUCKY LUCIANO AND HIS FRIENDS HAD STARTED IN 1929.

He was a two-time killer who had personally ended the lives of a wayward hustler named Louie DeMarco, in 1976, and of a disobedient mob associate named Vincent Falcone in 1979.

He had been involved in the planning of two more mob murders: the 1977 murder of Pepe Leva and the 1978 killing of Municipal Court Judge Edwin Helfant.

He was the nephew and constant companion of Nicodemo "Little Nicky" Scarfo, the newly appointed consigliere of the Philadelphia mob and one of the most feared gangsters on the entire East Coast.

He had rubbed shoulders with men like Angelo Bruno and Antonio "Tony Bananas" Caponigro, both now deceased, and had maintained long relationships with their successors, Philip "Chicken Man" Testa and Ralph "Blackie" Napoli.

He was feared and respected on the streets of Atlantic City and South Philadelphia. He was known to the men in North Jersey and in the social clubs in Little Italy.

He was a "good kid" in the eyes of Bobby Manna, the powerful Genovese family consigliere, and, most importantly, his bloodlines were pure: he was 100-percent Italian.

He was only 27 years old.

It was June 8, 1980, a few months after Ange got killed and Phil Testa became the boss. The Falcone trial was less than two months away. One day my uncle takes me, Chuckie, and Lawrence to Scannicchio's for lunch.

While we were eating he tells us, "Tomorrow's gonna be your day for this," and he rubs his index finger and his thumb together, meaning the button. He tells us, "Don't be nervous, everything's gonna go nice and smooth."

So the next morning we were up early, showered and shaved and wearing our best suits. The night before I had borrowed a car from a friend and parked it a few blocks away. We left the Cadillac in front of the office on Georgia Avenue. So me, my uncle, and Lawrence sneak out the back of Georgia Avenue through the alleys and we make it to the car that I had parked on Texas Avenue.

As we're driving, my uncle tells us the ceremony is going to be at a house in South Philadelphia belonging to Pete Casella's brother-in-law Johnny Cappello. I'm driving, my uncle's in the passenger's seat and Lawrence is in the back. We had to pick up Chuckie, and then head to Johnny Cappello's house. As we're driving, my uncle is telling us all about the ceremony and what to expect. Because this was a clean car, we felt comfortable talking in it.

Now it's summertime and it's scorching hot out and my uncle doesn't like air conditioning because it bothers his allergies. So we're driving, and me and Lawrence are dying with the heat while he's talking. He's as cool as a cucumber, but we are melting. I catch Lawrence's eyes a few times in the backseat and we gave each other the look, but we can't say nothing.

So we pick up Chuckie and we head over to Johnny Cappello's house. People were arriving as we were. Blackie Napoli and Patty "Specs" Martirano were there from North Jersey. Sindone was there with Chick Ciancaglini. Pete Casella was there. Santo Idone was there. Freddie Iezzi, Chickie Narducci, and his son Frank were there. Coo Coo Johnny Grande was there with his son Salvatore, whom we all called Wayne. Frank Monte was there. The Blonde Babe was there. Even my great uncles, the Piccolo Brothers. I can't even remember everyone else, but the house was packed. The whole organization was there, the whole mob. When we walk in everyone is hugging and kissing us—me, my uncle, Chuckie, and Lawrence. Then Phil Testa and Salvie arrived, and the ceremony begins.

Phil Testa starts off by introducing the guys who were getting made to everyone in the room. It was me, Chuckie, Lawrence, Salvie, Frankie Narducci Jr., Wayne Grande, Pete Casella's brother Anthony, Bobby Lumio, and the Blonde Babe, old man Pungitore who were getting made that day.

They then put all of us into a room in the house away from the *group and a few minutes later the person who is sponsoring you comes to the room and gets you and brings you back to the group.*

Now before the ceremony started, the house was like a big party: everyone was carrying on and it was very loud. But now you can hear a pin drop.

When it was my turn, my uncle came back and got me and walked me into the room. Everyone was standing around a big table and Philip Testa was at the head of the table. On the table was a knife and a gun. On one side of Phil Testa was Pete Casella, the underboss, and on the other was my uncle, the consigliere.

Phil Testa said, "Philip, do you know why you are here?" And I said, "No I don't," and the whole room erupts in laughter. Of course, I knew why I was there, but you were supposed to say that you didn't. It was like a running joke. He said, "These men at this table, do you know who they are and why they are here?" I said, "Yes, I do." He said, "Do you have any problems with any of the men in this room, or know of any reason why you should not be here today?" I said, "No I do not." He said, "Would you like to join this thing of ours?" I said, "Yes, I would." And he asked me to step forward, closer to the table.

He pointed to the knife and the gun and he said, "Would you use these to protect your friends?" and I said, "Yes, I would." He said, "Would you place this brotherhood before everything that you love in your life?" I said, "Yes, I would." He said, "If you had a wife or a child and they were on their deathbed and we needed you, would you leave them and join us?" I said, "Yes I would."

Phil Testa then said something in Italian and the men in the room formed a circle and held hands. He instructed me to go around the room and greet everyone. So I went around the table and shook hands and kissed each man on both cheeks. When I got to the head of the table, I kissed my uncle, and then I kissed Phil Testa. My uncle used the pin from a small gold tie clip to prick my trigger finger, and then he told me to cup my hands. He had a small piece of paper with a picture of a saint on it, and he lit the paper on fire and placed it in my hands.

Phil Testa told me to repeat after him, and he said, "May I burn like this saint if I betray my friends," and he told me to keep saying it and saying it until the flame burned out.

Then he told me to go back around the room and greet the men like I did earlier, only this time when I made it around the table and got back to Phil Testa, the circle broke and Phil Testa said something in Italian with the words amici *and* La Cosa Nostra, *which meant "friend" and "this thing of ours," and then he took my hand and the circle was formed again, but now I was a part of it. I was a made man.*

The ceremony was repeated for each of the remaining proposed members, and then Phil Testa addressed the group and the men toasted one another with glasses of homemade red wine, which was meant to symbolize blood in the same way that it is used in the Catholic Church.

Then the house full of men feasted on a giant spread of Italian food.

The celebration for three of those men—Nicky Scarfo, Philip Leonetti, and Lawrence Merlino—had a dark cloud over it. It was their upcoming trial for the December 16, 1979, murder of Vincent Falcone. If they were convicted, they could spend the rest of their lives in prison.

Thank God for the American Jury System

From the moment we got arrested on the Falcone murder, my uncle was working on ways to beat the case. The first thing we did was put together our defense team.

Harold Garber, who was around us and was very close with my uncle, would represent my uncle in the trial. I used Edwin Jacobs, and Lawrence used a Philadelphia lawyer named Bobby Simone. Bobby made a name for himself representing a lot of made guys in Philadelphia, and him and my uncle had become friendly.

Jury selection was set to begin in early September 1980. I had moved into the Claridge Hotel and Casino during the trial so that I wouldn't be distracted. This trial meant everything to us; it was literally life or death for us.

The State of New Jersey v. Nicodemo Scarfo, et al., got underway in the Atlantic County Courthouse on Main Street in Mays Landing, approximately 15 miles away from Atlantic City.

The prosecutor was a man named Jeffrey Blitz, and we knew he hated us. The judge was a man named William Miller, and they had brought him in from another county to try the case. In the beginning of the case, the judge granted a motion by one of the television stations that would have allowed the trial to be broadcast live on television each day. At the time this was unheard of. That's how big this trial was.

I remember pulling up the first day of the trial. We were in my uncle's Cadillac. A man named Ed Harrell who worked for Bobby Simone as a private investigator was driving the car and Bobby was in the front seat. Ed was an absolute gentleman. He was a black guy and had been involved with Martin Luther King Jr. in the '60s. How he ended up with Bobby, or with me, my uncle and Lawrence, I'll never know.

As we're pulling up, there were news cameras and reporters everywhere. My uncle said, "Jesus Christ, Bobby, are they here for us?" and Bobby said, "I'm afraid so."

Ed dropped us off in the front of the courthouse, and we walked through the crowd. Bobby was saying, "No comment," as we pushed our way through. Inside, we met Harold Garber and Ed Jacobs.

Now when it comes time for opening arguments, Harold was the first to go. He was representing my uncle. He got up and said, "Ladies and gentlemen, my name is Harold Garber and I represent Nicodemo Scarfo. The evidence in this case will show that Mr. Scarfo is not guilty. Thank you," and then he sat down. That was his whole opening argument. If my uncle could have killed him right there, he would have.

Ed Jacobs and Bobby Simone used their opening arguments to destroy the credibility of Joe Salerno, who was the State's star witness.

Nine months removed from that fateful night in Margate, where Philip Leonetti pumped two bullets into Vincent Falcone, Joe Salerno and his family had already been whisked away from Brigantine and placed in the Witness Protection Program and relocated to Topeka, Kansas, where they were given new names and new identities.

Now, wearing a bulletproof vest and under the guard of US Marshals carrying machine guns, Joe Salerno was back in town.

I remember when Joe Salerno took the witness stand, we were trying to ice him, trying to scare him. But he never once looked in our direction the whole time he testified, and he was no less than 10 feet away from us.

The prosecutor had him tell the story of how he met us and how I had loaned him money and how he had given my uncle the guns; he told them everything.

That night we all went out to dinner. Me, my uncle, Lawrence, Harold, Bobby, Ed Jacobs, and I think Chuckie was with us. We went to Caesars. We were discussing the best ways to attack Joe Salerno's credibility. We were all very focused on winning this trial; it was as if nothing else was going on around us.

Well except for the thing with Johnny Keys.

John "Johnny Keys" Simone had been a made member of the Bruno crime family for a number of years and operated out of the Trenton area. Simone, who was 70 years old, was a distant cousin of Bruno's and had formed a close relationship with the Gambino crime family in New York through a Trenton-based Gambino capo named Nicholas "Nicky" Russo, who reported directly to Gambino boss Paul Castellano and had been one of the Yardville 9 in the early '70s with Angelo Bruno and Nicky Scarfo.

Simone was sending messages to Castellano through Russo that he was interested in taking out Phil Testa and becoming boss of the Phila-delphia mob, much the same way Antonio "Tony Bananas" Caponigro had tried to do with Angelo Bruno.

But Caponigro and Bruno were now both dead.

Word gets back to my uncle that Johnny Keys was plotting against Phil Testa and was doing so through the Gambinos. My uncle reports this to Bobby Manna in New York, and Bobby says he is going to look into it. A few days later Bobby sent word down that he is sending a kid down named Sammy Gravano, who is with the Gambinos, to talk to us about it. He tells us we can trust him, that this Sammy is La Cosa Nostra *and respected by all of the Families in New York. Sammy was known as a hitter, a killer, and Bobby said to my uncle and me, "This guy is your kind of guy."*

So one night Sammy comes down and we meet him inside the lobby lounge at Bally's Park Place for a couple of drinks to get acquainted, and then we take him to Angelo's for dinner. It's me, him, and my uncle.

He tells us, "Look I don't know this guy Johnny Keys and quite frankly I don't give a fuck. He's trying to make problems for you and your family, then me and my crew are gonna make problems for him. I got the okay from Paul to whack this guy out for talking treason against your boss. Just give me some time and it will be done. Me and my crew are gonna handle this guy personally."

I could tell that my uncle was impressed by him and the manner in which he carried himself. He was very respectful and very straightforward, there no was bullshit with him. We ended up having a very nice dinner and spent a couple of hours talking about La Cosa Nostra. *Sammy knew this thing inside and out. That was the first time I met Sammy the Bull, and it wouldn't be the last.*

A few weeks later, the bullet-ridden body of John "Johnny Keys" Simone was found in a Staten Island landfill.

The hit team led by the up-and-coming Gambino family hit man, Salvatore "Sammy the Bull" Gravano, had kidnapped Simone from the parking lot of a posh country club on the outskirts of Trenton and drove him to a secluded area in Staten Island and pumped several bullets into the back of his head.

When we heard that Sammy's crew had killed Johnny Keys we were relieved. It gave us the opportunity to focus our attention on our trial.

Now this trial was live on TV every day. We had the highest ratings in the area. At the time, there was a show on TV called Shogun, *which was the No. 1 show, and we beat them in the ratings.*

But Joe Salerno was telling the jury everything about the night we killed Vince. Every detail. How I pulled out the gun, how I shot him, what I said. He gave the jury a play-by-play of everything that happened. I thought to myself: we're dead, we're finished.

When it's time for cross-examination, Harold and Ed Jacobs did a good job of going at him, but Lawrence's lawyer, Bobby Simone, destroyed him. Bobby made Joe Salerno look like a liar, even though every word he was saying was the truth.

Now Joe Salerno was the State's whole case. If we were able to neutralize him, we had a shot at winning.

Now when the State rested, we had a meeting. It was all the defendants and all the lawyers. We were in one of those little conference rooms in the courthouse.

Bobby Simone said, "I think I can win a Motion to Dismiss on behalf of Lawrence based on the fact that he didn't pull the trigger or order the murder. If I make the motion and win, me and Lawrence are out of the case."

Now like I said before Bobby was the best lawyer I have ever seen try a case. He had destroyed Joe Salerno on the stand. I wanted him in the case for closing arguments and so did my uncle.

My uncle asked the lawyers to step outside for a few minutes so that me, him, and Lawrence could talk privately.

My uncle said, "What do you want to do, Lawrence? Do you want Bobby to do that motion for you?" Now Lawrence knows if Bobby does the motion, he's probably going to win it and he would go home free. Lawrence knows that I am on the hook more than anyone, because Joe Salerno ID'd me as the killer. Lawrence turns to me and he says, "What do you think, Philip? What should I do?"

Now I'm torn. Because if I tell Lawrence to do the motion and he wins, Bobby Simone can't do the closing argument, and I thought my best chance of winning was Bobby speaking to the jury for all of us. The flip side is, Lawrence is my friend and if he can get out of this thing, then it's better for him.

I say, "I don't know Lawrence, that's a tough one."

Lawrence says to my uncle, "Nick, what do you think?"

My uncle says, "I'd hate to lose Bobby, but you do what you think is best for you."

We bring the lawyers back in and Bobby says to Lawrence, "So what are we doing about the motion?" And Lawrence looks at me and my uncle and says, "Fuck it. No motion. We win together or we lose together."

I was so relieved, I hugged Lawrence and kissed him on the

cheek. My uncle did, too. We went back into court feeling like we had a good chance at winning.

After closing arguments, we were feeling really good. Bobby was amazing. Harold waited until the end to tell me and my uncle that he knew one of the jurors, a guy who was a liquor salesman, and that the guy would not vote against us. So at best, Harold said the jury would be hung.

My uncle said, "You knew that this whole time and you wait until now to tell us?" This was the second time during the trial that my uncle looked like he wanted to kill Harold.

I remember Bobby said, "Is that why your opening argument was only 30 seconds," and everyone laughed. A few minutes later they told us that the jury had reached a unanimous verdict.

We all stopped laughing and everyone got very serious. We thanked the lawyers, and they rushed off into the courtroom. Then me, my uncle, and Lawrence spoke privately for a few minutes, and my uncle said, "I think we're gonna beat this thing."

We all hugged and kissed each other on the cheek and we went into the courtroom. My God, the place was packed. You couldn't even move. There were a million reporters trying to get in, but all the detectives who had chased us over the years had taken up most of the seats. We had a few supporters of our own that came every day to cheer us on.

There must have been 20 sheriff's officers all over the courtroom. It seemed like we were waiting forever for the judge to come out and read the verdict.

Then someone yelled, "All rise!" and here comes the judge. You could cut the tension with a knife. I've never been more scared in my entire life.

First, they read the charges off against Lawrence, and they say, "Not guilty." Then they read my uncle's charges and they say, "Not guilty." Then they get to mine and they say, "Philip Leonetti, not guilty."

Me, my uncle, and Lawrence all shake hands and shake hands with the lawyers and you shoulda seen the look on the faces of the prosecutor and the cops. My God. They looked like they were gonna cry.

As we were leaving, one of the reporters asked my uncle, "Is there anything that you'd like to say?" and my uncle looked into the television camera and said, "Thank God for the American jury system and an honest jury." I was standing right behind him when he said it and you can see me smiling on TV.

It felt like the weight of the world was off my shoulders. That night we had a big party on Georgia Avenue and everyone came to celebrate.

All the lawyers and their families came. Chuckie was there. The Blade was there. Saul Kane, Vince Sausto, Salvie, all the guys from the neighborhood, and all the knock-around guys who were with us around Atlantic City—they all came down.

At some point during the party, my uncle pulls me and Lawrence aside and said, "We got away with murder; we are very, very lucky. We gotta be more careful from now on."

But within weeks of the not guilty verdict, Little Nicky was back to his murderous ways.

Sindone was one of the guys who was involved in the plot to kill Ange, and him and my uncle hated each other. My uncle told Phil Testa that Sindone was a snake and that he couldn't be trusted. Phil Testa agreed.

So we set him up and Salvie took him to a house in South Philadelphia where Frank Monte was waiting inside to see him. When Sindone was shaking hands with Frank Monte, Chuckie Merlino shot him in the head and killed him. Chuckie hit him three times in the back of the head, and they dumped him in an alley behind a store in South Philadelphia.

Phil Testa immediately sent word out that Sindone's entire operation was to be split between his killers: Salvie Testa, Chuckie Merlino, and Frank Monte. Sindone's top lieutenant, Joseph "Chickie" Ciancaglini, who was now aligned with Testa and Scarfo, would also receive a piece of the action and would oversee what remained of Sindone's crew.

The year was almost over, but Little Nicky's killing spree wasn't.

John McCullough was the head of the roofers union in Philadelphia. He was a big Irish guy from Northeast Philadelphia and *he had been very close to Ange. He was the guy Ange wanted to let organize the unions in Atlantic City instead of my uncle.*

Now my uncle hated John McCullough. When I say hated, I mean he absolutely detested him. He used to call him "that big Irish cocksucker," or "the crew cut"—things like that.

Now when Ange was alive, John McCullough was untouchable because he was with Ange. But with Ange gone, John McCullough was vulnerable.

My uncle starts telling Phil Testa, "We gotta kill this guy, McCullough. He's interfering in the unions in Atlantic City and he's costing me money." So Phil Testa gives my uncle the okay.

When McCullough lost his bid to take over the unions through Ange, he started causing trouble in Local 54. He was trying to break the union and it was costing us a lot of money.

My uncle went to Raymond "Long John" Martorano, who was a member of our family and who was close to McCullough and told him, "I want you to help us kill this guy. He's no good." Long John says, "I'll do whatever you want me to do, Nick."

This was a way to test a guy's loyalty, and at the same time eliminate a rival and show the guy that you were the power, that you were the muscle.

This is how my uncle was. He wanted to kill everybody. Everyone was petrified of my uncle, because with him it was kill, kill, kill. He didn't give a fuck. There was no talking.

Even though Phil Testa was the boss, no one in our family was more powerful than my uncle. When the guys from New York wanted to discuss business with our family, they came and saw my uncle.

When it was time to whack somebody out, it was my uncle who was calling the shots. He would determine who was going to die and who was going to kill them.

So my uncle tells Long John, "I want you to use Al Daidone on this thing."

Now Al Daidone was part of the bartenders union out of Camden—the one with Ralph Natale—which was the other union that Ange was pushing to get into Atlantic City. My uncle figures this is a way of testing Al Daidone's loyalty as well, since at one time that union was opposed to my uncle.

He tells Long John that he will make Al Daidone a business agent for Local 54 if he helps out with the killing, and if he doesn't, that he will kill him instead.

As crazy as my uncle was, I guess you can say there was a method to his madness.

On Tuesday, December 16, 1980, a delivery van pulled up outside the home of Philadelphia roofers union boss John McCullough in the Bustleton section of North Philadelphia. The deliveryman was carrying poinsettias, the bright red flowers that are synonymous with Christmas, which was only nine days away.

McCullough's wife answered the door and let the deliveryman inside the home, and he placed two plants on the kitchen table. Standing a few feet away talking on a telephone that was attached to the wall was John McCullough.

McCullough nodded to the deliveryman, and the deliveryman nodded back. The deliveryman told Mrs. McCullough that he had one more plant in the truck and that he would be right back.

John McCullough saw that his wife had two dollars in her hand to tip the man upon his return and put his hand over the phone and said, "It's Christmas time, give him three."

When the deliveryman reappeared he was carrying the third poinsettia and placed it on the table with the others. Without hesitation he pulled out a .22 caliber handgun and fired six times into the head and neck of John McCullough at close range.

The union boss slid to the floor as a pool of blood surrounded him.

McCullough's wife screamed in horror as the gunman very calmly left the house, got back into his van, and drove away.

John McCullough would no longer pose a threat to Nicky Scarfo's control over the unions in Atlantic City. He was dead.

The night they killed McCullough, it was all over the news, the top story. My uncle was very happy until he learned that Long John didn't kill McCullough himself; he had used a civilian, some kid named Willard Moran.

As for Al Daidone, he always maintained he had nothing to do with the hit.

My uncle went nuts. "This motherfucker used a civilian? Some fuckin' Irish kid? Jesus Christ!"

Now my uncle wants to kill Long John for using this Moran kid to do the hit, but Phil Testa calms him down.

He says, "Nick, if we keep killing everybody, there won't be anyone left."

That year alone Angelo Bruno, Antonio "Tony Bananas" Caponigro, Alfred "Freddie" Salerno, John "Johnny Keys" Simone, Frank "the Barracuda" Sindone, and John McCullough had all been murdered as part of a mob power struggle.

And that's how 1980, the bloodiest year in the history of the Philadelphia mob, ended.

The Ides of March, Part II (1981)

Early in 1981, we learned that the US attorney's office in Camden was going to indict my uncle for illegal possession of a firearm by a convicted felon.

The case stemmed from a search warrant that was executed when they came to arrest us for the Falcone murder. They found a small .22 in one of my uncle's bedroom drawers.

We knew it was coming and we expected my uncle to do some time.

Now, at this time, I was starting to get more involved in some of the other unions in Atlantic City. We controlled all of them.

My uncle started giving me more responsibility now that I was made and with the fact that he was likely going to prison at some point on the gun case.

At this time I started to make some inroads with a local politician named Mike Matthews who wanted to become the mayor of Atlantic City. I had sent word to him that when the time was right that he and I would meet and we would discuss ways that we could help him get elected.

I also helped make a guy we knew named Joe Pasquale, the chief of police in Atlantic City.

We had the kind of power at that time where we could start a citywide strike with a single phone call and literally shut down the casinos. We also had the kind of power that if people didn't do what we told them to do, we'd kill them and everyone knew that.

That was one of the reasons my uncle was so big on the killings. When people knew that we are involved, all the games stopped because they knew that we weren't fucking around.

Around this time I got word that the president of one of the casinos wasn't going to sign a union contract with Local 54. I sent word to the president of the casino that if he didn't sign the contract that I personally would blow his brains out of his head.

He signed the contract the next day.

With Little Nicky slowing down slightly in anticipation of a federal prison term on the gun case, his nephew Philip "Crazy Phil" Leonetti was stepping in and running the day-to-day operations in Atlantic City.

While Scarfo and Leonetti were transitioning their power to the Jersey Shore, Philip Testa was losing his on the streets of South Philadelphia.

Basically, Chickie Narducci was back to his old tricks. The same stuff he was doing with Ange—the plotting against Phil Testa—he now started doing with the underboss, Pete Casella.

Narducci tells Casella that if they whack out Phil Testa and Casella becomes the boss that he would give Casella $1 million so he could retire to Florida and he could name Chickie Narducci the boss.

This is how bad Chickie Narducci wanted to be the boss. He was willing to pay $1 million for it. Now Chickie had two tons of money—he had millions of dollars, but he didn't have no real power and that's what he wanted.

Now Pete Casella doesn't have 30 cents to his name so when Narducci offers him the $1 million, he goes for it, and him and Narducci start the plot to kill Phil Testa.

After the McCullough hit, me and my uncle were pretty much staying in Atlantic City and focusing on our operation, on our business. Even though my uncle was consigliere, we weren't going to Philadelphia a lot so we were kind of out of the loop with what

Narducci and Casella were up to.

Now, you gotta remember: since the day my uncle came home from Yardville, I was literally by his side every day. Morning, noon, and night. Where he went, I went. This is going on eight or nine years at this point. All these meetings, all these killings, all of this plotting. I had been charged with murder twice, we had just beaten the Falcone case. I was literally exhausted. Now during our trial my uncle tells me and Lawrence, "If we win this thing, I'm taking you guys to Florida."

I gotta tell ya, I needed that trip and so did my uncle. In this life, it's not 9 to 5, it's 24-7, especially with my uncle. He never stopped.

So one day at the office my uncle tells me and Lawrence, "Let's go down there for a few days and relax. We'll get some sun, we'll have a good time."

This was the best news I'd heard in years, right up there with beating the Falcone case.

So we fly down to Miami and we are staying in a suite at the original Diplomat Hotel, which was in Hollywood, Florida. You shoulda seen this place; it was a five-star resort from top to bottom.

Me, my uncle, and Lawrence would sit at the pool and just relax, have a few drinks, and then we'd eat at the best restaurants in town. Even my uncle was relaxing. He said, "We need to get down here more often. This is the life."

Now the night we get back to Philadelphia, Chuckie is waiting for us at the airport. He has a look on his face. My uncle says, "What's the matter? What's going on?" Chuckie says, "Phil Testa says he needs to see you right away and it can't wait. I think it's the beef between him and Chickie." My uncle says, "Okay, let's go," and that was it, the vacation was over.

We head over to Phil Testa's restaurant on Bank Street in Old City for a meeting and when we get there it's Phil Testa, Frank Monte, and Salvie sitting in a back booth. It's me, my uncle, Chuckie, and Lawrence and we sit down in the booth.

Phil Testa says, "Nick, thanks for coming, I wouldn't have called you here if it wasn't urgent." My uncle says, "What's going on?"

So Phil Testa starts off by saying, "I think Chickie's making a move against me. I've been hearing things in the street, and on top of that, he came to see me last week and asked to borrow $50,000."

Now before we killed Sindone, Phil Testa borrowed $50,000 from him. That's how greedy these guys were. They'd borrow the money knowing the guy was gonna get killed, and then they wouldn't have to pay the money back.

That was the move that these guys did.

Now everybody knows the last thing Chickie Narducci needs is another $50,000—the guy is a multimillionaire. So Phil Testa is convinced that Chickie is doing to him, what Phil Testa did to Sindone.

My uncle says, "We gotta kill him. We gotta get him before he gets you."

Phil Testa seems relieved. He says, "Thanks, Nick, I knew I could count on you," and he gives my uncle a kiss on the cheek.

My uncle says, "We'll take a ride up tomorrow and figure this thing out. Don't worry about nothin','" and then we drove back to Atlantic City.

Our plan was to go back and see him the next day, but because of what happened a few hours later, that didn't happen.

The explosion could be heard blocks away. Like an earthquake, it rocked an entire city. Dozens of police cars, fire trucks, and ambulances raced to the scene, as did dozens of people from the neighborhood—onlookers, many huddled together dressed in their pajamas, wearing sweatshirts and wrapped in blankets.

After all, it was after three in the morning and the air was crisp, permeated by the unmistakable scent of a fire that was slowly burning from within the smoldering heap that had once been the well-kept home of man known to some as Philip Testa, but known to all as the Chicken Man, the boss of the Philadelphia mob.

Within minutes, more than a half dozen clean-shaven and nattily dressed men, wearing navy blue flap jackets with the letters FBI emblazoned in bright yellow across their backs, were on the scene. Unlike most of the spectators present, these men, agents assigned to the FBI's Organized Crime Unit, did not appear to have just woken up. It appeared quite the opposite; it appeared that these men never slept.

As the crowd of curiosity seekers swelled behind the yellow crime scene tape, sleepy-eyed reporters joined the crowd, the lights from their television cameras illuminating the sky.

Neighbors, friends, and family shrieked in horror when the gurney carrying a severely burned and mortally wounded Philip Testa was led from the rubble of his home to a nearby ambulance for the short trip to St. Agnes Hospital on Broad Street in the heart of South Philadelphia.

The Chicken Man was dead, literally blown to pieces by a homemade bomb made of nails as he walked through the front door of his house after a late night out on the town. It was a brutal death for a brutal man that highlighted the ruthless and grisly dark side of a life often glamorized and romanticized.

It was roughly three in the morning when Philip Testa returned to his home located on the 2100 block of Porter Street in South Philadelphia's posh Girard Estates neighborhood from picking up some late night collections. He double-parked his car and made his way up his porch and to his front door.

These would be the final steps of his life.

If the 56-year-old Testa had been paying closer attention, he would have noticed the suspicious black Volkswagen van parked across the street from his house with a young South Philadelphia pizza maker and wannabe wise guy named Rocco Marinucci behind the wheel.

Marinucci was known on the streets as Pete Casella's driver and protégé.

Even if Testa had realized what was going on around him, he probably couldn't have done much. Fate was already in motion.

From the second Testa got out of his car, he was in the crosshairs. Underneath his porch was a makeshift bomb made up of carpenters nails and 13 sticks of dynamite, rigged to a handheld detonator in the possession of Marinucci.

Most likely, he didn't feel a thing. The explosion happened in an instant. As Testa reached for his front door knob, Marinucci pushed a button and blew the Chicken Man into oblivion.

Reverberations from the blast registered for miles.

As the darkness of night gave way to the blinding bright light of dawn, many would casually dismiss the event with a shrug as "just another mob hit" as they read their *Philadelphia Inquirer* or their *Daily News* and sipped their morning coffee, but they were wrong.

This was anything but "just another mob hit"; it was the death of a sitting mob boss, the second such killing that had taken place in the city of Philadelphia in less than a year as a complex struggle over money and power became deadly. The City of Brotherly Love had become the City of Brotherly Blood.

The following year, New Jersey–born American rock icon Bruce Springsteen would release a song about it, immortalizing the event in pop-culture lore.

In the underworld, the killing of a mob boss like Philip Testa was akin to the assassination of a president. Like the earthquake that it resembled, the death of Philip Testa would produce seismic ripple effects and shake the foundation of the underworld in South Philadelphia and Atlantic City to its very core.

The ensuing chaos would last for the next three decades.

ACT TWO

The Dawn of a New Era

It was maybe three-thirty, quarter to four in the morning when I got the call from Salvie. He said, "Philip, they killed my father." I was in bed and I remember sitting straight up when he said it. I said, "Jesus Christ, Salvie, what happened?" And he said, "There was a bomb at the house and they blew him up, those motherfuckers blew him up." You could hear the sadness in his voice, but I also heard the anger, the rage. He said, "Philip, I swear on my mother's grave when I find out who did this..." And then his voice trailed off. I said, "Salvie, try and get some sleep. Me and my uncle will be up there in a few hours and we will figure things out." And he said, "Okay, Philip, you guys come to the house," and then we hung up.

So I get out of bed and I walk next door to my uncle's apartment and I go in and I wake him up. It was like four in the morning and he is dead asleep. So I'm nudging him and saying, "Uncle Nick, wake up," and right away the second he sees me he knows something's wrong and he says, "What happened?" and I told him.

I said, "Salvie just called, his father got killed, they blew his house up with a bomb." Without hesitation my uncle is out of bed and I follow him into his kitchen. His wife comes in and makes us coffee, and my uncle is just sitting there, staring straight ahead. Neither one of us are saying anything.

After a few minutes he takes a sip of his coffee and he leans in close to me and he says, "Do you know what this means?" and I nodded my head yes.

I knew that with Phil Testa dead, one of two things was gonna happen: either the guys who killed him were gonna try and kill us; or we were gonna try and kill them. Whoever was left standing, us or them, would take control of the family, the Philadelphia La Cosa Nostra.

We sat there for a few more minutes and my uncle was just staring straight ahead and I could tell by looking at him, he had a million thoughts racing through his head. This was it, this was kill or be killed for us, and it was like he was computing all of these different scenarios in his mind. Who he could count on; who he had to watch; who he had to kill.

He finished his coffee and got up from the table and without saying a word, he started walking back to his bedroom. As he's walking away he says, "I'm going back to bed for a few hours. Come down and get me around ten and we will head up to Philadelphia."

So I walk back over to my apartment, but my adrenaline is going and I can't get back to sleep. I'm lyin' there and now my mind starts racing, too.

I started thinking of everything my uncle had taught me about this life since I was a little boy. All of the rules. I knew that death and murder were a part of our life. I started thinking of Ange and how Caponigro had betrayed him and now they were both dead. I thought about Vince Falcone, about how me and him killed Louie DeMarco together, and then I killed Vince. I thought about Phil Testa; I knew that Salvie or my uncle would kill whoever had killed him. The killings never stopped.

I was thinking how in this life, one day a guy is your friend and the next day you're killing him or he's trying to kill you.

This was what La Cosa Nostra was all about, but now the stakes were much, much higher.

The March 15, 1981, bombing death of Philip "Chicken Man" Testa was the second time in less than a year that the boss of the Philadelphia–Atlantic City mob had been violently murdered, with the assassination of longtime don Angelo Bruno having occurred on March 21, 1980.

With Bruno and Testa gone, Nicodemo "Little Nicky" Scarfo was in prime position to assume control of the family and become boss; and his nephew Philip Leonetti, his protégé and heir apparent, was right by his side.

Every day since he got out of Yardville I was by his side. I drove him everywhere. Where he went, I went. I'd stay with him until he was in for the night and I'd be there at whatever time he needed me the next day.

That was my routine; that was my life in the beginning.

And at 10:00 a.m. sharp, a few hours after the death of Philip Testa, Leonetti was dressed and ready to drive his uncle to Philadelphia to pay their respects to Salvie Testa and his family.

Now when I come down to get him, he's in a suit and tie, his hair is perfectly in place and he seemed eager to get to Philadelphia. I don't think it was because he wanted to see Salvie and the family so much; I think it was because he knew guys like Pete Casella and Chickie Narducci would start making moves and he wanted to be there so he could see who was doing what.

My uncle says, "Get Lawrence and let's get on the road. I want to pick up Chuckie at his house, and then go see Salvie and his sister, and then we're gonna get to the bottom of this thing and see what's goin' on."

Now I know that things are tense. I mean, they just killed the boss less than twelve hours ago. So I say to my uncle, "Do we need these?" and I make my hand like a gun. And he says, "If we do, we can get them up there," meaning Philadelphia.

Remember, my uncle is out on bail on the gun possession case from the gun they found in his bedroom when they came to lock us up on the Falcone case. He knows that the cops know that we're driving up to Philadelphia. It's a 60-mile ride on the Atlantic City Expressway, a straight shot from Atlantic City right into South Philadelphia using the Walt Whitman Bridge. We could be pulled over and searched at any time.

So my uncle is being extra cautious. "I don't need no more headaches with those motherfuckers," he said, meaning the law, and we got in the Cadillac and headed to Philadelphia.

The news of the explosion that killed Philip Testa was the top story on local television and rumors of who had been behind it began to circulate on the mob-infested streets of South Philadelphia.

It takes us about an hour to drive up, and in the car no one is talking because we are always worried about listening devices. We get into the city and we drive to Chuckie's house and he meets us outside. At the time he was living around Ninth and Jackson. We park the car, and me, my uncle, and Lawrence get out so we can talk to Chuckie.

Chuckie goes right into what people are saying, "It was a nail-bomb. The word is it was the Irish and the roofers union, as pay-back for us killing John McCullough."

Right away my uncle is shaking his head no. He says, "No fuckin' way an Irishman is killing the boss of a La Cosa Nostra family. They're crazy, but they're not that crazy. Not in a million fuckin' years. No way."

So Chuckie says, "Well, who do you think did it?" And my uncle says, "Well, it didn't come from New York. It didn't come from North Jersey. It didn't come from the Irish. And we didn't do it," meaning us guys in Atlantic City, "so it had to come from up here," meaning South Philadelphia. Just last night he was telling us about his problems with Chickie Narducci, so I'm guessing he has a hand in this.

Then I said, "If Salvie gets wind of this, he'll kill Chickie right on the spot. He'll do it himself at the funeral, he don't give a fuck."

My uncle says to me, "Chuckie and Lawrence, we need to play dumb for now and see who does what. Who lines up with who. We need to keep Salvie calm and we need to find out exactly who did this, and then we will do what we gotta do," meaning kill them.

So we get in the car and we drive over to the house and Salvie is there with his sister and some members of his family. A few old-time guys that were around Phil Testa were also there.

We get out and we pay our respects, and Salvie looked like he was ready to kill a thousand guys. He said, "Nick, when I find out who did this, I'm doing them myself. I don't care who they are or who they're with."

My uncle put his hands on his shoulder and looked him right in the eye and said, "We're gonna get to the bottom of this, and who-ever did this is gonna get this," and he made the sign of the gun. "But we gotta sit back and see who was involved in this treason. We can't do anything half-cocked." Salvie just nodded.

While we're there a lot of guys start coming around. Guys like Joey Pungitore and Gino Milano, who were tight with Salvie. My uncle nudges me and says, "Look who's here, this treacherous cock-

sucker," and I look and in comes Chickie Narducci with his sons Frank Jr. and Philip. They pay their respects to Salvie and his sister Maria and then Chickie makes a beeline for my uncle.

He says, "Nick, isn't this awful? Those no good Irish motherfuckers did this to our friend."

Now my uncle knows that it's all bullshit about the Irish doing the killing, and he knows that in all likelihood Chickie Narducci was behind it. He knows, but at this moment he doesn't know enough that he's certain, and he wanted us to purposely play dumb.

My uncle says to Chickie, "What can we do, Chick? We gotta wait and see what happens. Just like with Ange." What my uncle was saying is, we gotta wait and see what New York says.

And Chickie kind of nods, but he looks confused by what my uncle said.

These guys like Chickie Narducci didn't get it. They thought they could pick who the new boss was, but only New York can do that and my uncle was the only guy that New York would speak to.

So we hang around the house for a little while and my uncle tells Salvie, "We're gonna be here for a few days for the wake and the funeral and we'll get to bottom of this."

In the days following Philip Testa's murder, three names emerged as his likely successor: Testa's handpicked underboss, Peter "Pete" Casella; his trusted friend and consigliere, Nicodemo "Little Nicky" Scarfo; and a renegade mob solider named Harry "the Hunchback" Riccobene.

My uncle was small, but Harry Riccobene was smaller. He was like 4'10" and weighed 110 pounds. We called him the Hunch because he had a hunchback. Him and my uncle had hated each other for years, but Harry had his own crew and he was the main guy in Southwest Philadelphia. They ran gambling, loan sharking, and extortion rackets like we did, but Harry and his crew were mainly known as drug dealers, and my uncle detested drugs and drug dealers, so that's one reason we didn't like him.

The other reason was that Harry never showed anybody any respect and that he didn't follow the rules. My uncle used to say, "The way he behaves, he's not Cosa Nostra."

Now Pete Casella, who Phil Testa picked as his underboss,

he, too, was a drug dealer. He had just gotten out of jail for selling
drugs. My uncle was the one who had Mickey Coco killed for selling
drugs to Frank Monte's kid. He always said, "Drugs and our thing,"
meaning La Cosa Nostra, *"don't mix."*

Scarfo's blind allegiance to *La Cosa Nostra*'s strict edict against getting involved in the distribution of drugs may have been admirable to some mob traditionalists, but rules were meant to be broken, and, in fact, Harry Riccobene and Pete Casella weren't the only mobsters who moonlighted as drug dealers.

Lucky Luciano, the architect of the national *La Cosa Nostra* syndicate and the first boss of bosses, was heavily involved with the distribution of drugs, as were his underboss, Vito Genovese, and Genovese's protégé, Vincent "The Chin" Gigante, who shared a cell with the powerful Mafia don inside the massive fortress-like federal penitentiary USP Atlanta following a 1959 conviction for heroin trafficking.

Following the murder of Angelo Bruno and the shift in power on the Commission, Vincent "The Chin" Gigante, the boss of the Genovese family, was now the boss of all bosses, the supreme leader of the Commission.

Scarfo knew that Gigante, whom he considered a personal friend, would nominate him over Casella and Riccobene.

When Ange got killed, the Chin wanted my uncle to become
the next boss, but my uncle declined and told them that Phil Testa
deserved it more. The Chin, through Bobby Manna, then ordered
Phil Testa to make my uncle the underboss or consigliere, and my
uncle became the consigliere.

Testa's choice of Pete Casella as his underboss would ultimately cost him his life.

Now in the days leading up to Phil Testa's wake, we were in
South Philadelphia every day—me, my uncle, Chuckie, and Law-
rence. We were using a bar at Ninth and Moyamesing called the
9M Bar, which was named after the streets it was on.

From the time I knew Chuckie, if he wasn't at his clubhouse on
Shunk and Sartian, you could find him at the 9M Bar. My uncle felt
safe there.

Now at the time, the captains in the family were Freddie Iezzi, Santo Idone, Joe Scafidi, Frank Monte, Johnny Cappello, and Chickie Narducci.

My uncle's captain before he became consigliere was Freddie Iezzi, so we knew that he was with us. My uncle went way back with Santo Idone and Joe Scafidi—back to the Reds Caruso murder—so we knew that they were with us, and Frank Monte was very close with my uncle and Phil Testa.

Remember, my uncle had Mickey Coco killed for selling drugs to Frank Monte's kid, so he was with us. We had everyone but Johnny Cappello and Chickie Narducci; they were with Pete Casella. None of the captains were backing Harry Riccobene.

My uncle had the support of four out of the six captains and he knew he had New York's support. But you gotta remember, not all these guys played by the rules. That's why Ange and Phil Testa were dead.

So we go to the wake and everybody's there, the whole organization. Members, associates, you name it. Everyone connected to La Cosa Nostra *was there.*

While we were there, Chickie Narducci comes up to my uncle and says, "Nick, Pete Casella wants to see you after the wake to sort some things out. We want you to come to John Cappello's house."

Now John Cappello, who was a captain, is Pete Casella's brother-in-law. His house is the house where I got made. These guys knew my uncle was making moves with the other captains and my uncle was now almost certain that Pete Casella was in on the plot against Phil Testa with Chickie Narducci. So this is it, this is the other side wanting to sit down with my uncle.

My uncle tells Chickie, "I'll be there. Me and Chuckie will come." And Chickie says, "Good, we'll straighten things out."

Now I'm standing there and I'm hearing all of this and I look Chickie Narducci dead in his eye and I say, "I want Johnny Cappello with me and Lawrence at the 9M Bar as insurance. He leaves when my uncle and Chuckie come back from the meeting. If anyone else but my uncle or Chuckie walk through that door, John Cappello will be dead before they get their guns out. Do you understand me?"

Now Chickie is taken aback and he has this stunned look on his face, and my uncle has a half a smile on his face, like he's proud I spoke up, and says, "That's what it is. John Cappello waits with my nephew until me and Chuckie get back."

Chickie kind of stammers a bit and says, "Okay, Nick, we just want to talk, that's it," and my uncle says, "Fine, we'll be there."

When Chickie was walking away I caught him giving me a look, I guess he felt that because he was a caporegime I shouldn't have talked to him like that because I was just a solider, and he was right. But if these guys weren't playing by the rules, why should I? I mean, Jesus Christ, they just whacked our boss out without approval from the Commission, and he's gonna give me the *malocchio* because he didn't like the way I spoke to him? My uncle sees what I'm seeing and he says, "Your whole life, what have I told you about these sig-gys? They are no fuckin' good. Greed and treason, that's all that's on their brain."

Now my uncle moves right into action. He grabs Blackie Napoli, who is at the wake, and tells him to leave the wake and drive up to New York and set up a meeting with Bobby Manna for the next day—the day of the funeral—to discuss being named boss of the family.

He told Blackie, "After you see Bobby, you turn around and drive back to the 9M and tell me what he said. You also tell him about this meeting at John Cappello's house, I want him to know everything. We're not going back to Atlantic City until you come back, I don't care what time it is."

Blackie says, "Got it," and he's out the door.

My uncle tells Chuckie, "Get two guns—one for Philip and one for Lawrence. I want a couple of guys with them at the 9M in case there's any trouble. I want everyone in that bar ready to go," meaning he wants everyone armed.

Chuckie says, "Okay, Nick," and he's out the door.

My uncle looks at me and Lawrence, and says, "This is it. You guys know what to do if there's any trouble," and we both nod.

We left the wake and went straight to the 9M and when we got there Chuckie was there with a few of his guys.

We walk in and Chuckie hands me and Lawrence pistols, and we sit at the bar and we're waiting for Johnny Cappello.

About a half hour later here he comes, and when he comes in, Chuckie frisked him for weapons. As Chuckie is checking him, he raises his hands and looks at my uncle and says, "Come on, Nick, is this necessary?" and Chuckie says, "He's clean."

My uncle says, "It's just a precaution, John, that's all," and him and Chuckie leave for the meeting.

While we're sitting there, John Cappello is trying to break the ice. He starts telling me and Lawrence the story about the Irish being behind Phil Testa's death. Me and Lawrence don't say nothing, and he's just talking and I'm staring him dead in the eye as he's talking.

I tell him, "You know if something happens to my uncle or Chuckie, you won't leave this bar alive. You know that, right?" And he looks at me and nods, and I say, "Let's have some drinks and see what happens," and after that I don't think he said two words the rest of the night.

Now, like I did with Chickie Narducci, I shouldn't be talking to John Cappello like that. But I'm thinking he's with the guys who killed Phil Testa. In my mind, I was thinking that those guys would have killed me, my uncle, Chuckie, Lawrence, Salvie, all of us, so in reality, I didn't give a fuck about none of them. On this day, the day of Phil Testa's wake, that was the first time in my life that I ever balked at the rules of La Cosa Nostra.

So we're sitting there and it seems like an eternity. A couple of guys were playing cards in one of the booths; a few more were watching TV. Two guys were sitting on stools by the front door and we had two guys outside the bar. Everybody had a pistol on them.

Me and Lawrence were sitting at the bar with John Cappello, and he started drinking. He knows his night's gonna end one of two ways: Door No. 1, he's going home; Door No. 2, I'm putting two bullets in the back of his head. There ain't no Door No. 3.

Me and Lawrence were milking our drinks because we had to stay alert in case there was trouble. It was very, very tense. The waiting became very monotonous and this John Cappello just keeps drinking as the hours pass by.

All the sudden, around midnight, the two guys by the front door are off of their stools and they are walking towards the door. The guys playing cards are on their feet. Lawrence starts walking towards the door. I got my gun in John Cappello's ribs and the door opens and in walks my uncle with Chuckie behind him.

I take the gun and put it back in my pants and my uncle walks right over to John Cappello and says, "Okay John, you can go now," and this guy is out the door like Flash Gordon.

Chuckie tells the guys in his crew to stand outside and that the only guy allowed in the bar is Blackie Napoli, who should be on his way back from New York with a message from Bobby Manna.

Lawrence makes drinks for all of us and we all toast, salud, *and my uncle tells us about the meeting.*

"When we got there, it was Pete Casella, his brother Anthony, that backstabbing cocksucker Chickie Narducci, John Grande and his son, and this kid, Rocco Marinucci. They checked us for weapons right when we got there.

"Rocco Marinucci was looking out one of the windows and listening to a police scanner and the rug in the room where we were meeting was rolled up. I think they were planning on blasting us, but they knew that you guys would have killed John Cappello."

Chuckie says, "If you guys didn't have him here with guns on him, we wouldn't be sitting here talking right now."

Lawrence chimed in and said, "Motherfuckers," and my uncle looks at me and says, "You caught Chickie off guard by asking for Pete's brother-in-law as insurance. If they had said no, then there wouldn't have been no meeting. They weren't gonna kill us and let him die as a result, so they tried Plan B, which was to try and trick us. These fuckin' guys think I started doing this yesterday. These cocksuckers, we'll show them."

My uncle says, "Pete Casella tells us that someone in New York told him that the Irish had killed Phil Testa and that he wanted me to retaliate." My uncle said Pete Casella was acting as if he was already the boss.

My uncle says, "I told him, Pete, that's not what I heard and I have a meeting set up for tomorrow in New York with Bobby Manna to tell him what I think is going on."

Chuckie says, "You shoulda seen their faces when Nicky said he had a meeting tomorrow with New York. The whole room got quiet and that was the end of the meeting."

So we're sitting there waiting on Blackie and all the sudden around 2:00 a.m. here he comes.

My uncle greets him with a hug and a kiss on the cheek when he comes in and says, "Well, how did it go?"

Blackie says, "He wants you up there tomorrow for a sit-down,"
and my uncle tells him, "Me and you are gonna go. We're gonna
have to miss the funeral, but this can't wait."

Blackie says, "Okay, Nick, I'll see you tomorrow and he leaves."
This poor guy had driven two hours down for the wake, two hours
up to New York to see Bobby Manna, two hours back to deliver the
message, and now another two hours to get home. But that's how it
was in this life. This wasn't a 9-to-5 job.

Chuckie and his guys walk me, my uncle, and Lawrence to our
car just in case the other side decides to take a shot, but they didn't,
and we drove back down to Atlantic City.

When we get home it's like four in the morning and my uncle
says, "Go upstairs and wake up [Dutch]. Tell him I need a car
around the corner first thing in the morning."

Dutch—as I will call him—was a guy that lived in our building
and ran errands for us. We let him stay there for free and gave him
$200 a week. He did odd jobs for Scarf, Inc. and Nat Nat, and he
always helped out my mother or grandmother. He was a good guy
and we didn't involve him in anything illegal.

So I go bang on his door and tell him what we needed and he
gets right up and gets a car and parks it a few blocks away on Flor-
ida Avenue so my uncle can leave the back way through the alleys
early the next morning without being detected.

While guys like Chickie Narducci and Pete Casella were playing
checkers, Nicky Scarfo and Philip Leonetti were playing chess. Each move
was calculated and measured, and in March 1981, Little Nicky and Crazy
Phil were one step away from running the entire Philadelphia–Atlantic
City mob.

Scarfo had just turned 52, and in a matter of days Leonetti would be 28.

Scarfo's meeting scheduled the next day with his old pal from Yardville, Bobby Manna, was at this point merely a formality.

The New King Is Crowned

The morning of the funeral, me and Lawrence get up early and we're getting ready to go to Philadelphia. My uncle's up and he's getting ready to head up to New York for his meeting with Blackie Napoli and Bobby Manna.

He's gonna go through the back alleys and get in the car Dutch had left for him so he doesn't pick up a tail. We were always careful, but going to New York you had to be extra careful. Guys like Bobby Manna and the Chin did everything top secret.

So my uncle says, "Tonight when I get back we will meet up for dinner. When you guys are up there today, keep your antennas up. I want to know who's saying what and who's gathering with who."

As Philip Leonetti and Lawrence Merlino were on their way to Philadelphia for Phil Testa's funeral, Nicky Scarfo was on his way to North Jersey to meet with Blackie Napoli and Bobby Manna in the back room of an Italian restaurant in Hoboken to discuss the future of the Bruno crime family and, more specifically, Little Nicky's future as its boss.

Ten years prior, the trio of Scarfo, Napoli, and Manna walked the track together at Yardville State Prison and discussed their future plans as mob leaders.

My uncle was very tight with those guys, ever since they were in Yardville together.

Scarfo told Manna everything he had learned about Phil Testa's death: the beef with Chickie Narducci, the rumors about the Irish, and his less-than-friendly meeting with Pete Casella the night of the wake.

Scarfo told Manna that he believed Casella, Narducci, and others not yet known to him were behind Testa's murder. Manna told Scarfo that whoever had killed Philip Testa did not have the permission of the Commission and, as such, the hit was unsanctioned.

As it had done with the unsanctioned murder of Testa's predecessor Angelo Bruno, the Commission would launch an immediate investigation to identify those responsible and make arrangements to mete out the appropriate punishment: death.

Sitting at the head of the Commission was Manna's boss and Scarfo's friend and ally, Vincent "The Chin" Gigante. Manna told Scarfo that he would schedule a meeting in a week and that both Scarfo and Casella would present their case to the Genovese hierarchy, which consisted of Gigante, Manna, and Anthony "Fat Tony" Salerno—the same individuals who presided over the investigation of Angelo Bruno's murder one year prior and who had ordered the gruesome torture killings of those involved.

This time around the Genovese would be without their minister of manipulation, Frank "Funzi" Tieri, who was on his deathbed in a prison hospital after being convicted of racketeering and sentenced to 10 years in prison.

With or without Tieri, the deck was heavily stacked in Scarfo's favor and Little Nicky knew it. In one week he would likely become the undisputed boss of the Philadelphia–Atlantic City mob.

That night, after his meeting with Blackie and Bobby Manna, me and my uncle went out to dinner at Caesars. I told him about the funeral and he told me about the meeting. He said, "For the next week, until I go to New York, we gotta watch our p's and q's. We're gonna stay close to home. This treachery, it may not be over."

For the next week, Scarfo and Leonetti stayed in Atlantic City and kept a low profile, shunning hastily called mob meetings in South Philadelphia and doing their best to avoid their usual haunts.

Back when Ange was boss and him and my uncle started having problems over the unions, we had heard that Ange had sent this big Irish guy from Northeast Philly down to Atlantic City and that this guy may have been looking to kill my uncle. We found out that he had a big tattoo on his arm and a couple people in the neighborhood described him to us and said they had seen him around Georgia Avenue, and he was asking people questions about us.

When my uncle found out about it, he went crazy. He knew someone who knew the guy and he told them, "You tell that Irish motherfucker if he ever steps foot in Atlantic City again, for any reason, I'm gonna chop him up and send him back to Philadelphia in six trash bags, one for each of his arms, one for each of his legs, one for his torso, and one for that big stupid fuckin' Irish head of his."

We never heard nothing about the guy from that point on. From that point on, everyone who came to Atlantic City checked in with us to let us know why they were in town.

This is back when Ange was the boss. My uncle even told Ange, he said, "I'm gonna cut your friend's arm off, the one with the tattoo, and I'm gonna send it you."

I remember Ange was steaming, but so was my uncle. This was towards the end, before Ange got clipped. Him and my uncle were beefin' over the unions.

Now several years later, with Scarfo on the cusp of assuming the throne, Atlantic City was crawling with wise guys looking to curry favor with Little Nicky.

It's like overnight every guy and their mother wanted to come to Atlantic City and see my uncle for one reason or another. This is in the days leading up to the meeting in New York.

It was me and Lawrence in the office, and we'd see this one and that one, whoever came. My uncle stayed upstairs in his apartment. He didn't come down to see anyone.

They were all coming to score points, and we knew it.

The day was finally here, it was finally time for the meeting with the Genovese leadership in New York.

The meeting was set for 1:00 p.m. inside Vincent "The Chin" Gigante's personal headquarters, the Triangle Social Club on Sullivan Street in New York's Greenwich Village.

Nicodemo "Little Nicky" Scarfo and Peter "Pete" Casella would sit before Gigante, his consigliere, Bobby Manna, and his front boss, Anthony "Fat Tony" Salerno, and learn their respective fates as Gigante, the *il capo di tutti capi* of the Commission, dictated the future of the Philadelphia–Atlantic City mob.

Me and my uncle are up early, dressed and ready to go. I'm driving him to New York for his meeting with the Chin. In addition to getting him up there on time, I also had to make sure we didn't pick up any tails.

The night before I told Dutch to take his car and to drive it to the Parkway and get off at the 7-N ramp. Me and my uncle were going to drive to the Parkway and we were going to get off at 7-S. The S is for South and the N is for North. There is a sharp bend where 7-S and 7-N are running parallel to one another. I told Dutch to pull his car over like he was broken down right at the bend, next to the divider.

Me and uncle come around the bend and there's Dutch, and his car is parked right where I told him and it's running. We slow down and we pull right up to the divider parallel to his car. Me and my uncle jumped the divider and got in his car and he jumped the divider and got in our car.

The cops who were following us knew we were in the Cadillac and that we were on the Parkway heading south. So they'd radio ahead and another car would pick us up with the surveillance. That was how they did it, but we knew their moves.

So now after the switch with Dutch, me and my uncle are in his car heading north on the Parkway, and Dutch's in our car heading south on the Parkway. I told him to go all the way to Cape May, which is the end of the Parkway, and turn around and come home. The cops would be following the Caddy and have no idea we weren't in it. By the time they figured it out, we'd be in New York.

Leonetti's plan worked. In addition to shaking a law enforcement tail, driving in a "clean" car gave Philip and his uncle an opportunity to talk freely for the nearly two hours it would take them to get to Greenwich Village.

My uncle knew they were gonna make him boss. I said, "You think they're gonna do to Pete what they did to Tony?"—meaning kill him. And my uncle shrugged his shoulders and said, "If it was up to me, I'd kill Pete, his brother Anthony, his brother-in-law Johnny Cappello, Chickie Narducci, and that fuckin' Rocco Marinucci. But it ain't up to me; it's up to this guy," and he stroked his chin, which is how we referred to the Chin.

As Scarfo and Leonetti got closer to New York, both men became more anxious, spotting in the distance the site of the World Trade Center's Twin

Towers and the Empire State Building as they prepared to enter the city through the Holland Tunnel.

> *Once we were in the city, my uncle started going over the protocol for the meeting. We were to first go to a restaurant in Little Italy, and then they would send for my uncle. He would go to the meeting and I would stay at the restaurant.*
>
> *When we got there we went into the restaurant and the first guy we saw was Benny Eggs.*

Venero "Benny Eggs" Mangano was one of Chin Gigante's closest friends and was the reputed underboss of the Genovese crime family.

> *Benny Eggs said, "Nick, it's good to see you," and he gave my uncle a kiss on the cheek. My uncle said, "Ben, I want you to meet my nephew Philip Leonetti, he is a friend of ours," and Benny shook my hand and gave me a kiss on the cheek and said, "So this is the young man I've heard so much about." He couldn't have been nicer to us.*
>
> *He tells us to have a seat and right away they start bringing over food and drinks. He says to my uncle, "Let's wait awhile for the other guy to get here, and then we'll get you over there," meaning the club where the Chin was.*

As Scarfo, Leonetti, and Mangano made small talk, at 12:45 p.m. sharp three Genovese soldiers walked into the restaurant and Benny Eggs excused himself from the table.

> *Now the meeting is scheduled for 1:00. Me and uncle get there at 12:00, and here it's 12:45 and Pete Casella is nowhere to be found.*
>
> *My uncle checks his watch and whispers to me, "I'll betcha this cocksucker ain't gonna show," meaning Pete. I just made a face back at my uncle like, no way, because that was a major no-no. If you got called to a meeting with the boss of the Commission and you didn't go, the penalty was death, no questions asked.*
>
> *So now Benny Eggs comes back and says, "I sent one of those fellas back to see what they want to do, if they want to get started, or wait a bit longer for the other guy." My uncle said, "Doesn't matter to me, Ben. Whatever you guys want."*

So five minutes later the guy comes back and whispers in Benny Egg's ear, and he says to me and my uncle, "It may be a little while."

Now we're just sitting there eating a little bit, having a couple of drinks, but this isn't the way it was supposed to be. All the sudden all these thoughts are racing through my mind. Were we getting double-crossed, like Caponigro did? Was I gonna wind up in the back of a car, like Freddie Salerno? Maybe they were gonna take us all out so they could have Atlantic City all to themselves.

My uncle's sitting there and I can see his antenna is up, but we can't talk because Benny Eggs is with us and he's telling stories and making small talk. But I know my uncle is thinking the same thing.

So next thing you know, it's three o'clock. Now my uncle knows the rules and so do I; we're not gonna say, "Hey what's takin' so long," or "Is there a problem?" So we're just sitting there.

What Scarfo and Leonetti did not know was that while Scarfo had his ace in the hole with Bobby Manna from their days together in Yardville State Prison, Pete Casella had made a similar connection with a powerful Genovese captain when the two men were doing time together on federal drug-trafficking charges.

At that very moment, the Genovese captain was pleading Casella's case to Gigante, Manna, and Salerno, trying to intervene on his behalf by either swaying the Genovese leaders to name Casella the new boss of the Philadelphia–Atlantic City mob or, at a minimum, spare his life in the event Gigante was looking to make an example, like he did with Antonio "Tony Bananas" Caponigro.

The whole time we're sitting there, the same guy who was running back and forth between Benny Eggs and the Chin keeps coming and going, whispering to Benny each time he does.

All the sudden the door opens and here comes Pete Casella and he has Rocco Marinucci with him. Benny gets up to greet him, and Pete introduces Rocco as a "friend of mine"—which means he's not Cosa Nostra, he's not made—and Benny's colors change and he won't shake Rocco's hand.

"You can't bring him in here," Benny says to Pete, and one of the Genovese guys barked at Rocco, "Go wait in the car," and Rocco was out the door. He never looked back.

It was almost four o'clock and Pete didn't even get a chance to sit down. And the guy who was going back and forth all day reappeared and whispered to Benny, and Benny said, "Okay, gentlemen, they are ready for you," and my uncle and Pete were being escorted towards the door. Benny said, "Nick, I'm gonna stay here with your nephew and teach him how to play cards," and we all laughed, everyone except for Pete. Pete looked like he was scared to death.

As Philip Leonetti and Benny Eggs Mangano played cards, Nicodemo Scarfo and Pete Casella were taken to the Triangle Social Club, which was only three blocks away.

The windows on the nondescript storefront were completely blacked out, and inside there were two chairs, one for Scarfo and one for Casella.

Sitting across from the two Philadelphia mobsters behind a table were the three Genovese leaders. Gigante was seated in the middle in his trademark bathrobe; the stone-faced Manna was to his left, and the dour-looking Salerno to his right, wearing his trademark fedora and puffing on a cigar that remained firmly between his teeth.

According to Scarfo, who later told Leonetti what happened inside the meeting, Gigante wasted no time with pleasantries and started the meeting by speaking directly to Casella in his rapid-fire New York cadence.

"Listen, we know what happened. Don't lie to us. If you lie to us, we can't help you. Tell us the names of everyone who was involved in this plot."

Scarfo told Leonetti that Casella answered the question directly.

"It was me. It was my idea. Me, Chickie Narducci, and Rocco Marinucci, and a kid Rocco knows."

Scarfo said Fat Tony took the cigar out of his mouth and barked, "This motherless fuck, the kid, does he have a name?" and Casella responded, "I don't know his name," and then hung his head in shame.

Gigante smacked the table, and Casella looked up at him, and then the don spoke, "You're finished. You are to retire immediately to Florida. You are forbidden from ever returning to Philadelphia. When you leave here, you get on a plane and you go. If you breathe a word of this to anyone, we will kill you, your brother, and your brother-in-law. Do you understand?"

Casella nodded his head and Gigante gestured for one of the Genovese soldiers to escort him out of the club. As Casella attempted to shake Gigante's hand, Gigante stared at him with disgust and spit on the floor in his direction, and Casella was whisked away.

With Casella gone, it was just Little Nicky and the three Genovese leaders. Again, Gigante got right to the point.

"Well, Nick, I don't see no one else here, so I guess that makes you the new boss," at which point Gigante stood and Scarfo approached the table and kissed Gigante on each cheek, as Manna and Salerno clapped their hands.

Scarfo would also kiss Manna and Salerno in a similar fashion.

Nicodemo Domenic Scarfo was now the undisputed boss of the Philadelphia–Atlantic City mob. He had just turned 52 years old and was strategically aligned with New York's Genovese crime family and Vincent "The Chin" Gigante, the most powerful mob boss in the nationwide crime syndicate known as *La Cosa Nostra, this thing of ours.*

The underworld in Philadelphia and Atlantic City would never be the same.

A Whole New Ballgame

T HAT NIGHT, WHEN SCARFO AND LEONETTI RETURNED TO GEORGIA AVENUE, THERE WAS A SMALL CONTINGENCY WAITING FOR THEM.

It was Chuckie, Lawrence, Salvie, and Frank Monte. I introduced my uncle to them as their new boss, and everyone was hugging each other and kissing each other on the cheek.

The five of us went down to Angeloni's for drinks to celebrate. My uncle told us, "We gotta let things settle a bit before we start making changes. We gotta do it right. One step at a time. This is a whole new ballgame."

Everyone was happy, but it seemed like Salvie was a little out of it. I think he was expecting my uncle to say our first order of business is we're gonna go kill this one or we're gonna go kill that one—the guys who had killed his father. But my uncle was saying we're gonna take things slow and let the smoke clear, which was definitely the right move for the organization.

Nicky Scarfo enjoyed a steady stream of visitors to his Atlantic City headquarters over the next few weeks, as members and associates of the Bruno crime family came to pledge their allegiance to the new boss.

Scarfo would also travel to Philadelphia and meet with the captains left over from the Bruno and Testa regimes to discuss the family's new hierarchy.

Nicky Scarfo would name his close friend Salvatore "Chuckie" Merlino as his underboss and Testa loyalist Frank Monte to the post of consigliere.

Within a few short months, Scarfo would name four new *caporegimes*: Joseph "Chickie" Ciancaglini, Salvatore "Salvie" Testa, Lawrence "Yogi" Merlino, and his 28-year-old nephew, Philip "Crazy Phil" Leonetti.

Scarfo kept his old captain, Alfred "Freddie" Iezzi, on board, but the old-timer was already semiretired. Scarfo also kept Bruno-era captains Santo "Big Santo" Idone and Joseph "Joe" Scafidi in place, but "took down" John "Johnny" Cappello, the brother-in-law of the recently deposed Pete Casella.

Scarfo also kept the treacherous Frank "Chickie" Narducci in place for the time being, but Little Nicky had already decided that Narducci's days were numbered for his involvement in the bombing death of Philip Testa.

Me, Chuckie, and Lawrence were the only ones who knew what Pete Casella had told the Chin about the plot to kill Phil Testa. My uncle was afraid if Salvie knew, or even Frank Monte, that they would kill Chickie Narducci immediately.

My uncle said, "We're gonna kill him; we're just not gonna kill him yet."

As March turned into April, Little Nicky and his new regime were in full swing, and business was good and it was about to get a whole lot better.

One day, me and my uncle are having lunch with Saul Kane and Lawrence, and Saul says, "Nick, I got an idea for you—you should start a street tax. The way it works is you tax everybody who is doing anything illegal, and you offer them the protection and sup-

port of your family in exchange for them paying the tax. I know it's been done in Chicago and real big in New York in the '30s and '40s. I think you could make a lot of money doing it."

My uncle's eyes lit up. He knew that we had the muscle to enforce it. He made a face at me and I made a face back at him, and we both smiled.

From that moment on, the imposition and collection of the street tax became our No. 1 priority and one of our biggest moneymakers.

As Scarfo was setting out to restructure the organization, each made member had to formally come in and sit down with the boss and the underboss and talk about what they had going on.

Guys had to come in and report what they had going on, who was doing what, so that we could figure out what was out there and what we were going to collect, both as tribute and as the street tax.

A lot of guys hadn't been paying Ange or Phil Testa the right amount in tribute for years, and some guys weren't paying at all. My uncle told everybody that came in the same thing: "Those days are over. You and your people are gonna pay what you're supposed to pay, or it's this," and he made the sign of the gun.

Scarfo had assembled a group of killers around him and everyone knew it. Despite that, there were those in the underworld who did not heed the new boss's warning.

Men like Chelsais "Stevie" Bouras, the leader of Philadelphia's Greek mob.

Bouras had blatantly balked at Scarfo's demand that he be forced to pay the mob's new street tax and Scarfo swiftly ordered his murder to send a message to anyone else considering not paying.

My uncle had Long John set it up because he was close to Bouras.

Raymond "Long John" Martorano, the onetime *aide de camp* to Angelo Bruno who had helped Scarfo murder union boss John McCullough in December 1980, set up a dinner party at a restaurant in Philadelphia and invited Bouras to join him and his wife and several other people for a night out.

Bouras brought his young girlfriend to the restaurant and everyone was having a good time until two men with ski masks entered the restaurant and motioned for Martorano and the others to move as they opened fire on Bouras, killing him with a barrage of bullets, and killing his young date who got caught in the cross fire.

The cold-blooded mob killing of Stevie Bouras sent the rest of the Philadelphia underworld scurrying to pay Scarfo's street tax, and Scarfo's crews were bringing in money, hand over fist.

> *Once we got it going good, we were bringing in $100,000 per month just in street tax money. Don't forget we still had gambling, loan sharking, and extortion operations, so on a good month we could bring in a half a million or more in cash.*

With Scarfo and Leonetti based in Atlantic City, Salvatore "Chuckie" Merlino and Salvie Testa were running the day-to-day operations of the family in South Philadelphia.

> *Things were great in the beginning, especially after we killed Stevie Bouras. Everyone was doing their job and we were making a lot of money. Everybody was paying. My uncle was happy and things were good.*

But hanging over Scarfo's head in the summer of 1981 was an imminent prison sentence stemming from his conviction on gun possession charges in connection with the .22 that was found in his bedroom drawer during the police raid following the Falcone killing.

As a convicted felon, Scarfo was facing several years in federal prison and was out on bail pending appeal. His lawyer, Bobby Simone, had told him that the appeal was a long shot, and that in all likelihood he would be in jail within the next twelve months.

The looming jail sentence did not stop Scarfo from ordering the murder of a South Philadelphia drug dealer and loan shark named Johnny Calabrese on October 6, 1981, because like Stevie Bouras, Johnny Calabrese balked at paying the Scarfo mob's street tax.

> *We approached Chickie Ciancaglini, who was close with Calabrese, and he set it up. Two guys from his crew, Tommy DelGiorno*

and Faffy Iannarella, were the shooters, and another guy named Pat Spirito was the getaway driver.

As Chick was walking Calabrese to his car, Tommy and Faffy came out of an alley and blasted him. He died in the street.

The Calabrese hit was the latest in a string of gangland murders that started with the Bruno killing less than 18 months before and garnered both a lot of publicity from the local media and a lot of extra scrutiny from law enforcement.

Three weeks after the Calabrese killing, Little Nicky turned his attention on an aging mob associate named Frank "Frankie Flowers" D'Alfonso.

Frankie Flowers wasn't a made guy, he was an associate and he made a ton of money with Ange. They were involved in a lot of things together, both illegal and legal stuff. So when my uncle becomes boss, he sends for Flowers and the guy doesn't come in. So my uncle tells Salvie, "I want you to give him a beating. Don't kill him, but shake him up. Make sure he knows that it's a new regime and he is going to pay like everyone else."

Scarfo knew that D'Alfonso was a huge earner, and Scarfo hoped that a beating at the hands of Salvie Testa would bring the old-timer around.

Salvie and Gino Milano, who was one of Salvie's guys, set up a meeting with Flowers and he falls for it and is walking to the meeting, which was going take place on the street in the Ninth Street Italian Market in South Philadelphia. As he's walking, Salvie and Gino jump out from behind a car, Salvie has a baseball bat and Gino has a steel bar, and they give Flowers a beating. They tuned him up pretty good.

When an ambulance crew found D'Alfonso, he was semiconscious and bleeding in the street. At the hospital it was determined that his skull had been fractured, his jaw had been broken, several bones in his face were broken, and one of his kneecaps had been shattered.

D'Alfonso would spend the next month in a South Philadelphia hospital recuperating.

By the time he was out, it was almost Christmas and Philadelphia's new mob don, Nicky Scarfo, decided to throw himself a party.

There was a place on South Street called La Cucina that we used to go to. Sam the Barber, who was with us, owned it. We rented the place out and threw a big party. Everyone in the family was there. You shoulda seen the spread: shrimp, lobster, champagne— the best of everything.

It was a great party.

Everyone who came brought my uncle an envelope for Christmas. Some envelopes had a couple hundred in them, some had a couple thousand.

By the end of the night, I think my uncle had made almost $100,000 just from the envelopes. Some guys would put a Christmas card in the envelope with a nice message for my uncle. He'd laugh as he was taking the cash out, he didn't give a fuck about the card or what they wrote. It was a shakedown. We weren't there to sing Christmas carols.

Towards the end of the night I'm sitting at a table with my uncle and Chuckie, and my uncle motions for Salvie to come over.

My uncle says to Salvie, "I think it's time," and Salvie says, "Time for what, Nick?" and my uncle says, "Your father, " and Salvie's eyes get real big.

My uncle says, "It's two guys," and he nods towards Chickie Narducci, who is standing a few feet away from us talking to some guys at the bar. "That's one of 'em, and the other one is the young kid with the pizza shop, Pete's friend."

Salvie nods his head and he's staring straight ahead in Chickie Narducci's direction, almost like he's in a trance.

My uncle says, "You handle it how you see fit. I want you to do this for your father and for this family."

Salvie's sitting there and his eyes had welled up with tears and he leans in and hugs my uncle and gives him a kiss on the cheek. He wiped his eyes and said, "Thank you, Nick," and he got up and, boom, he's out the door. I think his emotions had gotten the best of him.

Now when my uncle became boss, he didn't come back to Philadelphia and tell everyone what Pete Casella had said at the meeting with the Chin about who was in on the Phil Testa murder. The word going around was that New York had given Pete Casella a pass and that they had retired him to Florida and made my uncle the boss. That was it; that was the story.

No one knew that Pete had given up Chickie and Rocco Marinucci, except for my uncle, and the only people he told were me, Chuckie, and Lawrence. We knew, but no one else in the family knew.

Now we're at the Christmas party and my uncle tells Salvie and he gives him the okay to kill both guys.

It was a great way to end the year.

The Fine Art of Revenge

FRANK "CHICKIE" NARDUCCI WAS IN A BAD SPOT. WHILE IT APPEARED THAT THE MULTIMILLIONAIRE MOB CAPO HAD SURVIVED THE BLOODLETTING IN THE AFTERMATH OF THE BRUNO AND TESTA KILLINGS, NARDUCCI FACED AN ADVERSARY WITH GREATER MIGHT THAN LITTLE NICKY SCARFO: RICO.

Narducci was one of several defendants named in a 1980 racketeering indictment brought by the US attorney's office in Philadelphia aimed at dismantling the Bruno crime family.

The Racketeering Influenced Corrupt Organization (RICO) statute had become the federal government's most reliable weapon in the war against organized crime.

Within the scope of a RICO prosecution, the government first had to prove that the defendants were members of an organization and that the organization had engaged in illegal activities.

The government then had to show that each defendant had participated in at least two predicate crimes on behalf of the organization. Predicate crimes covered under the broad RICO statute included: facilitating illegal gambling operations; loaning money at usurious rates; the trafficking of narcotics; extortion; and acts of violence, including murder.

In theory, a low-level mob bookmaker who was also a loan shark could find himself facing more serious charges if other members of the organization had committed a murder on behalf of the organization.

The RICO indictment that charged Narducci, originally included Angelo Bruno and Philip Testa, but both men had died before the case was brought to court.

Jury selection began on January 4, 1982, inside the federal courthouse, located on Market Street, a few blocks away from Philadelphia's Old City neighborhood, which is one of the most historic areas in the United States.

Home to the Liberty Bell and the world famous Betsy Ross House, Old City is where the Declaration of Independence was first read and the Constitution of the United States was written.

In all likelihood none of this was on "Chickie" Narducci's mind as he and several codefendants left the courthouse after an exhausting fourth day of jury selection.

The kind of justice that Narducci was to face was not what our nation's forefathers had in mind.

That evening as Narducci parked his late model Cadillac half a block away from his South Philadelphia home and exited the car, he heard someone say, "Hey, Frank," and he turned around to see who was calling.

It was the Grim Reaper.

To Narducci's shock and horror, he was staring at Salvie Testa with a gun in his hand.

The mob's longtime gambling czar's luck was about to run out.

Testa pumped the first several shots into Narducci's face from point-blank range and Narducci's body crumbled into the street below him. Testa and another gunman, his best friend and right-hand man Joseph "Joe Punge" Pungitore, would then empty their guns into Narducci's fallen body as he lay bleeding and helpless wedged between his car and the curb, stuck in the gutter.

When it was over, Narducci was dead, having been shot ten times in the face, head, neck, and chest.

Salvie was on cloud nine after he killed Narducci. That's how much he hated him for what he had done to his father. He would brag about it and say, "I made sure he knew it was me and I gave him a second, so he knew what was comin'. You shoulda seen the look on his face when he knew I had him."

The revenge killing of Chickie Narducci could be justified by Narducci's involvement in the bombing death of Philip Testa.

But Scarfo's next killing seemed to be rooted in only pure evil and vindictiveness.

My uncle hated this guy from South Philly named Mickey Diamond. Hated him with a passion. This went back 15, 20 years. Mickey Diamond was close with Joseph "Joe the Boss" Rugnetta, who was Ange's consigliere before Caponigro, and Joe the Boss hated my uncle because my uncle once made a disparaging remark about his daughter. My uncle said she was ugly and Joe the Boss went nuts and wanted Ange to have my uncle killed, but Ange said no. This was in the late '60s, for Christ's sake, but ever since then my uncle hated both Joe the Boss and Mickey Diamond.

Now adding to this, around the same time frame, Chuckie Merlino had gotten into trouble with two old-time mob guys. Mickey Diamond had ratted Chuckie out to the old-timers, and they demanded a sit-down with Ange over what happened with Chuckie, and because Joe the Boss was the consigliere, it was his job to mediate the dispute.

Now at the time, Chuckie wasn't a made guy but my uncle was, and my uncle and Chuckie were best friends, so my uncle goes to the sit-down and represents Chuckie, he goes to bat for him. This Joe the Boss hated my uncle so much, his recommendation to Ange was that Chuckie should be killed. He wanted to kill Chuckie because Ange wouldn't let him kill my uncle. My uncle challenged him at the sit-down and this made Joe the Boss hate my uncle even more. These old-timers were all about respect.

So Ange tells Joe the Boss, he says, "We're not killin' the kid, not for this," meaning Chuckie, and Chuckie apologizes to the old-timers, and the whole thing is forgotten.

But the venom between my uncle and Joe the Boss continued until he died. I think he died in 1977. When Joe the Boss died, that's when Caponigro became the consigliere and Mickey Diamond kind of went with Caponigro.

Once Caponigro got killed, Mickey Diamond was basically out of it, he wasn't really in play.

So maybe a week or so after we killed Chickie Narducci, my uncle and I head to the Brajole Café for a meeting. I thought it was going to be just us and Chuckie, but when we get there it's Chuckie and Frank Monte. A few minutes later, in comes the old-timers who had the beef with Chuckie all those years before. Now all these years later, Chuckie is the underboss and these guys are semiretired. I'm thinking to myself, why is my uncle meeting with these two guys?

My uncle says to them, "Fellas, I need your help with something." Now if I don't know why they are there, I know that they have absolutely no idea why they are there. So they say, "Sure, Nick, what do you need?" And my uncle says, "It's about your friend Mickey Diamond," and he makes the sign of the gun and points it to the floor. "He's gotta go."

You shoulda seen the look on their faces; they looked like they were gonna cry. Chuckie even made a face at me like he couldn't believe my uncle wanted to kill Mickey Diamond after all these years, and he was going to make these two guys do it.

Now these guys know the rules—they know if they don't kill Mickey Diamond, my uncle's gonna kill them. But that was how my uncle was: he never forgot nothin' and he never forgave no one.

On February 25, 1982, Philadelphia police found the body of Dominick "Mickey Diamond" DeVito in the trunk of his car parked in a residential neighborhood in South Philadelphia.

DeVito had been shot in the head with a .38 and his body had been placed in plastic trash bags. His hands and feet had been tied behind him.

The DeVito killing was the 16th Philly mob killing in six years, and number 17 was less than three weeks away.

Around this time there was a message on a local TV channel in Atlantic City that played over and over for almost three days that said, "Nicky and Phil, you're next." It was handwritten on a piece of paper and was mixed in with some local advertisements. When we saw it, my uncle said, "What the fuck is this?" I later found out that an Atlantic City cop who lived to break balls was the one who wrote it, and him and his friend, another cop who loved to break balls, put it in the projector inside of Convention Hall as a joke.

There was nothing funny about what would happen next.

Salvie Testa had started 1982 off by killing Chickie Narducci, one of the men responsible for the bombing death of his father on March 15, 1981.

The other killer, Rocco Marinucci, thought that Scarfo and Testa were unaware of his involvement in the Philip Testa murder. That's because guys in Salvie Testa's crew had been referring burglary jobs to Marinucci, who in addition to making pizzas and nail bombs, was also a renowned burglar.

Right after Salvie killed Chickie Narducci, he went and grabbed Chickie's two sons, Frankie and Philip, and brought them in. He told them, "I killed your father, because he killed my father." Now Frankie and Philip were around La Cosa Nostra *all of their life through their father, so they knew the rules. Frankie was a made guy and he was part of Salvie's crew.*

Now when Salvie tells them this, they knew there is nothing they can say or do about it. If they tried to retaliate, or anything like that, we would have killed them both, and they knew it. So they accepted it for what it was and everyone moved on.

Now at the time, Frankie Narducci was tight with this Rocco Marinucci, the kid who made the bomb. So Salvie's crew, which included both Narducci brothers, are feeding this Rocco little jobs and Rocco and Salvie's guys are making money together, and Rocco thinks he's in the clear. But this is the trap. It's just like we did with the concrete union job for Vincent Falcone. And just like Vince, Rocco falls for it.

Salvie's guys tell Rocco, "We need you to help us open a safe. We think there's a couple million in there."

So Rocco and Salvie's guys go to the Buckeye Club in South Philadelphia, which is Frankie Narducci's place to go over the plan to get the safe and get the tools they needed. Rocco is thinking: this is it, this is the score of a lifetime. Now this whole time, Rocco is dealing with guys in Salvie's crew, but never Salvie himself.

So they get to the club, they go inside, and the lights are out. Frankie says, "Must be a bad bulb." The other guys come in and Rocco is asking them if they brought flashlights so they can see, because the place is pitch black. Frankie says to Rocco, "There's some flashlights in the backroom and there's a light switch back there, see if that's working." Rocco finds a string hanging from the ceiling and he pulls it, and a dim light goes on, and as Rocco turns around, instead of seeing the flashlights, he sees Salvie Testa.

The Grim Reaper would strike again.

Testa and his crew, who were known in law enforcement circles as the Young Executioners, lived up to their name by tying up Marinucci and brutally torturing him for several hours before putting him out of his misery, but things didn't go quite as Salvie had planned.

> *Salvie told me afterwards that he bought a bag of M-80s and cherry bombs, like the firecrackers you see on the Fourth of July. He wanted to torture this kid within an inch of his life, and then when he was ready to kill him, he wanted to put the fireworks in his mouth and keep setting them off until he died. But the problem was the saliva in his mouth made it difficult to light the firecrackers, so they kept beating him and beating him every time they wouldn't light.*
>
> *So finally, Salvie pulls out a gun and empties it into this kid's head. Then they stuffed three of the firecrackers into his mouth to send a message that the killing was payback for what happened to Salvie's dad.*

The firecrackers weren't the only message that Salvie Testa and his Young Executioners crew would send; they purposely committed the murder on March 15, 1982, the one-year anniversary of Philip Testa's death.

In less than a year, Nicodemo "Little Nicky" Scarfo had established his burgeoning organization as the most ruthless regime in the history of the Philadelphia mob. Gone were the Docile Don days of Angelo Bruno. Nicky Scarfo was a gangster, and the men around him were stone-cold killers.

> *This is exactly what my uncle wanted. He wanted people to be afraid of us, and they were. Everyone was scared to death.*

And for good reason.

Scarfo and Leonetti had turned Atlantic City into the Wild West of the 1970s, with several high-profile gangland killings, and now they were doing the same in the streets of South Philadelphia.

The Prelude to a War

A S FAR AS APPEARANCES GO, HARRY "THE HUNCHBACK" RICCO-
BENE COULD NOT HAVE BEEN LESS INTIMIDATING. BARELY FIVE
FEET TALL, WITH A SQUEAKY VOICE, A LONG, BUSHY WHITE BEARD
AND, AS YOU MIGHT EXPECT FROM HIS NICKNAME, WALKING WITH A
SLUMP DUE TO A CURVATURE OF THE SPINE HE HAD HAD SINCE BIRTH,
RICCOBENE DIDN'T LOOK LIKE MUCH TO CONTEND WITH.

He was.

Born in Sicily on July 27, 1909, Harry Riccobene came to the United
States with his family as a young boy, settling in South Philadelphia and
quickly gravitating to a life of crime. Law enforcement records indicate he
was inducted into the mob by Prohibition-era don Salvatore Sabella when
he was only 17 years old. Benefiting from the early experience of plying
his trade in the underworld, he became an expert and well-respected racketeer by the time he reached his 30s, making money from a variety of illicit
endeavors and keeping himself continually in the good graces of whoever
was running the show in the Philly mob by always giving them a little taste
of his action.

That was until Nicky Scarfo took over.

Scarfo wasn't satisfied with prior arrangements.

He wanted more than a little taste of the Hunchback's vast riches.

When he became boss in the spring of 1981, Little Nicky made it known
to Riccobene, a onetime underworld ally, that he expected a nonnegotiable
set percentage of his monthly cash intake to be collected as part of Scarfo's
aggressive underworld street tax.

Despite the killings of John Calabrese and Stevie Bouras, and the
violent beating of Frank "Frankie Flowers" D'Alfonso—all of whom had
balked at paying Scarfo's street tax—Riccobene, the seasoned old-school
mob vet, scoffed at Scarfo's demand.

Over the years, Riccobene had built up a strong power base. He surrounded himself with a loyal and well-stocked crew of thugs, thieves, and
fellow racketeers who answered to him and to him only. He, in essence,

oversaw a family within a family. This fact made him believe he could challenge Scarfo in a street war. And that's exactly what he did.

> *We started having problems with the Riccobenes in 1982. Harry refused to pay the street tax and he was thumbing his nose at my uncle. This drove my uncle crazy. He used to say, "This guy thinks he's gonna make a jerk off outta me? We'll see about that."*
>
> *We tried everything to bring him in and get him on board, but Harry was a stubborn old-time siggy, and he made it clear that he didn't acknowledge my uncle as his boss and he wasn't going to pay us.*
>
> *He left us no choice. We had to kill him.*

Scarfo decided to send his consigliere, Frank Monte, and the treacherous Raymond "Long John" Martorano to see Harry's younger brother, Mario "Sonny" Riccobene, with an order from Scarfo that Sonny help in setting up his brother to be killed.

The move backfired.

Instead of joining the assault against his brother, Sonny Riccobene went to his brother and warned him of the pending plot to kill him and who was involved.

The Hunchback's response was loud and left little doubt that he was more than willing to go toe-to-toe with Little Nicky.

A few weeks later, on May 13, Frank Monte was gunned down while standing in front of his car at a South Philadelphia gas station by Joseph Pedulla and Victor DeLuca, two hit men in Riccobene's crew who had been lying in wait for the mob consigliere in a parking lot across the street from the gas station with a powerful scope-fitted rifle.

The Riccobenes had struck first.

Nicky Scarfo was incensed.

The war was on.

An Old Foe Returns

S IF A STREET WAR WITH HARRY RICCOBENE IN SOUTH PHILA-
DELPHIA WASN'T ENOUGH, NICKY SCARFO AND PHILIP LEONETTI
SOON BECAME SADDLED WITH A NEW PROBLEM FROM AN OLD
FOE IN ATLANTIC CITY.

Now right around the time we started beefing with Harry, Frank Gerace gets word to us through Bobby Lumio that he needs to see me and my uncle.

Frank Gerace was a bartender who we knew, and we made him the president of Local 54, which was the biggest union in Atlantic City representing the hotel and restaurant workers in the casinos. At the time they had like 15,000 people in the union and they were strong, but we made them even stronger.

Bobby Lumio was a made guy who my uncle put in a powerful position at Local 54. He was the secretary-treasurer and was on the executive board. He also lived in one of our apartments on Georgia Avenue.

At the time, Bobby was dying. He had real bad cancer, and the doctors had only given him a few months to live.

Bobby tells me one day, "You gotta get with Percy," meaning Frank Gerace, "He has a problem with Joe Salerno."

I say to Bobby, "Joe Salerno the plumber? They got him in the Witness Protection Program. How's he making trouble for Frank Gerace?"

I'm thinking maybe his medicines got him loopy, because Joe Salerno isn't around anymore, and I don't think he planned on coming back because he knew we would have killed him.

So Bobby's lying there in the bed and he says, "You gotta get with Percy."

So the next day I send for Frank Gerace and I have him meet me down in Margate near a place that I had on Adams Avenue. When he gets there I tell him what Bobby had told me, and he says,

"It's true, Philip. Joe Salerno is gonna testify against me at a hearing with the state. They are trying to get me out of Local 54 because they are saying I am with you and your uncle and Joe Salerno is their main witness."

I told Frank I would talk to my uncle and we would figure things out.

Now this is bad. We made a lot of money from Local 54. We were getting 50, 60, sometimes $100,000 a month, all of it in cash. If Frank Gerace got bumped out, it was going to be a problem for our family.

I knew my uncle was going to go nuts when he found out. Winning the Falcone murder trial wasn't enough for him. He wanted to kill Joe Salerno for testifying against us, but we couldn't get to him because he was in the Witness Protection Program.

Every time we were around the Narducci brothers, Frank and Philip, my uncle used to ask them, "You guys seen Salerno around?" because Joe Salerno's family lived right near where the Narducci's lived. When Frank or Philip would say no, my uncle would go into a tirade about Joe Salerno, calling him a "no good rat motherfucker" or calling him a "cocksuckin' rat" and he would tell them, "If that motherless fuck ever shows his face, it's this," and he'd make the sign of the gun, "I don't care who he's with. He could be with the pope and it's this," and make the sign of the gun.

So the next morning when I pick up my uncle, I tell him about my conversation with Bobby Lumio and Frank Gerace. He went berserk about Joe Salerno. He said, "This motherfucker wants to keep trying to hurt us, we're gonna hurt him. We're gonna see how he likes it. This no-good rat motherfucker." He was irate. One, because he was gonna testify against us again, and two, because this time it could cost us a lot of money.

He said, "Today, when we go see Bobby, I want him to get to the bottom of this." We were on our way to Philadelphia to see Bobby Simone, who was representing my uncle on his appeal of the federal gun charge.

The whole ride up, we're not talking, because we never talked in the car or even near the car, but every 10 minutes or so my uncle would say, "This motherfucker," or mutter something to himself about Joe Salerno. I'm riding next to him and he's talking to himself like a crazy person.

So we get to Bobby's office and he tells my uncle that if he doesn't win the appeal on the gun case that he was looking at two years in prison, and he'd have to do about 18 months.

It was almost like my uncle didn't hear a word Bobby said. He said, "Look, Bob, I'm not worried about the gun case. If I have to do the two years, I'll do the two years. I need you to look into this thing for me," and he told him all about the thing with Joe Salerno and Frank Gerace.

Bobby said, "Okay, Nick," and he started talking about the gun case again and my uncle waved him off and said, "Bob, we need to focus on this thing with Joe Salerno. We can worry about the gun case later."

Bobby told us to give him a few days to see what was going on.

During this time, Bobby Lumio was in a real bad shape. He was on his deathbed. One of the last things he said was, "Tell my friend I will miss him." He was talking about my uncle. This was on his deathbed.

So after Bobby dies, my uncle hears what he had said and my uncle said, "I don't give a fuck about him; nobody's gonna miss him." This was a guy who was with us, a made guy, who while he was dying was looking out for us by tipping us off about the thing with Joe Salerno and Frank Gerace. But now that Bobby was dead, he couldn't do anything for my uncle. That's how he thought. That's how evil of a guy he was.

So about a week later Bobby Simone comes down to see us and we walk up to the boardwalk and he tells us that Joe Salerno is scheduled to testify before the state and that if things go bad, Frank Gerace is going to be removed as the president of Local 54 and that there could be an indictment for labor racketeering charges.

My uncle looks at me and shakes his head and says, "These fuckin' rats, we gotta do something here. We can't just sit back and watch. We gotta take action."

I didn't know what to say; what could I say? Joe Salerno was in the Witness Protection Program. It's not like he was in Atlantic City or South Philadelphia and we could kill him. We had no idea where he was.

A week later, under the protection the United States Marshals Service, Joe Salerno would testify before the New Jersey State Casino Control Commission about Local 54 and its connections to Nicky Scarfo, Philip Leonetti, and the mob.

His testimony touched on his relationship with Scarfo, Leonetti, the Merlino brothers, and mob killer Nicholas "Nick the Blade" Virgilio in the late 1970s, and each of their relationships with the union, and then went on to detail once again the night that Philip Leonetti murdered Vincent Falcone.

As Salerno testified, he wore a dark hood over his head with holes cut out around his eyes, so that his identity could remain a secret. There were more than a dozen armed US Marshals in and around the building where Salerno was testifying, which was located at the corner of Tennessee and the boardwalk in Atlantic City, less than two miles from Scarfo's Georgia Avenue headquarters.

Salerno's testimony included a story about an incident in which Nicky Scarfo lost his temper at Bobby Lumio, a high-ranking official of Local 54, after Lumio made a joke that Scarfo didn't find funny.

According to Salerno's testimony, Scarfo said to Lumio, "Let me tell you something, I got you your job and I got that other big fat jerk off downstairs his job, and don't you ever fuckin' forget it."

Based in large part on the testimony of Joe Salerno, Frank Gerace was disqualified from having any further association with Local 54, as were several of his top associates, which meant that Nicky Scarfo and Philip Leonetti no longer controlled the union through Gerace.

So after we get the news that Frank Gerace is out, my uncle is furious. He was so full of venom against Joe Salerno. He said, "Do you believe this motherfucker? Can you believe what he did to us? We can't let this stand." He was enraged.

The Summer of '82

NICKY SCARFO WAS A VOLATILE, HOMICIDAL MANIAC ON A GOOD DAY, BUT THE CLIMATE AROUND HIM IN THE SUMMER MONTHS OF 1982 MADE HIM AN UNTAMED BEAST WHOSE PENCHANT FOR BLOOD AND VIOLENCE HAD REACHED AN ALL-TIME HIGH.

As if the murder of his trusted aide Frank Monte and the war with Harry Riccobene weren't enough, Scarfo had just lost control of the biggest union in Atlantic City and the riches that came with it, which amounted to almost a million per year in tax-free cash and the unbridled power that came from controlling a union with thousands of members.

Add to that the two-year federal prison sentence that was hanging over his head on the 1979 weapon charge and Little Nicky wasn't exactly in what you'd call a good place.

Plus his allergies were bothering him.

My uncle's allergies were real bad and when they were bothering him, forget about it, he was the most miserable human being on the planet. Everybody would stay away; that's how bad he was.

Now around this time, we had our hands full and my uncle was unbearable, the worst I'd ever seen him.

One day my uncle says to me, "Let's take a walk," and we start walking up Georgia Avenue towards the boardwalk. We were going to meet Salvie and Philip Narducci in front of Convention Hall.

As we are walking my uncle starts telling me a story about the Blade getting drunk in the casino and starting a fight and causing this big scene. I figure he's gonna tell me to go to the casino and straighten it out.

He says, "This fuckin' guy is an embarrassment, the way he conducts himself with the drinking and all this nonsense, I've had it up to here with him and I am done with his shenanigans. I want you to take him for a walk down the alleys behind the house and I want you to kill him right there in the alley, leave him in the gutter where he belongs with all his drinking."

I'm thinking to myself, "Jesus Christ, with everything we got goin' on, now we're gonna start killing our own guys? What are we doing?"

After flippantly ordering the murder of Nicholas "Nick the Blade" Virgilio, one of his oldest friends, Nicky Scarfo was about to cross an even more sinister line with his next murder plot.

So now we're on the boardwalk and Salvie and Philip were there waiting for us. Like clockwork my uncle says to Philip, "You seen that cocksucker Joe Salerno around?" and Philip says, "Not the kid, but I see his old man all the time. He owns a motel down in Wildwood." It was almost like I could see the lightbulb go off in my uncle's head. I could read him like a book, I knew what was comin' next.

Without hesitation my uncle says to Philip, "I want you to go see the old man, and when you do, it's this," and he makes the sign of the gun. "We're gonna teach these animals a lesson."

Philip says, "Okay, Nick," and Salvie shoots me a look like, "What the fuck is this?" This was against the rules and what we were supposed to stand for. Joe Salerno's father was a civilian; he wasn't involved with us or this thing and now we're gonna kill him because of something his son did. I knew this was a big, big mistake, but with my uncle there was no questioning him.

My uncle then turned to Salvie and said, "Everybody connected to our friend, the dwarf," meaning Harry Riccobene, "it's this," and he makes the sign of the gun. "All of 'em, his whole regime. You're in charge, get it done."

In a span of about 15 minutes, Nicodemo "Little Nicky" Scarfo had ordered the murders of Nicholas "Nick the Blade" Virgilio, Joe Salerno Sr., Harry "the Hunchback" Riccobene, and everyone connected to Riccobene's crew.

My head was spinning. It was like he wanted to kill everyone and everything around him. It was a never-ending cycle with him.

Wasting no time carrying out Scarfo's orders, Salvie Testa drafted a list of everyone connected to the Riccobene faction and ordered that they be killed on sight.

Within days, Salvatore "Wayne" Grande, an ambitious Scarfo assassin and trusted member of Salvie Testa's Young Executioners crew, caught the Hunchback all by himself on a South Philadelphia street corner, standing in a phone booth.

The Hunchback was a sitting duck.

Wayne Grande ambushed Riccobene, blasting him with five shots from a revolver at close range, but miraculously, the 73-year-old Hunchback was able to wrestle the gun away from the 28-year-old Grande before he could finish the job.

When Philadelphia police arrived moments later they found Riccobene leaning against the phone booth, bleeding and holding his assassin's gun.

When he was asked how he was able to wrestle the gun from his would-be killer, the Hunchback responded, "He was done with it, so I took it."

Riccobene would later tell associates he knew that the weapon was a six-shot revolver and had counted the five shots that had hit him. Knowing that there was one bullet left, Riccobene stated he took the gun and attempted to shoot his assailant with the sixth bullet, but the gun was empty.

So far, Harry the Hunchback was winning the war and he was about to return fire with a strike of his own.

While Scarfo's gunmen were out looking to kill everyone who was part of the Riccobene faction, the Riccobenes were out looking to kill the men aligned with Scarfo.

In late July, Joseph Pedulla and fellow Riccobene loyalist Victor DeLuca found Salvie Testa eating clams while sitting on a wooden crate in the middle of the famous Ninth Street Italian Market, and hit him with multiple shotgun blasts fired from their passing car.

The hit team of Pedulla and DeLuca had previously killed Scarfo's consigliere, Frank Monte, and now had wounded his street boss.

The spry and vibrant Testa had half of his left shoulder blown off, but like the Hunchback, he survived the attack and after some time in the hospital, he was back on the street leading Little Nicky's assault on Riccobene and his renegades.

Shortly after the shooting of Salvie Testa in the Italian Market, Joey Grande, a Scarfo hit man and the brother of Wayne Grande, fired multiple shots at Riccobene as he sat behind the wheel of his Mercedes on a South Philadelphia street corner. However, once again, the old man survived, failing to take a single bullet.

Things were at a standstill. Tensions were increasing and the local press was having a field day as the streets of Philadelphia were engulfed in an all-out mob war.

But killing Harry Riccobene wasn't the only thing on Nicky Scarfo's mind.

A few weeks later on August 9, 1982, Joseph Salerno Sr. was in the office of the motel he owned in Wildwood Crest, which was a short distance from the beach and the famous Wildwood Boardwalk, which was one of the most popular destinations at the Jersey Shore.

The NO VACANCY sign was lit, yet a young man was pacing outside the office door wearing a jogging suit and a hooded sweatshirt. He was 19-year-old Philip Narducci, the son of the late Frank "Chickie" Narducci.

When Joe Salerno Sr. opened the door, Narducci took a handgun out of his pocket and fired two shots at him, one of which struck him in the neck.

Salerno Sr. was not only alive, but he was able to talk to the paramedics who arrived on the scene and took him to the hospital.

While Philip Narducci, the young would-be mob assassin, had failed to kill Joe Salerno Sr., Nicky Scarfo's message had been delivered: If you betray me, I will find you and kill you. And if I cannot find you, I will kill your family.

This ominous message still haunts many today, including Philip Leonetti, more than two decades after the shooting of Joe Salerno Sr.

The shooting of Salerno Sr. made front-page news in Philadelphia and all throughout South Jersey, and the headlines were the kind that Little Nicky loved.

> *The day after the shooting, there were more cops following us than ever. They were everywhere. My uncle said to me, "Look at all these cocksuckers watchin' us. They got nothing better to do." I knew we had made a big mistake when my uncle ordered the hit on Joe Salerno's father, and I think my uncle did, too, but he would never say it.*

If Scarfo didn't know that trying to kill the father of a federally protected witness was likely to draw the ire of law enforcement, he would get the message loud and clear less than a week later, when the FBI arrested him on Georgia Avenue and whisked him away.

We were standing in front of the office when all the sudden here comes the cops up the street. It was a one-way and they were coming in both directions. Like five or six cars. It was just me and my uncle. There's like 20 guys. They all got guns.

My uncle says, "What the fuck is all this?" and they moved in and grabbed him, handcuffed him and threw him in the back of one of the cars. They grabbed me, but they let me go once he was in the car. They were only there for him. Before they pulled off I heard him say, "Call Bobby" and that was it, they were gone. It was the FBI; I knew he was in trouble.

The US attorney's office in Camden had filed a motion to revoke Scarfo's bail pending appeal because they claimed to have evidence that he had violated the conditions of his bail by associating with convicted felons. The judge took the unusual step of issuing a body warrant for Scarfo in lieu of scheduling a hearing first.

Scarfo was taken directly to the Camden County Jail and placed in solitary confinement to await his hearing.

The next day I went to Philadelphia to see Bobby Simone and Bobby told me, "This is because of what happened down in Wildwood. There's too much heat."

I told Bobby, "You gotta get me in to see my uncle. I need to talk to him."

Two days later Bobby arranged for me to visit my uncle inside the jail. It had been almost ten years since I had visited my uncle in jail, when he was in Yardville, and I found myself thinking of how much had happened over those 10 years. How many guys had been killed, all the stuff we had done, and how things seemed to be spiraling out of control. Then my uncle suddenly appeared on the other side of the glass and picked up the phone. I could tell right away he was agitated.

He started complaining right away. He said, "Tell Bobby to get me out of this place right away. This place is a fuckin' toilet and I cannot stay here. Tell him I don't give a fuck where they send me. They can send me to Russia, I don't give a fuck, but I cannot stay here."

I said, "Okay, I'll go see him."

My uncle takes his finger and points at me and says, "On this side, and the guy over the bridge on that side. Got it?" and I nodded my head, yes.

He was saying he wanted me to run everything on this side of the bridge, meaning New Jersey, while he was gone, and he wanted Chuckie to run everything on the other side of the bridge, meaning Philadelphia.

He then took his hand and held it out like he was trying to demonstrate someone's height. He made the height very low, and I knew immediately that he was talking about Harry Riccobene.

He said, "Tell your friend over there that I said him and his friends need to start acting right and stop playing games."

He's looking at me through the glass and his eyes are really big as he is saying it, meaning for me to tell Salvie that him and his crew need to start killing the Riccobenes and to stop botching the hits.

My uncle always talked in circles, but I knew what he was saying because I knew what he was thinking.

Then he said, "Bobby says I'm lookin' at a year and a half," and he shrugged his shoulders like he didn't give a fuck, but I know he did. My uncle hated jail. All he ever did was bitch and complain when he was locked up.

Now he's going on about the food, the guards, the noise, the black kids with their boom boxes, the dust, and all I'm thinking is how great it is going to be to not have to deal with him for the next 18 months. I couldn't wait for them to ship him the fuck out; I was hoping they'd send him to Alaska.

Two days later Nicodemo Scarfo's bail was revoked and he was immediately driven to the Philadelphia International Airport, where he boarded a plane with two US Marshals and was flown directly to El Paso, Texas, and sent to the La Tuna Federal Correctional Center to serve his sentence.

Little Nicky was a long way from Atlantic City and would stay there for the rest of 1982, for all of 1983, and into 1984.

In his absence, the murder and mayhem would continue.

But for his nephew Philip Leonetti, life was about to change.

Taking a Break

The day after they shipped my uncle to Texas, I remember waking up and I couldn't have been happier. I felt free for the first time in my life. I can't even describe the feeling, it was as if I had beaten cancer and had a new lease on life. I remember going up to the boardwalk and walking all the way from Georgia Avenue down to the end of the boardwalk in Ventnor, as if I didn't have a care in the world.

I was just walking and staring out at the ocean. At that moment I didn't give a fuck about my uncle, Harry Riccobene, the mob, none of it. It was like I was living a different life.

That night I took my girl out for a nice dinner at the Knife and Fork, which was one of the best restaurants in Atlantic City. I was constantly running around, day and night with my uncle, 24-7. He never shut down, so I never shut down. And now here I was, relaxing, having a night out. I couldn't remember the last time I had been out with her where I wasn't worried about what time I had to get home or what time I had to meet someone for my uncle.

My girl told me that I was smiling the whole night.

Philip Leonetti's girlfriend was accustomed to his daily routine, as she lived directly across the street from the Scarfo compound on Georgia Avenue.

She was also somewhat familiar with the life of a mobster, as she had once dated Vincent Falcone and was dating him when Philip killed him in December 1979.

She was the one who came by the office and asked if I knew where Vince was right after I killed him. Maria. Me and her started dating a few months after I killed Vince, and at the time she had no idea that I had killed him. We never talked about him; it was as if he had never existed.

In addition to having a steady girlfriend for more than a year, Philip Leonetti had something else in his personal life: an eight-year-old son.

Philip Jr. was born in March 1974, right before my 21st birthday. I wasn't much of a father in the beginning, because I had put La Cosa Nostra first, which is what you are supposed to do when you take your oath.

This thing is supposed to come before everything, even your family and your own kids, and for me, it did. But now I was starting to have second thoughts about this life, mainly because I was so sick of being around my uncle and just the way that he was—all the killings, all of the treachery.

Maria and I started taking Little Philip places like the movies, the Ocean City Boardwalk, the Philadelphia Zoo—things I would never do when my uncle was around. He'd go crazy if he found out I took my kid to the zoo. He would have said, "What are you, a jerk off, goin' there and lookin' at animals?" But I was having the time of my life with Maria and Philip. I never felt so alive in all of my life.

Just as Philip Leonetti was starting to get accustomed to life without his uncle, a phone call from an angry and agitated Nicky Scarfo from a Texas prison would snap him back to reality.

I was in my grandmother's apartment with my mother and Little Philip and the phone rings and my grandmother asked me to pick it up, and it says, "You have a collect call from Nick." I almost got sick to my stomach hearing his voice.

I accepted the charges and before he was connected the operator said, "This call is from an inmate at a federal institution and it will be monitored and recorded," and the next thing I hear is him screaming into the phone, "Where the fuck have you been? I've been trying to get you for two fuckin' weeks and you are nowhere to be found. Did you go to Philadelphia? Did you do what I asked? I'm sittin' down here like a jerk off while you're out gallivanting." I cut him right off and said, "I've been busy with Scarf, Inc. I've got a couple new jobs." And he says, "Fuck Scarf, Inc. and fuck those jobs." He is still hollering into the phone, and I hand the phone to my grandmother and say, "Here, you talk to him," and I left the house.

When I got outside, I knew my uncle was steaming. I had never talked to him like that or even talked back to him. But I was sick and tired of all of his ranting and raving.

TOP, LEFT: Philip's parents, Pasquale and Annunziata (Nancy), on their wedding day in 1952 with Philip's uncle, Nick Scarfo. **TOP, RIGHT:** Philip as a baby with his godmother and his Uncle Nick. **BOTTOM:** A nine-year-old Philip (front row, third from left) and members of the 1962 St. Mike's basketball team.

TOP: The "gangster" Nicodemo "Little Nicky" Scarfo on the streets of South Philadelphia in the late 50's. **BOTTOM:** The Scarfo compound located at 26-28 North Georgia Avenue in the Ducktown section of Atlantic City, as it appeared in the 80's.

TOP: Philip with his mother, Nancy, and his grandfather, Philip Scarfo, in the early 70's. **BOTTOM:** Nicky Scarfo with his mother Catherine inside their home on Georgia Avenue in the early 80's.

TOP: Philip visiting mob enforcer Nicholas "Nick the Blade" Virgilio at New Jersey's Bayside State Prison in Leesburg in the early 70's. **BOTTOM:** Philip with his cousin Nicky Scarfo Jr. at Casablanca South in Fort Lauderdale in 1987.

TOP: Philip with his cousin Christopher Scarfo, his uncle's oldest son, at a family wedding in 1986. **BOTTOM:** Philip and Nicky Jr. behind the wheel of *The Usual Suspects* as "Little Nicky" and "Nick the Blade" relax on the back of the boat off the coast of Atlantic City in 1986.

Nicky Scarfo, the jailed-for-life former boss of the Philadelphia/Atlantic City mob, behind bars at USP Marion in the early 90's.

TOP: Philip "Crazy Phil" Leonetti, the former underboss of the Philadelphia / Atlantic City mob, behind bars at FCI Phoenix in the early 90's. **BOTTOM:** Mob jester Anthony "Spike" DiGregorio and "Little Philip" inside the Scarf Inc. office on Georgia Avenue.

Philip Leonetti back on Georgia Avenue in December of 2011, visiting his former home for the first time since 1996.

While I'm standing outside the office, who comes walking up the street but the Blade. Now according to my uncle, I'm supposed to kill him. I say, "Hey, Nick, want to grab something to eat?" And he says, "Sure, Philip," and we walk to Caesars. Me and him had been there a few times and we were there together on the night that Ange had gotten killed.

While we're eating, the Blade says, "I know your uncle's mad at me." I say, "Nick, my uncle's mad at everybody. He's mad at me, too," and we both started laughing.

And he said, "I know, Philip, it's just hard for me sometimes."

You see, the Blade had a young son who had drowned and died and the Blade used to carry a picture of him around and he would get fall-down drunk and talk about what had happened with his son, and then after awhile, he'd start trouble and get into a fight.

I understood why he was the way he was. It wasn't his fault.

Philip Leonetti was no longer his uncle's robot. He started thinking for himself and making his own decisions.

And killing Nick the Blade wasn't going to happen.

A few days later Chuckie drives down from Philadelphia and me, him, and Lawrence go to Angeloni's for dinner. He says, "Bobby Simone came to see me. He talked to your uncle and your uncle wants you and Bobby to go down to Texas to see him."

I said to Chuckie, "Hey, Chuck, you wanna come down with us, we'll have a good time," and Chuckie said, "He didn't ask for me, just you and Bobby," and we both laughed.

If anyone knew my uncle besides me, it was Chuckie. He and Chuckie had been hanging since the '50s. Chuckie knew my uncle like the back of his hand.

I think, like me, Chuckie was enjoying not having my uncle around.

So the next day, I'm in the office and the phone rings, and it's my uncle. It's the same routine with the collect call, only this time, when he gets on he's not screaming. He says, "I'm glad I got you. How are things going? How is Scarf, Inc.?" Now I know he could care less about Scarf, Inc., but this is his way of breaking the ice a little bit. I say, "Scarf, Inc. is good; everything is good." He says,

"Good, I'm glad to hear it." He says, "I want you and Bobby to come down and see me. You'll like it down here. It's right on the border of Mexico. The Rio Grande is right there." I say, "Oh, yeah?" And he says, "Yeah." I tell him, "We will set it up and get down there before Christmas," and my uncle seemed happy with that.

I'm thinking to myself: now we're making small talk. I think my uncle knew I was getting sick of all of the bullshit.

Then I told him I had dinner with Chuckie and Lawrence, and he asked how they were doing—again more small talk—and then I couldn't help myself. I said, "Guess who else I had dinner with?" And he said, "Who?" And I said, "The Blade." He said, "You had dinner with him?" I said, "Yeah, we went to Caesars. He apologized for all of that trouble and he's trying to clean his act up."

Now by saying this, I am telling my uncle that I am not going to kill the Blade. Surprisingly, my uncle says, "Good, good. Tell him I said hello and tell him I said to knock it off with the drinking and to start coming around more."

While Nicky Scarfo seemed to be somewhat humbled by being away from his gang, Philip Leonetti knew that it, like his little break, wouldn't last long.

I knew it was only a matter of time before he was screaming and yelling again, that's just how he was. In the meantime, it was back to work for me.

Business as Usual

WITH NICKY SCARFO TUCKED AWAY IN A DUSTY FEDERAL PRISON OVER 2,000 MILES AWAY IN EL PASO, TEXAS, HIS LONGTIME FRIEND AND UNDERBOSS SALVATORE "CHUCKIE" MERLINO WAS CALLING THE SHOTS ON THE STREETS IN SOUTH PHILADEL-PHIA, WHILE HIS 29-YEAR-OLD NEPHEW, PHILIP LEONETTI, WAS OVERSEEING THE FAMILY'S NEW JERSEY OPERATION.

On most days I was in the office or I was taking meetings with guys in restaurants. I'd usually have either Lawrence or Saul Kane with me, and sometimes the Blade.

Blackie Napoli was coming down from Newark twice a month to bring my uncle's money and the guys from Trenton were coming down once or twice a month.

I was meeting with the Taccetta brothers, who were with Tumac Accetturo and the North Jersey branch of the Lucchese crime family, and I was seeing a lot of "Sammy the Bull" Gravano who was with the Gambinos. Me and Sammy started getting real close. He'd always stop by the office if he came to Atlantic City, and me and him would go out to dinner.

When all of these guys would come down to Atlantic City, out of respect they would check in with my uncle. Now with him gone, they were checking in with me.

We'd go out to dinner, we'd talk about who was doing what, who was making moves. Most of the time I'd get an envelope with cash, usually a few thousand dollars, as tribute money for my uncle.

Even with Little Nicky behind bars, the Scarfo mob continued to earn—and earn big. Leonetti estimates that he collected almost $3 million in cash for his uncle during the 17 months that he was behind bars.

The street tax money coming down every month from Phila-delphia could range from $50,000 to $100,000—it depended on what was going on.

Don't forget, we still had our bookmaking and loan sharking operations and we were involved in a million other deals. Making money wasn't a problem for us.

I'd always pick the money up directly from Chuckie and I'd bring it home and I would count it out with Nicky Jr.

Without fail, no matter what the amount was, it would always be light a few hundred dollars. I knew Chuckie wasn't skimming three or four hundred dollars; he was making tens of thousands of dollars himself. I believed it was his son Joey who was robbing the money.

Joey Merlino was always a no-good kid. He was a punk even as a teenager, 18 or 19 years old. He was constantly starting trouble in Atlantic City, and my uncle would always make me straighten it out. He would bet with bookmakers who were with us and not pay them when he lost, then he would lie and say that it wasn't him. On top of that, I believe he was robbing the money that was coming down from Philadelphia to Atlantic City for me and my uncle.

Around that time I wanted to kill him, but he was Chuckie's son and I know there was no way my uncle would sanction it. At that time my uncle liked this kid very much because the two of them were very much alike, and Joey was always respectful around my uncle. Plus, Chuckie was my uncle's best friend and he was the underboss, and Joey and Nicky Jr. were also the best of friends.

I thought he was no good and, if I could have, I would have killed him.

While Philip Leonetti was busy in Atlantic City, Salvie Testa and his Young Executioners crew were still on the front lines of the Scarfo mob's war with the Riccobene faction.

A couple times a week my uncle would call and say things like, "Did Salvie clean that boat yet? Tell him to get the boat clean," which was his way of saying tell Salvie and his guys to get the Ricc-obenes. He would say, "Tell him the whole boat, top to bottom, clean the whole thing," which meant he wanted everyone dead—Harry and his whole crew.

In December 1982, Harry "the Hunchback" Riccobene was jailed on a parole violation for possession of a handgun during a traffic stop. Already convicted on a slew of federal racketeering chargers, the Hunchback was out on an appeal bond when he violated.

Riccobene was immediately whisked away to jail and, like his arch nemesis Nicky Scarfo, the Hunchback was forced to command his assault effort from behind bars.

Right before Christmas, me and Bobby Simone flew down to Texas to see my uncle, like I had promised him. He seemed to be in good spirits because he knew we were making a lot of money, but he was still hell-bent on killing all of Harry's guys, even with Harry in jail.

When we got down to Texas and went to the jail, they would only let Bobby in and told me I was prohibited from having any unsupervised contact with my uncle. I said, "No problem," and I told Bobby to meet me back at the hotel when he was done. Truth be told, I was okay not seeing him, I actually preferred it. I was enjoying my time away from him, especially my time with Maria and Little Philip.

I decided to drive around a little bit and, boy, was I out of place. It was all cowboys and Mexicans down there. I felt like I was on another planet. I knew my uncle couldn't have been happy in there and now I knew what he meant when he said that the other prisoners in La Tuna were "not our kind of people."

My uncle had told me that the whole place was full of Mexican guys and black guys. He said, "There's not two white guys in this whole fuckin' place." The Mexican Mafia was very big down there, and there were a lot of fights in that jail, a lot of stabbings.

My uncle kept to himself while he was in there, but he had two Mexican guys who were with him the whole time he was there. He called them his pistoleros, and they served as his bodyguards.

He'd have me send money to put on their books or do things for their families. These guys were dirt poor but they were loyal, and like my uncle, they were stone killers. My uncle told me when he got out, he said, "I wish I had ten more guys just like them."

So I'm back at the hotel and I'm in the lobby having a drink, and in comes Bobby back from the prison and seeing my uncle. I say,

"Hey, Bob, how did it go?" And he says, "You know how he is," and we both smiled. He said, "Let me go upstairs and freshen up a bit and I'll be right down."

Bobby and I were staying in the best suite in the hotel, but, remember, we were in El Paso, not Beverly Hills.

Five minutes later Bobby pages me and he's out of breath and I can barely make out what he's saying. He tells me that when he put the key in the room he sees two guys in the room dressed like maintenance workers, and that they seemed startled to see him and hurried out of the room once he arrived.

Now my mind is racing, I'm thinking, "Is this a hit? Was someone there to kill me?" There was no reason to kill Bobby—he was our lawyer. No one wanted to kill him, except maybe the prosecutors and judges he dealt with.

But I was a captain in La Cosa Nostra *and my uncle was the boss, and here I am, 2,000 miles away from Atlantic City. Like Harry Riccobene in that phone booth, I realized I was essentially a sitting duck.*

Two minutes later Bobby's down in the lobby and I tell him, "We're out of here, we need to pack our bags and go back home," and Bobby agrees. We were supposed to be there all weekend and Bobby was supposed to go see my uncle the next morning.

We went to the room and packed our stuff and drove right to the airport and got on the first plane back to Philadelphia.

On the plane I tell Bobby, "That was either a hit or the FBI trying to bug our room; either way I don't like it," and Bobby agreed.

When he arrived in Philadelphia, Leonetti rounded up Chuckie Merlino and Salvie Testa and told them what had happened in El Paso.

We all agreed that we needed to be on guard and make sure everybody in the family was on point. The next day, my uncle called and wanted to know what happened with the second visit and he was stunned when I told him what had happened in the room. I could hear it in his voice. He said, "Jesus Christ, did you get a look at them?" and I told him, "No, only Bobby saw them." He said, "You made the right move leaving. Make sure everyone back home tightens their belts. I don't like what I'm hearing here."

It was never determined if this was a botched hit attempt on Philip Leonetti or the FBI attempting to plant a bug in his hotel suite, but it was determined that the two men inside the hotel room were not maintenance workers.

We checked it out at the hotel and they told us there was no work being done in any of the rooms, and Bobby contacted a lawyer down there to look into it and the lawyer told him the same thing.

Life in the mob was certainly unpredictable.

Cleaning the Boat

FROM BEHIND BARS NICKY SCARFO WAS SENDING MESSAGES TO HIS NEPHEW PHILIP LEONETTI AND TO HIS STREET BOSS, SALVIE TESTA, TO "CLEAN THE BOAT," AND TO MAKE SURE THEY CLEANED "THE WHOLE BOAT, TOP TO BOTTOM."

Scarfo wasn't referring to the boat that Testa kept in a Ventnor marina, nor was he talking about the cabin cruiser he and Leonetti had docked out by Harrah's Casino in Atlantic City. He was cryptically instructing Testa and his Young Executioners crew to finish the Riccobene War by killing anyone and everyone connected to rival Harry "the Hunchback" Riccobene, who, like Scarfo, was behind bars.

As 1983 got under way, the Scarfo mob was back to doing what it did best: killing people.

On January 27, the body of Robert Hornickel, a low-level South Philadelphia drug dealer who had run afoul of Scarfo's street tax, was found in the trunk of his car.

With Harry "the Hunchback" Riccobene locked up, his brother Mario "Sonny" Riccobene was running the gang. This made him Salvie Testa's No. 1 target, as the Scarfo mob hit men escalated their murderous efforts to appease their jailed boss.

Pat Spirito was one of the guys in Ciancaglini's crew. I never liked him; I thought he was a crybaby and didn't think he was much of a gangster. But he was a decent earner and he led one of the crews that was out collecting the street tax.

Salvie gave Pat and his crew the Sonny Riccobene contract. At the time Pat had Nicky Crow, Charlie White, and Junior Staino in his crew, and they all reported to Ciancaglini.

That was about to change.

We were getting reports that Pat and his guys were dogging it, not doing what they were ordered to do. None of them guys in that crew were killers, except for Charlie White. Pat, the Crow, Junior— they were all neighborhood guys, knock-around guys. They weren't gangsters.

So one day I'm with Chuckie, Salvie, and Ciancaglini, and we decide that Pat Spirito needs to go, that we need to kill him to send a message to everyone in our family that we mean business, and that an order is an order.

I knew my uncle wanted to kill Pat since the day he made him. After he got made, Pat came up to my uncle and said, "You know, Nick, you should think about making Patty Specs a captain," and my uncle just stared at him, like he couldn't believe this guy who just got made was telling him how to run the family. When he walked away, my uncle said, "Do you believe the balls on this fuckin' guy?" And Chuckie said, "Nick, maybe we should get one of them suggestion boxes and let the guys gives us ideas on how to run things, like they do at restaurants." Me and Chuckie were laughing and my uncle said, "Where do these fuckin' guys come from?"

So Chuckie ordered the Crow and Charlie White to kill Pat.

A few weeks later, on April 29, Charles "Charlie White" Iannece, who was armed with a .38, shot Pasquale "Pat the Cat" Spirito in the back of the head as he sat in a parked car in South Philadelphia with Nicholas "Nick the Crow" Caramandi.

As the war with the Riccobenes continued, it became obvious that the Riccobenes were losing their momentum. Harry the Hunchback was in jail, as were his top two soldiers, Joseph Pedulla and Victor DeLuca, both of whom were locked up for the attempted murder of Salvie Testa.

Botched or aborted hits from both sides ensued for the next several months, until a Scarfo hit team supervised by Testa pumped multiple gun shots into Riccobene solider Frank Martines as he got behind the wheel of his truck to drive to work on a foggy October morning in 1983.

Two of the shooters on the hit team that got Martines were the Narducci brothers, Chickie's sons Frank Jr. and Philip.

Frank Jr. had helped Salvie Testa set up and kill Rocco Marinucci in retaliation for Marinucci's involvement in the bombing that killed his father, Philip "Chicken Man" Testa.

Frank Narducci Jr. gladly assisted Testa, despite knowing that Testa had personally murdered his father, Frank Sr., for the exact same reason that Marinucci had been killed—because the elder Narducci had also been involved in the murder of Philip Testa.

Philip Narducci was the gunman who shot Joe Salerno Sr. in Wildwood Crest on direct orders from Nicky Scarfo himself, despite the fact it was Scarfo who had ordered his father killed only six months earlier.

In a piece of twisted, blood-soaked underworld irony, Joe Salerno Sr. had been one of the first neighbors to find Chickie Narducci as he lay dying in the gutter, and the elder Salerno even went and got a neighborhood priest to come and read Narducci's last rites.

Now, the Narducci brothers were two of Scarfo's go-to soldiers, members of Salvie Testa's Young Executioners crew.

> *They were two of Salvie's top guys and my uncle had told them both before he went to jail that he wasn't going to hold them responsible for what their father had done. So despite the fact that we killed their father, they were with us.*
> *The reality is, they didn't have a choice.*

Years later, a witness who would testify against Scarfo, Leonetti, and the Narducci brothers would tell FBI agents that he was baffled as to how the Narduccis could swear blood allegiance to the man who had killed their father. "Never in a million fuckin' years will I understand that one," the witness would say in one of his debriefing sessions.

Frank Martines would survive the October 1983 ambush, but the incident served to break the street war wide open in favor of Scarfo and would foreshadow similar events with different outcomes over the next two months.

On November 3, Philip Narducci and another member of Salvie Testa's Young Executioners crew, Nicholas "Nicky Whip" Milano, the younger brother of Testa's close friend Eugene "Gino" Milano, shot and killed Sammy Tamburrino, a Riccobene loyalist, who had previously been aligned with Scarfo.

Tamburrino was killed in a Southwest Philadelphia arcade that served as his headquarters, and the killing took place in front of his mother, who stood and watched in horror.

When Tamburrino decided to shift his allegiance from Scarfo to Riccobene, he did so in an effort to make more money, by filling the void that was left when the Hunchback, Joseph Pedulla, and Victor DeLuca went to jail.

Tamburrino had become close with Sonny Riccobene, and he and Frank Martines stood to inherit what remained of the lucrative Riccobene crew if Sonny Riccobene were to join his brother Harry behind bars.

Mario "Sonny" Riccobene had been arrested and charged in a massive 1980 federal racketeering case. Riccobene's codefendants included Angelo Bruno, Philip Testa, Chickie Narducci, and Pat Spirito, all of whom were killed either before the trial or prior to sentencing.

Sonny Riccobene's brother, Harry the Hunchback, was also convicted. The bail he put up while his appeal was pending got revoked when Philadelphia police discovered a gun in his car during a routine traffic stop.

Only Sonny Riccobene and Scarfo capo Joseph "Chickie" Ciancaglini remained free on bail, pending appeal, but both knew their days as free men were numbered.

A month later, Scarfo's men would finally hit the jackpot, finding and killing one of the Hunchback's own flesh and blood—his brother Robert "Bobby" Riccobene.

After stalking him the entire day of December 6, a Scarfo death squad—made up of Charles "Charlie White" Iannece, Joseph "Joey Punge" Pungitore, and Francis "Faffy" Iannarella—caught Bobby exiting his car in the presence of his elderly mother.

Similar to the Tamburrino hit, Little Nicky's men disregarded the callousness of rubbing out someone in front of his mother and attacked their prey on site.

Armed with a shotgun, Iannarella, a young, street-savvy, second-generation South Philadelphia gangster, approached Riccobene and his mother. When Riccobene spotted Iannarella, he took off, jumping a nearby fence in an attempt to escape the onslaught.

His efforts would prove futile.

Taking aim at his fleeing target, the former US soldier, who had been decorated for his service in Vietnam before enlisting in Nicky Scarfo's *La Cosa Nostra* army, Faffy Iannarella blasted Riccobene to oblivion with a shot to the back of the head, dropping Bobby Riccobene as he was trying to climb the fence.

As Iannarella retreated to the waiting getaway car, he was confronted by Riccobene's mother, who tried to wrestle the shotgun from him.

The scene was eerily reminiscent of the time her son Harry had wrestled a handgun from his assailant in a phone booth following an attempt on his life.

Iannarella would take the butt of his shotgun and strike Riccobene's elderly mother in the face, sending the hysterically crying woman crashing to the ground.

In a sick and perverted way, the murders of Bobby Riccobene and Sammy Tamburrino in front of their mothers, like the shooting of Joe Salerno Sr., highlighted what had become the Scarfo family's specialty: raw, vicious, visceral, in-your-face, wanton violence.

Honor and respect seemed to be a thing of the past.

I wasn't happy when I found that these two guys had been killed in front of their mothers. And I didn't agree with the shooting of Joe Salerno's father. But you have to understand, the Riccobene guys were trying to kill us, so it was kill or be killed. This was a war in every sense of the word. Just like my uncle was ordering us to kill them from his jail cell, the Hunchback was doing the same from his. Everyone knew the stakes were life or death.

Scarfo, on the other hand, was ecstatic following the two high-profile mob murders.

He would get the Philadelphia Inquirer *in the mail, but it was always a few days behind. We couldn't talk on the phone and say, hey, we killed Bobby Riccobene today. So he'd make a comment and*

say, *"How about the Eagles, they are playing terrific aren't they?"*
That's what he would say if he was happy with what we were doing.
If he wasn't happy it would be, "How about these fuckin' Eagles,
the whole team is lousy, from top to bottom. They need to get rid
of everybody and start over." That meant he was disgusted that we
weren't doing our jobs.

Following the shooting of Frank Martines and the murders of Bobby Riccobene and Sammy Tamburrino, the Riccobene faction seemed to be on its last leg.

But a wounded animal is a dangerous animal, and Harry's gang wasn't done yet.

A few days after Bobby Riccobene's murder, Salvie Testa was driving through South Philadelphia with members of his Young Executioners crew, Joseph "Joey Punge" Pungitore and the Milano brothers, Gino and Nicky Whip.

Their car became boxed in by another car that was loaded with four Riccobene soldiers, who jumped out of their car and opened fire in broad daylight.

Luckily for Testa and his men, nobody was hit in the fusillade of bullets, and it proved to be one of the last assaults in the carnage-filled conflict that had rocked the underworld in South Philadelphia.

There would be, however, one more casualty in the Riccobene war.

A few days after Harry's guys tried to kill Salvie and Joe Punge,
I drove up to Philly with Lawrence to go see a jeweler I did business
with on Jewelers Row. It was a few weeks before Christmas, and I
was going to pick up a watch for Maria.

Me and Lawrence met Salvie at Virgilio's and we went and saw
the jeweler. I think we may have had Faffy with us.

As we were leaving we passed by a jewelry shop that was
owned by Sonny Riccobene's son Enrico. Salvie said, "Let's go in
there and see what's on this kid's brain," meaning to see what he
was thinking.

I knocked on the window and I saw Sonny's son coming
towards the door, and then he froze when he saw who it was. I said,
"Come on, we just want to talk to you," and I saw him retreat to
the back of the store.

With these jewelry stores, you had to be buzzed in; you couldn't just walk in the store.

A few seconds later a guy who worked there came to the window and said, "If you don't leave, we're calling the police." So we left.

Moments later, Enrico Riccobene walked into his office at the rear of the store and put a pistol to the side of his head and pulled the trigger. He was so frightened by the site of Philip Leonetti and Salvie Testa that he killed himself.

He was 27 years old.

Salvie Testa was now bragging, "We don't have to kill these guys anymore; they do it themselves."

When the news of his nephew's suicide reached him in prison, Harry the Hunchback's heart and will were shattered.

Things had gone too far.

Both his brother and now his young nephew were dead.

He was ready to give in and wave the white flag.

During the first week of 1984, the Hunchback sent word to what remained of his crew that the war was over.

Nicodemo "Little Nicky" Scarfo had won the war.

The victory entitled Scarfo to everything that belonged to the Riccobenes, a treasure trove of illegal operations that he and his men would devour and add to their already overflowing stable of cash-cow rackets.

But all was not well in the ranks of the tumultuous Scarfo mob, despite the fact that it had won the Riccobene war and that Little Nicky was set to be released from prison in a matter of weeks.

Those in Scarfo's inner circle didn't know it yet, but the plot would soon thicken and was about to get even more treacherous than it already was.

Falling Apart

BY JANUARY 1984, NICKY SCARFO HAD BEEN THE BOSS OF THE PHIL-
ADELPHIA–ATLANTIC CITY MOB FOR APPROXIMATELY 34 MONTHS,
AND SPENT 17 OF THOSE MONTHS—OR HALF OF HIS TENURE TO
THAT POINT—BEHIND BARS IN A FEDERAL PRISON IN EL PASO, TEXAS.

The crime family he had left was not necessarily the crime family he was returning to at the end of his prison sentence.

Simply put, the Scarfo mob was in tatters, with many of Scarfo's top guys facing legal problems of their own, some of the charges stemming from incidents that occurred while Scarfo's men were drunk.

For starters, Scarfo's longtime friend and underboss, Salvatore "Chuckie" Merlino, had been arrested on suspicion of drunk driving in Margate, and during the course of his arrest, the drunken mob under-boss had offered the arresting officer a bribe in the form of his expensive gold watch as the entire episode was captured on videotape. Merlino was booked on attempted bribery and DWI charges, and faced as many as 10 years in state prison.

Merlino's brother Lawrence had been arrested and charged with disorderly conduct after he got drunk at a wedding and then made terroristic threats to a Philadelphia police officer. Like his brother Chuckie, Lawrence was also facing state prison time.

Despite promising to clean up his act, Nicholas "Nick the Blade" Virgilio was back in trouble after a drunken incident at an Atlantic City casino, where during a fight, he threatened to kill a man. The twice-convicted murderer was sent to state prison for three years as a result.

Scarfo's own son, Nicky Jr., was facing an underage-drinking rap following an arrest in Atlantic City.

Scarfo capo Joseph "Chickie" Ciancaglini had lost his appeal on federal racketeering charges and was hauled off to federal prison, as was his codefendant, Mario "Sonny" Riccobene, who headed what was left of the Riccobene gang.

Both Raymond "Long John" Martorano and his son Cowboy were facing federal drug charges, and rumors were abound that Long John would soon face charges for his role in the murder of union boss John McCullough after it was reported that the triggerman Willard "Junior" Moran was cooperating with the Philadelphia District Attorney's office.

Saul Kane was also under investigation on federal drug charges.

Frank Gerace was facing charges that he had embezzled union funds when he was the head of Local 54 and allegedly funneled those funds to Scarfo and Leonetti.

Even Scarfo's attorney, Bobby Simone, was facing a federal prison sentence after getting indicted for income tax evasion.

But the worst news Scarfo was to hear dealt with his own nephew, Philip Leonetti, who had been indicted on extortion charges stemming from his involvement in a corrupt land deal with the mayor of Atlantic City.

Now while all of the stuff with the Riccobene's was going on in Philadelphia, I started getting involved with some new things for our family in Atlantic City.

A few years earlier I had been approached by a guy named Frank Lentino—who had been a Teamster, and then was with us in Local 54—about getting involved with a local politician named Mike Matthews, who wanted to become the mayor of Atlantic City.

Mike Matthews sent word through Frank Lentino that he wanted our help in getting him elected. We had given him almost $200,000 for his campaign and had helped him win by getting all of the unions to support him.

One of the first things he did for me was to make a guy who we were close with the chief of police. His name was Joe Pasquale, and me and my uncle both knew him and liked him. We trusted him and he always looked out for us.

Now when I was meeting with Mike Matthews, one of the trade-offs for our support was that we would get a piece of what they called the H tract, which was a 78-acre parcel of land that the city was going to sell to a casino developer for millions of dollars.

It had been a landfill, the site of the city dump. But this was going to be a major score for all of us—me and my uncle, as well as Matthews and Frank Lentino, who had set the whole thing up.

Everything seemed great.

But it wasn't.

The casino developer who had promised to pay Matthews and Lentino the kickback money that would be used to pay Scarfo and Leonetti turned out to be an undercover FBI agent.

Before long, Leonetti, Lentino, and Matthews were all indicted and looking at lengthy federal prison sentences.

Nicodemo Scarfo would be named as an unindicted coconspirator.

It seemed that the only high-ranking member of the Scarfo mob that didn't have legal problems was Salvie Testa, Scarfo's street boss and the leader of the Young Executioners crew.

But Salvie Testa had other problems.

Following the shooting incident in the Italian Market, the handsome young mob captain started dating the beautiful, dark-haired daughter of family underboss Salvatore "Chuckie" Merlino.

Pretty soon the two lovebirds were engaged and a wedding date was set.

The underworld was abuzz at the thought of the Merlino and Testa families, both mob royalty, being aligned through marriage.

Everyone seemed to be happy for them; well, almost everybody.

One day my uncle called the office from jail, and I told him that Salvie had gotten engaged to Chuckie's daughter. When I said it, there was dead silence on his end of the receiver.

I knew that he wasn't happy about it. I knew that his paranoia would start, and he would go through every possible scenario of what could happen if Salvie married Chuckie's daughter. Would they form an alliance and try to overthrow him? Would they try to kill him? Could he ever fully trust that they weren't plotting against him?

These are all of the thoughts that went through his head in the 15 seconds of silence on the phone. That is how his sick mind worked.

But Scarfo's worries were for naught, as Salvie Testa would soon break off the engagement, leaving both Chuckie Merlino and his daughter embarrassed and furious.

The once-solid relationship between Nicky Scarfo's underboss and his street boss was now irrevocably shattered.

And Little Nicky couldn't have been happier.

Back in Business

My uncle was set to be released from prison right around New Year's Day in 1984, but the feds didn't let him out. Bobby Simone and Nicky Jr. flew down to Texas to see what the issue was. After a few days Bobby sorted everything out, and my uncle's release was back on and scheduled for January 20.

A bunch of us flew down to El Paso to be there when he got out. It was me, Chuckie, Lawrence, Salvie, Bobby Simone, Nicky Jr., Harold Garber, Chuckie's son Joey, Tory Scafidi, and a few others. We took several suites at the Marriott and we had one giant party in that hotel. We must have spent 20 grand on food and liquor that weekend.

I remember having mixed feelings about my uncle coming home. I knew it meant that my life was going back to the way it was before he went to jail, running around all day, all of the chaos. But that was the life I had chosen, or I guess had been chosen for me. I didn't have the option of saying, hey, I want to go to college or I want to be a doctor. This was the path that I was put on as a young boy. There was no way to change that. I was born and raised in this thing, in La Cosa Nostra.

So the day he gets out of jail, we take a limousine to the prison. It was me, Lawrence, Nicky Jr., and Bobby Simone.

My uncle comes out and he's wearing a red Windbreaker and a pair of sunglasses and he has a box containing his belongings. The first thing he says is, "Let's get the fuck out of here," and we start heading towards the car. The news media, the FBI, and even the Texas Rangers were there, and everyone was taking pictures. Not the baseball team, the cops. They were wearing the ten-gallon hats and had the stars on their chest, the whole nine yards.

As we're walking, my uncle nods in their direction and says, "Get a load of these jerk offs in the cowboy hats."

I knew from my uncle's demeanor that he had not changed one bit during his 17 months in El Paso. He looked very fit and had a deep tan.

Back at the hotel everyone made a big deal when he got there and we had a good time. He seemed like he was in a good mood. He pulled me aside at one point and asked me about the money I had collected while he was away. I told him it was just under three million and he was happy. He then pulled me away even further and said, "What's going on with Salvie and Chuckie?"

I told him Chuckie wasn't happy that Salvie broke off the engagement but that Chuckie hadn't said too much about it. He said, "We gotta keep our antennas up on this one; I don't like this situation."

I knew right there that my uncle was spooked about the possibility of Salvie marrying Chuckie's daughter, and then with the engagement being broken off, it seemed like he was even more spooked.

I can't explain it, but he was always thinking like that. Nothing was simple. Everything had a subplot, and the subplots had subplots. It would make you dizzy listening to him.

Meanwhile, 10 feet away, Chuckie Merlino, Salvie Testa, and the rest of those gathered to celebrate Nicky Scarfo's release from prison were having a great time and oblivious to what was going on in Scarfo's head.

To the others, this was just a party. But with Nicky Scarfo, nothing was ever what it seemed.

It was a scene fit for a king. News cameras were everywhere. Photographers snapped shots of his every move. Nicodemo Scarfo's long-awaited homecoming at the Philadelphia International Airport caused the level of commotion usually reserved for the arrival of a head of state or an A-list celebrity.

And in a lot of ways, it was appropriate. Scarfo had become both.

He was the undisputed head of the Philadelphia–Atlantic City *La Cosa Nostra*, and his notoriety had made him one of the nation's foremost celebrity gangsters.

Always impeccably dressed and groomed, the 55-year-old Scarfo had become a media sensation, a precursor to the flamboyant John Gotti, who was then still a lowly solider in New York's Gambino family.

As the cameras flashed and reporters followed his entourage, Little Nicky was carrying himself with a swashbuckling swagger and regal flair not typical of someone who had just been released from prison.

I think in many ways my uncle had become even more self-centered and more self-absorbed during the 17 months that he was away. His ego was a thousand times worse than it was before.

Flanking Scarfo as he walked from the airport terminal to a waiting fleet of white limousines were his top two lieutenants, Philip Leonetti, who was 30 years old, and Salvatore Testa, who was 27.

When Scarfo was away in El Paso, Leonetti and Testa worked together to look after his empire with ruthless efficiency, proving their merit as future leaders in *La Cosa Nostra* and as possible heirs to Scarfo's throne.

But therein was a problem.

Beneath the surface and all of the smiles, backslaps and kisses on the cheek, Scarfo was an evil and vindictive despot who maintained an unquenchable thirst for blood as a means of both obtaining and keeping power.

While Scarfo loved every minute of it, Leonetti was growing tired of it.

There was a time in my life when all I wanted was to be with my uncle and to be with La Cosa Nostra *and live that life 24 hours a day, 7 days a week, 365 days a year, just like my uncle.*

It's all that I knew.

But when he went away and I started living my own life, waking up every day and making my own decisions, I started to resent both my uncle and what being involved in La Cosa Nostra *was doing to my life. I felt like I had no life being in the mob, no identity.*

I realized that I was a lot happier doing things with Maria or doing things with Philip Jr. than I was doing things with my uncle, but I was trapped. Once you are in this life there's only two ways out: jail or death. There was no retiring or quitting.

I felt stuck.

And then there was the pure sport of it.

La Cosa Nostra *was my uncle's whole life. He lived for* this thing. *Every day was just like the day before it. Where are we getting money? How much are we getting? Whose making what moves? Who do we have to watch? Who do we have to kill? That was our routine, day after day after day.*

If you made a big score and made him a lot of money, the second he was done counting the money he would say to me, "This guy thinks he's a big shot now; all the sudden he's J. D. Rockefeller," or "We gotta watch him so he doesn't get too big for his britches."

The guy just hands you a bag with $200,000 in it and ten minutes later you're burying the guy. It didn't make sense, but that's how he was.

If he ordered you to kill someone and you did it perfectly and you got the guy just like he asked, he'd say to me, "Now this guy thinks he's Al Capone because he killed a guy."

As quickly as he would build somebody up, he'd already be bringing them down.

Nowhere would this be more evident than with the next mobster who found himself in Nicky Scarfo's crosshairs.

So when we get back to Atlantic City, my uncle stayed in for a day or two, just to get his bearings straight. On the third or fourth day he had me set up a full day of meetings at Scannicchio's so he could talk to everyone and see what was going on.

He told me to bring down Chuckie and Bobby Simone, and he wanted to see Blackie Napoli from North Jersey. He was going to meet with everyone separately and he wanted an hour or two blocked out for each meeting.

I said, "Do you want me to bring Salvie down?" And he said, "I don't think we need to." Now this gets my antenna up, because the whole time my uncle is gone, it was mainly Salvie and his guys who were out there shooting it out with the Riccobenes, and Salvie was also heavily involved in the street-tax collections. I found it strange that my uncle wasn't bringing him down to meet with him, too.

He tells me, "I want you in on these meetings," which means I gotta sit there all day.

The first guy down was Blackie Napoli. When my uncle was away I was meeting with Blackie once or twice a month, and he was bringing my uncle's tribute money down. Now Blackie was getting up there in age and he wasn't as sharp as he used to be, but him and my uncle went way back, even before they were in Yardville together.

My uncle wastes no time in telling him, "These envelopes you sent down while I was away, they were light. What are you guys doing up there? Did you forget how to make money or are you guys just giving it away?"

When my uncle became boss, remember, it was him and Blackie who first went to see Bobby Manna the day after Phil Testa's wake. My uncle always knew that Blackie was letting Bobby Manna and the Genovese take more than they should in North Jersey, but my uncle felt like Blackie had given away the store up there when he was in jail.

Then my uncle told Blackie, "We're gonna tighten our belts up there, no more free lunches for anyone. I don't care who they are with," and Blackie left. I could tell he was disappointed, because he thought he had done a good job while my uncle was gone.

When he left my uncle said, "I'm taking him down. He's getting too old. He's losing his fastball. I'm gonna keep him up there, but I'm putting Patty Specs in charge up there. Bring him down tomorrow and tell him I want to see him."

Patty Specs was a guy named Pasquale Martirano who had been with the North Jersey branch of our family dating back to the days when Ange was boss.

The next one in was Bobby Simone. My uncle seemed very concerned about Bobby's tax case, and Bobby talked about it a little bit. My uncle then went through the litany of criminal charges that everyone in the family was facing—from Chuckie's bribery case to my thing with the mayor—and asked Bobby to explain every possible scenario of everyone's individual cases.

This went on for like two hours. My uncle was just asking hypotheticals. Towards the end he said, "I can't depend on anybody in this entire borgata. Everybody's drunk, stupid, or incompetent. I should go get six black guys from North Philly and start a new gang. They'd be better than what I got right now."

Now I can't say anything, but what I'm thinking is: you just came home from jail, you got $3 million sitting in a safe, everybody you wanted us to kill is dead, and you're still complaining?

So after Bobby leaves, Chuckie comes in. Chuckie's telling him everything that had been going on in Philly while he was away. He says to my uncle, "We never filled Frank's spot after he got killed," *meaning the consigliere position. "And with Ciancaglini in jail, we are down a capo."*

My uncle says, "I'm gonna put my uncle Nick in as consigliere," meaning his mother's brother "Nicky Buck" Piccolo. Now, me and Chuckie both know how bad my uncle hates his Uncle Nick. He hated him and his brothers his whole life. He used to say they were no good, that they mistreated him and always tried to hold him back. Now he's gonna make him the consigliere. The position of consigliere is very important in La Cosa Nostra. The consigliere is the counselor, someone to settle disputes in the family and someone who can advise the boss. The consig is the third most powerful position in the family, behind the boss and underboss. Bobby Manna was the Chin's consigliere and Bobby was the Chin's eyes and ears. My uncle is gonna make his uncle the consigliere, a guy he hated his whole life—it didn't make any sense. It's almost like he was saying, "I don't need a consigliere, 'cause I ain't askin' nobody their opinion or how to settle disputes." My uncle settled almost every dispute with a gun, but that wasn't what La Cosa Nostra was about. When my uncle got out of La Tuna, this thing started to become my thing with him.

Then he says, "And as for Chickie's crew, let's leave things the way they are for now. Too many chiefs and not enough Indians," which was his way of saying he wanted more soldiers and less captains. He wanted to keep all the power for himself.

Then he says to Chuckie, "What . . . about . . . Salvie?"

It was like he said it in slow motion, like a movie. I couldn't believe it. I immediately felt sick. I knew at that very second that my uncle had decided that he was going to turn on Salvie and was now going to make a case for killing him.

Leonetti's intuitions would prove to be spot-on.

Dead Man Walking

ONLY DAYS OUT OF JAIL, NICKY SCARFO WAS ALREADY PLOTTING HIS NEXT KILL, AND THIS TIME, INSTEAD OF SALVIE TESTA DOING THE KILLING, HE WOULD BE THE ONE GETTING KILLED.

Prior to this, Philip Leonetti had been Nicky Scarfo's prized pupil and had never seriously questioned his uncle's leadership. He was in many respects the perfect soldier, the perfect protégé.

But by putting a hit out on Salvie Testa, Little Nicky had gone too far, even for Crazy Phil.

Nicky Scarfo's increasingly erratic behavior had shaken Philip's faith in his uncle, and his blind allegiance to *La Cosa Nostra*, to the core, turning his world upside down.

For the first time in his life, Philip was seriously reconsidering his path in life. Being his uncle's protégé had worn him down, both physically and emotionally, and he didn't know how much more he could take.

My uncle went crazy with the power when he became the boss. It was like he got drunk off of it. He became so full of jealousy and hatred that he had turned into something out of a horror movie. This wasn't a thing of honor or respect anymore. It wasn't even about the money.

It was all about the power.

Bodies were falling everywhere. He wanted to murder everyone and everything around him. It wasn't enough for us to kill our enemies. We were now going to start killing our friends.

He used to say, "The only way to hold on to the power is to kill anyone who stands in your way." That's the kind of mentality he had on everything. He was just looking for excuses to kill guys. And the more power he got, the crazier and more paranoid he became.

My mother used to call him Adolf behind his back, that's how bad it was.

He would get angry and tell a whole group of guys, "Don't fuckin' test me 'cause I'll bring in a squad of guys from New York and wipe everybody in this room right off the fuckin' map. I won't leave none of you guys standing."

He's talking about killing our whole family and these guys knew he'd do it. And guess what, he would have. I didn't understand it. Before we were only killing bad people. Now, we're killing everybody. It didn't make sense.

Now we're gonna kill Salvie? He was one of us. He loved my uncle. He believed in this thing, La Cosa Nostra. He killed for it and he almost died for it. Salvie looked up to my uncle as almost a second father.

Right before Phil Testa died, we were having dinner and he turned to my uncle. I'll never forget it, he said, "Nick, if God forbid something were to happen to me, please be sure and always take care of Salvie."

And my uncle said, "God forbid that would happen, I would treat him as one of my own."

That kept replaying over and over in my head, when he said that he would treat Salvie as one of his own, and now he's gonna have him killed.

Who was gonna be next? Me?

Several factors contributed to the animosity that Nicky Scarfo felt toward Salvie Testa in those early months of 1984.

Salvie Testa had ruffled Scarfo's feathers when he became engaged to Chuckie Merlino's daughter. Despite the fact that both Testa and Merlino were like family to him, the increasingly paranoid mob dictator saw it as a power play by either Testa or Merlino—or perhaps both—and became obsessed with stopping the marriage.

Salvie Testa's stock had been on the rise in the underworld since he personally avenged the death of his father by murdering two of the men responsible in such sensational fashion. Testa was, in a lot of ways, like a younger version of Scarfo himself. He had developed a loyal crew of killers with the Young Executioners, and he enjoyed an almost rabid, rockstar-type following among many in the Philly underworld.

All of this made Scarfo see Testa as a potential threat to his power, and this paranoia would ultimately lead to Testa's brutal downfall.

The tipping point in Scarfo's betrayal of Salvie Testa came in April 1984 after an article in the *Wall Street Journal* referred to the ruggedly handsome and charismatic Testa as the "fastest-rising mobster in the United States."

When Testa got cold feet and broke off the engagement to Merlino's daughter, the always-plotting Scarfo saw an opportunity to manipulate the situation and turn his inner circle, and ultimately the rest of the family, against Testa for disrespecting the daughter of the underboss.

Both Chuckie and Salvie loved my uncle. They were both loyal. They would have never gone against him, but he had it in his head that Salvie marrying Chuckie's daughter meant they were teaming up to eventually challenge him.

So when things started to go south with Salvie and Chuckie's daughter, my uncle used it to play both sides against each other and turn Chuckie against Salvie, which he can then use to get Chuckie to back his plan and help him kill Salvie.

What a lot of people didn't know was that right before Salvie broke off the engagement, Salvie talked to my uncle on the phone when he was in prison and he basically asked my uncle for permission to end it with Chuckie's daughter. Salvie was trying to do the right thing. He wasn't trying to disrespect Chuckie or his daughter. They were both young. It didn't work out; that's all it was.

Now my uncle's telling him from jail: "You don't gotta marry her. You should do what you want, spread yourself around. Don't worry, when I come home I'll talk to Chuckie. He'll understand."

At the same time, he's in Chuckie's ear telling him that what Salvie was doing had dishonored his daughter, was a slap in his face, and that he shouldn't stand for that kind of disrespect to his daughter and his family.

This cocksucker was stirring the pot. He wanted Salvie to think he was okay with it; meanwhile, he was getting Chuckie all worked up about it.

My uncle started to say things about Salvie like, "This kid is getting too big for his britches" or "This kid's acting like he wants to be the boss—we'll see about that." Or he would say, "This kid is full of treason" or "This kid's foolin' with drugs," or "These siggys are always up to something." And all of it was nonsense.

I remember that whole summer, Salvie was on edge. He knew that something was up, he just didn't know what it was. And here

I am, one of his best friends and there was nothing I could do to help him.

I wish I could have saved him, but I couldn't.

By the summer of 1984, Nicky Scarfo's plan had worked. Not only was Chuckie Merlino backing his play, he was supervising the plot.

At one point, Nicky Crow and Charlie White had the contract, but they couldn't get it done. Then Faffy and Tommy DelGiorno had it, but they couldn't get it done either.

Salvie's antenna was up and even though he was a lot younger than all of those guys, he knew the street 100 times better. He wasn't gonna be an easy mark.

Killing the leader of the Young Executioners crew wouldn't be easy.

Attempted hits were set up to kill Testa at various locations, including: a South Philadelphia health club where he worked out; a beauty salon he owned; mobster Faffy Iannarella's house, where a baby shower had been scheduled; a mob gathering at Tommy DelGiorno's condominium on the Ocean City Boardwalk; aboard Salvie's boat, which was docked in Ventnor; and an exit ramp in Northfield coming off of the Garden State Parkway. But all of the plans failed.

The setting of the next plot to kill Salvie Testa showed just how far the Scarfo mob had deteriorated.

Joe Punge was Salvie's best friend. Joe Punge had a brother, Anthony, who was with us. They were part of Salvie's crew. Their father, old man Pungitore, who we called the Blonde Babe, was a made guy and had been around since Ange was boss.

The Blonde Babe's sister died, Joe Punge's aunt, and the whole family was going to the wake, which was in South Philadelphia, to pay their respects. My uncle was very big on this. Nobody ever missed a wake.

Chuckie had gotten involved in the planning of Salvie's murder and decided he wanted to bang him right there in the funeral parlor at the wake and that he wanted Tory Scafidi, who hung around his son Joey, to do the shooting.

And guess what, my uncle loves the idea. This is how crazy we had gotten. We're gonna shoot a guy inside a funeral parlor during a wake for an old lady. Are you kidding me? That's honorable? That's respectful?

So what happens is the night before Tory got into a fight at a bar and he got pinched. When my uncle finds out about it he went nuts. He said, "These fuckin' kids, you can't count on 'em for nothin'."

But as in the Hollywood gangster film life that life in the Scarfo mob had come to resemble, the show must go on.

So Chuckie assigns the killing to Charlie White, and he tells Charlie White to bring a .38 to the funeral parlor, which he did.

The plan was to shoot Salvie inside the bar area. This funeral parlor had a little lounge, and there was a small bar that was separate from the room where the body was.

But when we were there, the place was packed; you couldn't even move. We are all at the bar—me, my uncle, Chuckie, Lawrence. Salvie was 10 feet away from us. My uncle told Chuckie, "Call it off, this place is no good," and Chuckie made eye contact with Charlie White, who was across the room waiting for the signal, and Chuckie shook his head no, and Charlie White just disappeared into the crowd.

So now it's time to leave, and they have a receiving line outside for the Pungitore family, and we all go through it together, one at a time, the whole mob. As we are going through the line, the guys are gathering near our car so that they can greet my uncle and Chuckie, the boss and the underboss, as a sign of respect. Me, my uncle, Chuckie, and Lawrence were the last four guys in the line—it was Lawrence, Chuckie, then my uncle, then me. I was always in front of, next to, or behind my uncle—we never deviated from that. I was his eyes, making sure no one was sneaking up on him.

So we are going through the line of our guys and everyone is there lined up, the whole mob: Faffy, Tommy Del, the Narducci brothers, Nicky Crow, Charlie White, the Milano brothers, the Grande brothers, Joe Ligambi, even the Pungitores left their receiving line to come over and pay their respects. All the other guys were there and all the way at the end of this line was Salvie. He was standing right next to the limousine we drove up in.

So we are going through the line and we are hugging and kissing everyone, and we are now coming up to Salvie, and when Chuckie goes in to kiss him, he grabs both of Salvie's cheeks and kisses him square on the lips for like 10 seconds, and then pulls away and is looking at him with a crazy look in his eye. Salvie looked stunned and all the guys around, their mouths were hanging wide open.

It was the kiss of death.

Salvie knew after that my uncle was going to kill him. There was no more doubt about it.

Scarfo decided it was time to up the ante and he called for another meeting with Tommy DelGiorno to discuss a revised plan to murder Salvie Testa.

My uncle tells Tommy, "Give the order to Joe Punge." Now Joe Punge was Salvie's best friend, he was his right-hand man. They were together every day since they were kids. The whole time this is going on, nobody in Salvie's crew knew we were going to kill him. They knew there was some tension, but no one knew exactly what was going on.

A few days later, Tommy Del comes back and he says to my uncle, "Joe Punge said he'd do it, but he doesn't want to pull the trigger." My uncle laughed and said, "What's the fuckin' difference?"

The plot to murder Salvie Testa had become more sinister by enlisting Joseph "Joe Punge" Pungitore, Testa's best friend, to lure him into what was to be a death trap.

Joe Punge knows the rules. If he tells Salvie or he drags his feet, my uncle will kill him, his brother, and his father, because they are all connected to La Cosa Nostra.

Pungitore enlisted two other members of the Young Executioners crew to carry out the killing of their friend and leader.

Joe Punge brought Wayne and Joey Grande in on the plot, and he set up a meeting at a candy store on Passyunk Avenue in South Philly, and when he and Salvie arrived, Wayne pulled out a gun and shot Salvie in the back of his head. I heard that Wayne then stood over him and shot him again to make sure he was dead.

He was.

Hours later, another crew of bloodthirsty Scarfo mobsters would go to the candy shop and retrieve Testa's corpse, which was then loaded into a van and dumped on the side of a trash-strewn road in a wooded area just outside of Washington Township, New Jersey, a 20-minute ride from South Philadelphia.

Later that night Nicky Scarfo hosted a mob feast at an Italian restaurant in South Philadelphia, where members of the gang toasted Testa's murder. Scarfo also introduced his gang to the two Mexican *pistoleros* who had watched his back in El Paso, after he had Leonetti fly the two men up for the celebration.

I hadn't seen my uncle that happy since we killed Vincent Falcone. The whole thing made me sick to my stomach.

The following day, September 15, 1984, authorities found the body of "the fastest rising mobster in the United States" hogtied and in a ditch off of Sicklerville Road in Camden County, about 50 yards from the Atlantic City Expressway.

Testa's tennis whites, the clothes that he was wearing at the time of his execution, had been so badly stained by blood that they had turned a crimson red.

It was a macabre scene and told you everything you needed to know about life in the Scarfo mob.

Nobody was safe.

Heading South for the Winter

A S 1984 DREW TO A CLOSE, THERE WAS A LOT MORE GOING ON IN AND AROUND THE SCARFO MOB BESIDES THE MURDER OF SALVIE TESTA.

Harry "the Hunchback" Riccobene, who was serving concurrent sentences on a federal racketeering conviction and a state charge on unlawful possession of a handgun, got dealt even worse news when he learned that three of his top aides—Joseph Pedulla, Victor DeLuca, and his own brother, Mario "Sonny" Riccobene—had worked out deals with the feds and were set to testify against him in a new racketeering indictment that included the 1982 murder of Scarfo family consigliere Frank Monte.

Harry "the Hunchback" was likely going to die in prison.

Two other Scarfo associates, Raymond "Long John" Martorano and Al Daidone, met similar fates after both had been arrested and convicted of the December 1980 murder of union boss John McCullough, with both receiving life sentences as a result, which would later be overturned.

Like Riccobene, Martorano and Daidone had been betrayed by one of their own. Willard "Junior" Moran, the triggerman in the McCullough hit, pled guilty and cooperated in the prosecution of both men.

Atlantic City mayor Michael Matthews and former Local 54 official Frank Lentino were convicted in federal court in connection with their scheme to siphon money from the sale of the old city dump known as the H tract to a would-be casino developer who turned out to be an undercover FBI agent.

Matthews was given the opportunity to cooperate against Philip Leonetti, who had also been indicted in the scheme, but the mayor told the FBI that, while he was afraid of Nicky Scarfo, he was "petrified" of his nephew, Philip Leonetti.

Without Matthews's testimony, the case against Leonetti fell apart and the charges were dismissed.

The disgraced former mayor was ultimately sentenced to 15 years in federal prison.

The family's underboss, Salvatore "Chuckie" Merlino, wound up pleading guilty to the bribery case out of Margate and was sentenced to four years in New Jersey state prison. Merlino's lawyer promptly filed an appeal and Merlino remained free on bail pending his appeal.

Deciding that he'd had enough of Atlantic City and South Philadelphia for a while, Scarfo took a long vacation to South Florida during the winter of 1985 to relax and to clear his head a little bit.

Philip Leonetti and Lawrence Merlino would join him on the excursion, much like they did following their acquittal for the Falcone murder in 1980.

Me, my uncle, and Lawrence went down to Florida for almost three weeks. It was nice. We sat on the beach all day and ate at the best restaurants at night. We were staying at a condominium in Turnberry, which was a little ways from Miami. I loved these vacations. I needed them. We all did.

While we were there I said to my uncle, "We should get a place down here." My uncle loved the idea and told me and Lawrence to start looking at houses.

We found a place in Fort Lauderdale that was owned by a guy from Philadelphia who was a real estate developer. It was a gorgeous, sprawling hacienda-style home right on the water. My uncle loved it. He had me pay the guy $650,000 in cash, and we bought the place. We named it Casablanca South and we had a little sign made up that said that and we put it on the front of the house. The place was gorgeous. It had a pool, a boat slip—the whole nine yards.

Scarfo's South Florida shopping spree wasn't done.

We bought a white Rolls Royce Silver Shadow that we drove whenever we were there. We brought our boat up from Atlantic City which was a 40-footer and we docked it right behind the house. We named the boat, The Usual Suspects, and I was the captain of the boat. No one drove that boat except me.

My uncle put a guy who was with us named Anthony "Spike" DiGregorio in the house and he maintained it all year when we weren't there. He would cook Italian food, make homemade red wine, and tell stories all night. We would eat, drink, and laugh all night when Spike was around, even my uncle. He used to say to me, "Where the fuck did we find this guy?" sometimes as he was wiping tears out of his eyes from laughing so hard. Spike was a character and one of the best guys you could ever meet, but he was also a degenerate gambler and a con man. He'd rob anything he could get his hands on and he owed everybody and their mother money.

One time a guy told me a story that he went to Spike's mother's house in South Philadelphia to see Spike and he needed to borrow $5,000. He said Spike brought him in the house and listened to him and why he needed the money, and then said to the guy, "Do you see that woman in there," and he pointed to his mother who was in the kitchen cooking, "I love her more than anything on this planet, but guess what, if she asked me for $5,000 I wouldn't give it to her." The guy told me he was going back and forth, begging Spike for the money because he knew Spike had just made a score, and within a few minutes Spike had turned the whole thing around and was now asking the guy if he could borrow money off of him. The guy said to Spike, "Spike, if I had money to loan you, I wouldn't be in your living room asking to borrow $5,000," and Spike said, "You have a point there." It was a never-ending comedy routine when Spike was around, and my uncle put him in charge of the house in Florida.

When we were down in Florida, we were relaxing every day. The pool, the beach, the boat, we'd go out drinking, we'd go to dinner. Life was great when we were down there. Even my uncle was relaxed.

It's almost like I forget how bad things really were when I was down there. I guess I blocked it all out.

Eventually Scarfo's South Florida home became a retreat for the rest of his crime family members. Many of them had never ventured outside of Philadelphia, New Jersey, and New York. Their gracious host, who happened to be the most violent mob leader in the country, welcomed everyone to his lavish home and did his best to make it a family-friendly destination for the members of his gang.

I would bring Little Philip down. My uncle would have Chris, Nicky Jr., and his son Mark down there. Other guys would bring their sons or their nephews. I think my uncle was using Florida to bring everyone together and keep everyone together and strengthen our family.

With all of the killing and all of the treachery going on around us, there wasn't a whole lot of joking going on. But one time when we were down in Florida, it was me, my uncle, Nicky Jr., Spike, and a guy we were friendly with named Sam the Barber. Sam the Barber owned La Cucina, the restaurant on South Street in South Philadelphia that we used to go to. Now Sam wasn't a made guy, but he was with us and he was very close with Spike. My uncle had put Sam in charge of the renovations at the Florida house and my uncle ended up spending close to $100,000, and Sam was overseeing all of it. When it was done, the place looked amazing and my uncle was very happy. One night after dinner, my uncle stands up and makes a speech thanking Sam for everything he did in getting the house ready and he tells Sam he wants to give him something to show his appreciation and he takes out a medal, like you would get in the army. Now while he is talking to Sam and getting ready to give him the medal, Spike gets right in on the joke and starts saluting my uncle, like my uncle was a general. Even Sam's going for it and he starts crying, because he's so happy that he made my uncle proud. Me and Nicky Jr. were off to the side and we were trying to keep our composure, but we were pissing ourselves. It was really funny. My uncle would only act like that down in Florida—that was the only place that he would ever slightly let his guard down, and that was usually because of Spike and all of his antics.

As the winter hiatus came to an end, Scarfo, Leonetti, and the entire mob were back home in South Philadelphia and Atlantic City.

It wasn't long before Little Nicky had set his sights on his next target.

Memories

SHORTLY AFTER BECOMING BOSS IN 1981, NICKY SCARFO BEGAN HAVING PROBLEMS WITH AN OLD-SCHOOL SOUTH PHILLY MOB ASSOCIATE NAMED FRANK "FRANKIE FLOWERS" D'ALFONSO.

D'Alfonso had been closely aligned with former boss Angelo Bruno and had a lucrative working relationship with Bruno. The two men dabbled together in such ventures as bookmaking, loan sharking, real estate development, casino junkets, and even a closed-circuit television business.

Bruno and D'Alfonso made a lot of money together, but Angelo Bruno was dead. And Nicky Scarfo, the new boss, felt that he was entitled to not only the money that D'Alfonso had been paying to Bruno, but an even larger share.

When D'Alfonso balked, Scarfo ordered him beaten within an inch of his life, and had called on Salvie Testa and Testa's sidekick, Gino Milano, to carry out the beating. But there was a problem.

Salvie came back and told my uncle that every time him and Gino thought they had Flowers, he was always with the Geator and they didn't want to do the beating in front of him.

The Geator with the Heater was a popular Philadelphia area disc jockey named Jerry Blavat, who was primarily known for spinning oldies records on his radio show; for his nightclub, Memories, in Margate; and for the record hops he held at catering halls and nightclubs in South Jersey and Philadelphia.

When Ange was boss, the Geator was around him a lot. He'd be at parties or gatherings we would attend, and we got to know who he was. When Ange died, the Geator was hanging around Frankie Flowers, who had been real close with Ange.

So around this time, Salvie and Gino are trying to give Frankie Flowers the beating my uncle ordered, but the Geator was always hanging around Flowers and getting in the way of what we were trying to do.

A week later, Testa and Milano finally caught him alone and, armed with a baseball bat and steel pipe, ambushed D'Alfonso on a South Philadelphia street corner, beating him so badly that Frankie Flowers would spend the next several months in the hospital.

D'Alfonso got the message.

He started paying Scarfo's street tax, and for a while Scarfo seemed content with their arrangement. But as time elapsed, D'Alfonso began to pay less and less, and then stopped paying altogether.

Little Nicky decided it was time to send D'Alfonoso another message, only this time, instead of bats and pipes, the messengers would be carrying guns and orders to kill.

In the summer of 1985, my uncle decides that he had had enough of Frankie Flowers and wants to kill him. But Flowers did business with Benny Eggs in New York who was the Chin's underboss, and my uncle goes through the proper channels and reaches out to Benny Eggs and the Chin through Bobby Manna, who was the consigliere. My uncle sent word that he wants to kill Flowers, and the message we got back from New York was: do what you gotta do. So we banged him out as he was walking down the street near the Italian Market in South Philly. They hit him five times, and he died right there in the street. My uncle loved it. He said, "Every once in a while, you gotta show people this," and he made the sign of the gun. "It keeps 'em in line."

The July 1985 murder of Frankie Flowers served as a reminder to everyone that failure to pay the Scarfo street tax would result in death.

In the weeks that followed the D'Alfonso murder, the cash was pouring in faster than it ever had before. The Scarfo mob was making money hand over fist.

You have to remember, all the shake money, the money we got from the street tax, went into what we called the Elbow, and it was divided between my uncle—he would take half—and me, Chuckie, Lawrence, Salvie, and Ciancaglini would split the other half. But

Salvie was dead and Ciancaglini was in jail, so the Elbow was now just the four of us.

The new arrangement should have made Leonetti and the Merlino brothers extremely wealthy, but the despotic Scarfo began to exhibit a new trait: unbridled greed.

One day my uncle tells me to go to Longport to see Felix Boc-chino, who was an old-timer who used to be around Tony Bananas before he got killed. Everyone called him Little Felix. So I meet up with him at a coffee shop and he gives me a shopping bag with $180,000 in cash inside. He made a score and this was my uncle's end and the money for the Elbow. I take the bag back to Georgia Avenue and I bring it to my uncle in his apartment, and he says, "Don't tell Chuckie or Lawrence about this; let's keep this between us, and for the time being, I'm gonna hold on to your end." Now what am I gonna do, argue with him?

By this time my uncle was a multimillionaire. He stashed cash all over the place. We built a fake wall in his apartment and we had a safe behind the wall. And we were hiding it in his furniture. We'd cut a hole in a couch or a chair, put $100,000 in there, and sew it back up. So the last thing he needed was to rob my end or what was supposed to go to Chuckie and Lawrence. But he did. He kept all that money for himself.

A year after the death of its street boss, Salvie Testa, the Scarfo mob was still trying to reorganize to fill the void that came with losing someone of Testa's caliber.

When Salvie died, a lot of things changed. For starters, he was one of our top guys and you can't replace a guy like that with a guy like Tommy Del, who was now one of the guys running the day-to-day operations in South Philadelphia, which is what Salvie did when he was alive. My uncle also broke up Salvie's crew, which is one of the other reasons he wanted to kill Salvie. He didn't like all them young guys together.

Me and Lawrence were the only capos on the street at the time, but we were both based in Atlantic City. But as time went by, Law-

rence was around less and less and was doing more with his rebar company, Nat Nat, and was starting to really build the business and make good money. This bothered my uncle when Lawrence wasn't around as much, and he would say, "Where's Lawrence been?" and I would tell him that Nat Nat just got a new job or something and my uncle would make a comment like, "So now he don't want to hang around us? He's too good for us? He wants to go legit?" The truth is, I think Lawrence had gotten sick of being around my uncle and La Cosa Nostra and he was trying to do his own thing, trying to break away a little bit.

At that time, Chuckie was still the underboss, but he had that four-year jail sentence hanging over his head and he started drinking very heavily around this time. Chuckie always drank ever since I can remember, but now in the fall of 1985, he was drunk all the time. And not just drunk, I mean fall-down drunk. One night my uncle and I went to dinner at Angeloni's and he asked me what my thoughts were regarding Chuckie and Lawrence. I'm sitting there thinking: here we go again, now this sick fuck wants to kill the two guys we were closest to, Chuckie and Lawrence. I mean Christ almighty, we just killed Salvie, so why not? Let's kill everybody. Who gives a fuck? I couldn't believe what I was hearing. This guy had lost his fuckin' mind. This was not the La Cosa Nostra that I had swore an oath to, had killed for, and had dedicated my life to.

So I looked my uncle square in the eye and I said, "Uncle Nick, Chuckie and Lawrence have been with us since the beginning. They have always been loyal. We've got nothing to worry about with either one of them. They are both solid." When I'm saying this to him, he could tell by looking into my eyes and the way I was talking, how serious I was. I think my uncle was surprised that I voiced my opinion like that, but to be honest, I had to. Enough was enough. I couldn't take another killing like Salvie's. As close as we had been to Salvie, we were even closer with Chuckie and Lawrence.

Don't forget, my uncle had wanted me to kill the Blade, too. These were our top guys who had been with us since the beginning. Me and Lawrence were together almost every day, and my uncle and Chuckie had been like brothers for almost 40 years. My uncle and the Blade went back even further. Right away my uncle backed off of it and said, "Let's keep an eye on 'em and make sure they are not up to something," but I could tell he was steamed that I wasn't "yessing" him like I always did.

At that very moment I made a promise to myself that if my uncle brought this up again and started to move forward with any plans to kill to Chuckie or Lawrence, not only was I gonna step in and stop it like I wish had done with Salvie and I had done with the Blade, but I was gonna do something that me or someone else should have done a long time ago.

I was gonna kill my uncle.

The Underboss

AS 1985 CAME TO A CLOSE THERE WAS YET ANOTHER MOB HIT THAT MADE NATIONAL NEWS, ONLY THIS TIME IT HAD NOTHING TO DO WITH NICKY SCARFO, PHILIP LEONETTI, OR THE PHILA-DELPHIA–ATLANTIC CITY MOB.

On December 16, Big Paul Castellano, the boss of New York's Gambino crime family, was gunned down outside of the now infamous Sparks Steakhouse as he arrived for a prearranged meeting with several underlings. Castellano's underboss, Tommy Billotti, was also gunned down. The bodies of both men, two of the nation's most powerful gangsters, were on the street, riddled with bullets and covered in blood, much to the horror of the throngs of Christmas shoppers who had also lined the same midtown Manhattan street.

Castellano, who had been close to former Philadelphia–Atlantic City mob boss Angelo Bruno, was gunned down in a palace coupe orchestrated by an ambitious underling named John Gotti and one of his top lieutenants, a man that Leonetti knew well, Salvatore "Sammy the Bull" Gravano.

My uncle and I had dealt with Castellano a couple of times, and he helped us with the murder of Johnny Keys by authorizing Sammy to do it, but that's about it. My uncle used to say that Castellano reminded him of Ange, meaning that he was more of a businessman and less of a gangster. That's the same thing that Sammy used to say about Castellano. He'd say, "This guy ain't a street guy like us, like your uncle. This guy thinks we're fuckin' IBM and not the Gambino crime family."

Around this time I was hearing a lot about John Gotti, most of it coming directly from Sammy. John and Sammy had become very close and Sammy would say to me, "John's like us Philip, he's a gangster's gangster. You and your uncle are gonna like this guy."

Me and Sammy had become very close and we would go out drinking together or go out to dinner when he would come down to Atlantic City. I helped him when he got assigned the contract on this guy Frankie Stillitano, who everybody called Frankie Steele in 1981 after Frankie killed Nick Russo's son in Trenton.

My uncle and Nick Russo had always been close; they were in Yardville together. We used to call him the Reverend. Nick Russo ran the Gambino family's operations in Trenton. Our family also had a presence in Trenton, and everything was always smooth between the two families because Nick was an absolute gentleman.

Now Frankie Stillitano was a cowboy, a renegade and he had some problems with Nick Russo and ultimately Nick Russo's son. One night after they had an altercation, Stillitano opened up on them as they left a bar in Trenton and he shot Nick Russo and killed his son.

The Gambinos were looking to kill Stillitano, but no one could find him. He went into hiding. Sammy came down and saw me and my uncle and he asked us for our help in trying to find him. This was after Sammy and his crew had done the Johnny Keys hit while we were on trial.

Scarfo and Leonetti knew that Frankie Stillitano had connections to a loose-knit group of Irish gangsters that worked out of Northeast Philadelphia.

We found him and shot him in the head and left his body in the trunk of a car at the Philadelphia Airport.

Sammy came right down to thank us for whacking this guy out. That's the kind of guy he was—he was very big on respect. Now a few days after Castellano gets killed, Sammy comes down and he tells me and my uncle that everything is okay in New York and that after New Year's he wants us to come up to Staten Island to meet his new boss—which we knew was John Gotti, but Sammy didn't tell us who it was. I had heard from Blackie Napoli that Sammy was going to be part of the new Gambino administration, either under-boss or consigliere.

As the NYPD and the FBI investigated the murders of Castellano and Billotti in New York, Nicky Scarfo was busy throwing his annual Christmas party in South Philadelphia.

Everybody was there and everybody brings an envelope, that's how it was.

The party was great, but Chuckie was fall-down drunk; I'd never seen him that bad and my uncle was furious. I mean Chuckie was the underboss and the underboss can't behave like that—it makes the family look bad, and with my uncle it was always about appearances and his reputation.

After the party, when we were driving back to Atlantic City, I could tell that my uncle was steaming about Chuckie, but we were in the car so he is not going to say anything. The next day we go for lunch at the Brajole Café and he says, "I can't take any more of this guy's drunkenness. It's an embarrassment to me, and it makes us look weak."

Now I had already voiced my opinion about a month or so prior, so my uncle knew where I stood in regards to killing either Chuckie or Lawrence. And regardless, Chuckie was going to jail in a couple of weeks; he had to do the four years on the bribery case.

I said, "Maybe we should have a sit-down with them; but Chuckie and Lawrence are solid and they always have been," and I'm looking him dead in his eye as I'm saying this, just like I did that night at Angeloni's. I wanted him to know that I was absolutely against killing either one of them, and that my position had not changed and it wasn't going to change. We finished our lunch and didn't discuss it any further.

Now you have to understand that I had to be very careful with my uncle, because if he thought for a second that I wasn't 100 percent with him, or that I was going against him, he would have had me killed in a heartbeat. The fact that I was his nephew and his own blood meant absolutely nothing to him if he thought I was challenging him as boss—which I was by not backing him up on his plans to take out Chuckie and Lawrence.

A few days after Christmas, Scarfo, Leonetti, and the entire Philadelphia–Atlantic City mob, including the Merlino brothers, headed down to Casablanca South for another winter retreat in Florida.

As the Scarfo mob enjoyed their two-week holiday of fun in the sun, Little Nicky was growing increasingly frustrated with his underboss and his out-of-control binge drinking.

When we were down there, Chuckie's drinking got even worse. He was drunk the whole time we were there. I could tell my uncle had had it with both him and Lawrence and was now starting to get angry with me because of the position I had taken. Everything was fucked up at this point, nothing was right. Everything seemed off.

Philip Leonetti knew that changes were coming, he just didn't know what they would be or who may be dying as a result.

A few days after we got back to Atlantic City, my uncle set up a meeting with Bobby Manna in North Jersey and I drove him up. Every time we met with Bobby Manna, it was something serious. So we are sitting there and I have no idea what this was about. It was just me, my uncle, and Bobby, and my uncle says, "Bobby, I'm thinking of taking Chuckie down and putting my nephew up. What are your thoughts? Do you think he's old enough?"

What my uncle was saying is that he wanted to demote Chuckie, from underboss back down to solider, and he wanted to elevate me from captain to underboss. I think he wanted Bobby's opinion because I was so young. I was only 32 years old. Bobby said, "Nick, if you feel he knows the rules and he knows how this thing works, then I don't think how old he is really matters much. Plus, don't forget, Luciano, Lansky, and Capone were all in their twenties when they started this thing, so I don't think age really matters." And my uncle just nodded and looked at me and patted me on the back of the head.

A week later, Nicodemo Scarfo called a meeting and announced to the members of his crime family that Salvatore "Chuckie" Merlino and his brother Lawrence Merlino were being "taken down," and that his nephew, Philip Leonetti, was now the new underboss of the Philadelphia–Atlantic City mob.

Neither of the Merlinos was invited to the meeting.

My uncle addressed the family and said, "I am going to give Chuckie a break here. I've known him a long time. I know that he is going to jail in a few weeks. I'm going to let him go to jail and clean his act up, sober up. If he does that, we will welcome him back into this family when he comes home. If he does not, it's this," and he did the sign of the gun. "For him, his brother, and maybe his son."

At 32 years old, Philip Leonetti became the youngest underboss in the modern-day history of *La Cosa Nostra*. He was the No. 2 man behind his uncle, Nicodemo "Little Nicky" Scarfo, one of the most powerful Mafia dons in the United States, and he couldn't have been less happy about it.

I was numb; I didn't have a feeling one way or the other. By this time I was so sick of my uncle and all of his treachery that I didn't even want to be around him anymore, let alone be involved in La Cosa Nostra. *That's how bad it had become.*

Following the murder of Salvie Testa and his uncle's betrayal of Nick "the Blade" Virgilio and the Merlino brothers, Philip Leonetti had seen enough to believe that eventually his uncle would turn on him.

If we had made it a few more years, he would have turned on me and tried to have me killed, I have no doubt in my mind about it.
One time, my uncle and Nicky Jr. got into an argument and Nicky Jr. was talking fresh to my uncle. I was right there, but I

didn't say a word. When Nicky Jr. left, my uncle turned to me and started hollering, "You need to teach him that he can't talk to me like that," and I still didn't say anything. Very quickly my uncle's colors change and he says to me, like he just figured out the answer to his own question, "I see what it is—you want him to get in trouble. You want me and him to be at odds. I see what it is with you." This is how sick he was. In his mind, he thought I wanted him and Nicky Jr. to argue and to fight because it would be better for me, which was the last thing on my mind.

As Leonetti began to settle into his new position as underboss, Scarfo placed the relatively inexperienced duo of Francis "Faffy" Iannarella and Tommy DelGiorno in charge of the family's street operation in Philadelphia and entrusted them with delivering the news to the Merlino brothers that they had been taken down.

My uncle said to me, in a very aggressive tone, "If I have to see either one of them guys," meaning Chuckie or Lawrence, "if either one of them try and come down here and see me, I am ordering you to kill them on the spot. And that is a direct order from me to you. I'm not your uncle saying this, I am your boss in La Cosa Nostra. *If you don't want to see them dead, tell them to stay the fuck in Philadelphia and clean their acts up."*

It was as if my uncle was saying that he spared their lives because I had spoken against it, but he was warning me that they were on very thin ice.

The very next day I get a call in the office from Chuckie. He says, "Philip, what's going on? He took us down and now he won't see me." I told him, I said, "Chuck, just stay in Philadelphia, be with your family, go do your sentence, and everything will be okay." And he said, "What did I do? I didn't do anything. I just want to come down and talk to him and straighten things out before I go to jail." And I said, "Chuck, please don't come here, please don't. Be with your family, go to jail, and everything is going to be okay, but please, do not come here, Chuck. I'm begging you."

Salvatore "Chuckie" Merlino had been around Nicky Scarfo for over 30 years and he knew by the tone of Philip Leonetti's voice in imploring him not to come to Atlantic City that Leonetti was warning him of Scarfo's desire to kill him if he did.

Merlino spent the next few weeks in South Philadelphia, and then turned himself in a few weeks later on February 21, 1986, to begin serving his four-year prison sentence.

His brother Lawrence apparently got the memo, too, and avoided Scarfo, Leonetti, and Georgia Avenue at all costs.

I didn't save Chuckie and Lawrence's life with that call, I saved my uncle's. Because there was no way I was killing either one of them, and if push came to shove, I was going to kill my uncle. I was absolutely disgusted with him. Because at that point, if I had disobeyed his direct order to me to kill either one of them, he would have had me killed, and then he would have killed them. That's how bad things were at this time. We weren't a family anymore.

The Scarfo mob, which had thrived with Chuckie Merlino as underboss and Salvie Testa as street boss, was no longer.

Testa had been murdered on Scarfo's orders, and Chuckie Merlino was behind bars and stripped of his rank.

Nicholas "Nick the Crow" Caramandi was a solider in the Scarfo mob, a made man following his participation in the 1983 murder of Pat Spirito.

The Crow was a con artist, a flimflammer. He wasn't a gangster, but he always had some scheme goin'—and once in a while, whatever he was doing would hit pretty big and we would make a lot of money, so my uncle kind of tolerated him.

He started to get involved in Philadelphia, shaking down construction companies so they could get their projects done without any interference. You have to understand that all the unions were under our control and we could shut projects down with a phone call, so these guys would pay us so that we wouldn't bother them.

Around this time Caramandi became acquainted with a Philadelphia city councilman from South Philadelphia named Leland Beloff and Beloff's aide Robert Rego.

We knew Leland Beloff. He came every year to our Christmas party and always paid his respects to my uncle if we saw him out somewhere. In turn, we would have the unions support him during his elections and he would do little favors for us from time to time.

So as the Crow starts getting more involved with the construction stuff, he comes into contact with Beloff, who as councilman had a lot of influence over what projects would go forward and what projects would not. So one day, the Crow comes down to see my uncle and he asks for permission to start doing business deals with Beloff, and my uncle gives him the okay, but says, "Be careful. Use your head."

In April 1986, Nicodemo Scarfo and Philip Leonetti were the boss and underboss of the Philadelphia–Atlantic City mob. Scarfo was 57 years old and Leonetti was just 33.

As they tried to reshuffle their own family hierarchy following numerous deaths, demotions, and incarcerations, the New York Families were going through the same type of bloodletting that Philadelphia had gone through in the early 1980s following the deaths of Angelo Bruno and Philip Testa.

After Paul Castellano got killed in New York, John Gotti became the boss of the Gambino family, and he made Frankie DeCicco his underboss and he named Sammy the Bull his No. 3, his consigliere. This was their new administration. Even though our family was aligned with the Genovese, with the Chin, and Bobby Manna, we always had a working relationship with the Gambinos, the Luccheses, the Colombos, and the Bonnanos, who were the other Families in New York.

But what happened was, the Chin had a strong relationship with Paul Castellano, in the sense that, while they weren't the best of friends, they didn't get in each other's way and they would help one another from time to time. When Gotti killed Castellano, the Chin decided to kill Gotti in retaliation and made a pact with the Luccheses and their boss, Vic Amuso, that they were going to kill Gotti and put another guy in there to run the Gambinos so that they would be able to control the family, using the new boss as their puppet. This would avenge Paul Castellano's death and

make the Chin even stronger, because he would essentially con-
trol both the Genovese and Gambino Families and have absolute
control over the Commission, and it would have made Vic Amuso
and the Luccheses the second most powerful family in New York
behind Chin's. The Chin hated John Gotti and wanted to elimi-
nate him at all costs.

On April 13, 1986, a low-level Genovese associate walked toward a parked car outside of the Veteran & Friends Social Club in the Dyker Heights section of Brooklyn. Very casually, he placed a bag containing a powerful homemade bomb underneath the car.

Inside the club, new Gambino boss John Gotti, his underboss, Frankie DeCicco, and his consigliere, Salvatore "Sammy the Bull" Gravano, were scheduled to attend a meeting, and when the meeting was done, the men were supposed to drive back to Gotti's headquarters, the Ravenite Social Club in the Little Italy section of Lower Manhattan.

Gotti's would-be bomber sat in a parked car just up the street with a full view of the Veteran & Friends Social Club and the car with the bag of explosives under it that belonged to Frankie DeCicco.

The hit planned for Gotti and DeCicco was eerily similar to the bombing death of Philip Testa in March 1981.

As DeCicco and another man believed to be Gotti approached the car, the bomb was detonated, killing DeCicco instantly and wounding the other man, who turned out not to be John Gotti.

The Chin's plan had failed and now Gotti and the Gambinos were on high alert.

My uncle and I had been told by Bobby Manna that John Gotti
did in fact get the Commission's permission to kill Paul Castellano,
but I didn't believe it and it never made any sense to me. I think
Bobby told us that because the Chin never wanted to be connected
to the killing of Frankie DeCicco and the attempted killing of John
Gotti. By telling us that Gotti had gotten the okay, it took suspicion
away from the Chin being involved in the bombing. They used the
bomb to make it look like the siggys did it because they were close to
Castellano. The use of explosive devices was against the rules of La
Cosa Nostra. I remember thinking to myself: this fuckin' Chin ain't
so crazy; he's the shrewdest of them all, and the most deadly.

Another person who told both Scarfo and Leonetti that John Gotti had gotten permission from the Commission to murder Paul Castellano was Gotti himself.

A month or so after Frankie DeCicco got killed, my uncle and I went up to a house on Staten Island belonging to Sammy the Bull's brother-in-law, and Sammy the Bull formally introduced us to John Gotti as the boss of the Gambino family. After DeCicco got killed, Sammy became the underboss. Gotti said to my uncle, "Nick, I wanted you to know that I got the okay and I did this thing right," and my uncle said, "I'm sure you did, John."

For the next several hours, the bosses and underbosses of the Gambino crime family and the Bruno–Scarfo crime family got acquainted with one another over drinks and a homemade Italian feast.

It was just the four of us. Gotti and my uncle talked about how similar Ange and Castellano were, in the sense that were racketeers and not gangsters, which is exactly what me and Sammy had said all along.

After a while, Gotti said to me, "My friend Sammy here has told me a lot about you," and then he said to my uncle, "Your nephew here has quite a reputation for such a young man." My uncle said, "He's been with me since he was a boy and he knows this thing as well as I do." Gotti said, "You did good with him. You should be proud to call him your nephew and underboss. We need more young men like him in La Cosa Nostra. But these young kids today, this generation, they're not like us, Nick. There's no one left to teach them the rules and show them the parameters of what this thing is all about."

Gotti spoke very fondly of his mentor, Aniello Dellacroce, and my uncle talked the same way about Skinny Razor, and you could tell that Gotti felt the same way about La Cosa Nostra that my uncle did. All in all, it was a great meeting.

When we got back to Atlantic City, my uncle said of Gotti, "He's sharp. I now know why our friend," and he stroked his chin, meaning Gigante, "doesn't like him."

The Beginning of the End

T HE RULES AND PARAMETERS THAT GOTTI SPOKE OF INCLUDED ONE EDICT THAT MEMBERS OF *LA COSA NOSTRA* ROUTINELY IGNORED: THE PROHIBITION AGAINST PARTICIPATING IN THE DISTRIBUTION OF NARCOTICS.

> *Dealing drugs was an absolute violation of the rules. Plain and simple. My uncle and I were 100 percent against anyone who sold drugs or used drugs. When my uncle became boss, he brought everyone in and told them the rules.*
>
> *A few days after that meeting, Raymond "Long John" Martorano asked to meet with my uncle, and I arranged for them to meet. Long John said, "Nick I just want to make sure we are on the same page regarding the policy on drugs," and my uncle said, "I don't understand what you're asking," and Long John said, "Ange had the same policy, but he and I were heavily involved in the drug trade. We made a lot of money selling drugs together."*
>
> *My uncle and I were both shocked, and my uncle said, "You and Ange sold drugs together?" and Long John said, "Nick, the entire time Ange was boss, he was the biggest drug dealer in Philadelphia. Him, Phil Testa, and Caponigro, that's where they made most of their money."*
>
> *My uncle changed his tone and said very seriously, "Raymond, listen to me. If anyone in this family is involved with drugs from this day forward and I find out about it, it's this," and he made the sign of the gun.*

By the summer of 1986, various members of the Scarfo organization had successfully circumvented the edict against being involved with the distribution of drugs by shaking down drug dealers and loaning them money, which in essence, financed their operations.

My uncle said it was okay to shake down the drug dealers with the street tax and it was okay to lend them money with our loan sharking operation, but we were forbidden from getting directly involved with what they were doing.

Many *La Cosa Nostra* bosses—like Lucky Luciano, Vito Genovese, and even Vincent "The Chin" Gigante—had been convicted of dealing heroin in their younger days, and black drug dealers were making piles of money selling cocaine in the 1980s. Several members of the Scarfo organization became directly and indirectly involved in the manufacturing and distribution of methamphetamine—more commonly known as "meth" or "crank" or "speed"—by obtaining and reselling phenyl-2-propanone (P2P) to "cookers" who used P2P oil to make meth.

A gallon of P2P could be obtained overseas for under $2,000 and resold to dealers in the United States for $20,000, or more.

It was an offer that some in the Scarfo mob couldn't refuse.

The first sign of trouble came when Saul Kane got indicted for labor racketeering with Stevie Traitz and the roofers union, and then got indicted on a federal drug case, which was nonsense. Saul told me he never sold drugs a day in his life, and I believe him to this day.

The feds alleged that Kane, who was 51 at the time, was the leader of an international drug operation that specialized in importing P2P into the United States, and then wholesaling it to various drug operations. The indictment alleged that the operation made an excess of $24 million. Almost as quickly as Saul Kane and several of his top associates were rounded up, one of them began cooperating, and Kane was held without bail.

Several other alleged Philadelphia meth dealers were rounded up in separate indictments that charged them with importing P2P and distributing meth, and shortly after they were charged, several of these individuals began to cooperate and point the finger at various made members of the Scarfo mob, including Ralph "Junior" Staino, Charles "Charlie White" Iannece, Thomas "Tommy Del" DelGiorno, and Nicholas "Nicky Crow" Caramandi, as being directly or indirectly involved in importing, manufacturing, and distributing both P2P and methamphetamine.

Indictments were being prepared, but for tactical reasons they were kept under seal.

In addition to his involvement in the P2P case, Nicholas "Nick the Crow" Caramandi had not heeded Nicky Scarfo's warning about "being careful" in his dealings with Philadelphia City councilman Leland Beloff. The Crow was caught trying to extort $1 million from a prominent Philadelphia land developer, using and mentioning his connections to both Leland Beloff and Nicky Scarfo in his dealings with a representative for the developer, who was actually an undercover FBI agent.

On June 27, 1986, Caramandi was arrested, but 11 days later the charges against him were dropped.

The Crow comes down to Atlantic City to see my uncle and tells him that the case is bullshit and that's why the feds dropped the charges. But my uncle spoke to Bobby Simone and Bobby told him that he thought the feds were going to reindict the case down the road and that their ultimate goal was to include my uncle in the indictment, even though my uncle never met the developer or the undercover agent. My uncle didn't seem to be too concerned about it and neither was I.

Another problem Nicky Scarfo was having at the time was with Tommy DelGiorno, one of the men supervising his mob's street operation in South Philadelphia.

The same thing that had happened towards the end with Chuckie was happening with Tommy Del. He was drunk seven days a week and my uncle took him down, just like he did to Chuckie. My uncle said to me, "We gotta get this thing back on track, from top to bottom." He knew that our organization was in bad shape.

What Scarfo had no way of knowing at that time was exactly how bad things actually were.

With Tommy DelGiorno taken down from captain to solider, the 39-year-old Francis "Faffy" Iannarella became the family's new Philadelphia street boss.

There was just a sense that things were falling apart around us. It's hard to explain, but the regime just wasn't the same. After Salvie got killed, and then the thing with Chuckie and Lawrence, it just kept going downhill from there.

And things were about to go from bad to worse.

US v. Nicodemo Scarfo, Philip Leonetti, et al.

IN OCTOBER 1986, NICHOLAS "NICK THE CROW" CARAMANDI WAS REARRESTED IN THE EXTORTION CASE INVOLVING WILLARD ROUSE, THE REAL ESTATE DEVELOPER HE TRIED TO SHAKE DOWN FOR A MILLION DOLLARS. HE WAS HELD IN A PHILADELPHIA PRISON WITHOUT BAIL.

At Caramandi's bail hearing, the US attorney laid out for the judge the government's belief that Caramandi was a career criminal and made member of the Scarfo mob, while also claiming that Caramandi figured prominently in both the P2P case, which remained under seal, and the 1983 murder of Pat Spirito.

Caramandi, who had known Scarfo since the early 1970s, understood that the volatile mob boss was furious that Caramandi had talked so recklessly in mentioning both Scarfo's name and *La Cosa Nostra* when dealing with the man he was trying to extort, who was both an FBI agent and was wearing a wire.

My uncle had told him to be careful and use his head, but the Crow decided to act like a gangster, which he wasn't, and he started shooting off at the mouth, playing a role and he buried himself.

On November 3, 1986, the New Jersey Attorney General's office unsealed an indictment against Nicky Scarfo, Philip Leonetti, and 16 others, charging them with racketeering, money laundering, and bookmaking. The backbone of the case was a series of secretly recorded wiretap conversations in which a drunken Tommy DelGiorno openly discussed mob business and expressed his dissatisfaction with his mob superiors, namely "Little Nicky" and "Crazy Phil."

On the eve of the indictment being announced, detectives from the New Jersey State Police visited DelGiorno at his South Philadelphia home and played the tapes for him in an effort to turn him into a cooperating witness.

Tommy Del knew that once Scarfo and Leonetti heard the tapes, he would become a dead man walking, as the two mob leaders predictably made bail shortly after they were arraigned, posting $400,000 and $300,000 respectively. The other 16 defendants named in the indictment were given court dates for early January.

A week later, Tommy DelGiorno became the first made member of the Scarfo mob to defect from *La Cosa Nostra* and enter into an agreement to cooperate with the government.

Three days later, Nicholas "Nick the Crow" Caramandi would become the second.

Both men were now cooperating with the FBI and the US attorney's office in the multiple investigations that were ongoing against Nicodemo Scarfo, Philip Leonetti, and the entire Philadelphia–Atlantic City *La Cosa Nostra*—investigations which included all of the unsolved mob murders that Scarfo and Leonetti had ordered and participated in dating back to their early Atlantic City days in the late 1970s up through the Frankie Flowers murder in July 1985.

> *I remember Bobby Simone came down after the news of Tommy Del and Nick the Crow broke and said, "Nick, it's not good," and my uncle knew it. My uncle said, "How long before they come to get me?" and Bobby said, "It could be a day, could be a week, could be a year, but they're definitely coming."*
>
> *The next day, me and my uncle went to Angeloni's for lunch and the mood was very somber. He knew his days were numbered. He told me, "If they lock me up and I can't make bail and you're not in the cell next to me, you're in charge for as long I'm locked up. You will get*

messages either directly from me, through Bobby, or through Nicky Jr." I tried to lighten the mood by saying, Uncle Nick, you think any jury is gonna believe Tommy Del or Nicky the Crow? It'll be just like the Falcone case with Joe Salerno. We'll get the best lawyers and we will fight them and we will win, just like we did before.

Now at this time, between the two of us we had almost three million dollars, and my uncle said, "You're right, fuck 'em. Fuck Tommy Del, fuck Nicky the Crow, and fuck the feds. Fuck 'em all. We ain't laying down for none of them."

As the feds meticulously debriefed DelGiorno and Caramandi in separate locations, they were obtaining an insight into the dark world of *La Cosa Nostra* under the despotic Nicodemo "Little Nicky" Scarfo.

Right before Christmas of that year, 1986, me and my uncle headed down to Florida to Casablanca South for a few days. Spike was down there and he tried to cheer us up, but it was gloom and doom ever since we found out that those guys had flipped. I went back to Atlantic City right before New Year's 1987 and my uncle stayed down there a few more days with his girlfriend at the time, who we all called Chicago.

On January 7, 1987, the remaining 16 defendants in the New Jersey State racketeering indictment were all arraigned and subsequently released on bail. Among those charged were Faffy Iannarella, Scarfo's Philadelphia street boss; Joseph "Joe Punge" Pungitore; Joseph Grande and his brother Salvatore "Wayne" Grande—all four of whom were allegedly involved in the Salvatore Testa murder—and Joseph Ligambi, the alleged triggerman in the Frankie Flowers murder.

This arraignment took place five years to the day that Frank "Chickie" Narducci was ambushed and murdered by Salvie Testa and Joseph "Joe Punge" Pungitore for his role in the murder of Testa's father, Philip Testa. Those five years essentially defined the rise and the fall of Little Nicky Scarfo's Mafia empire.

The next day, January 8, 1987, would mark Nicodemo Scarfo's final day as a free man.

As the 57-year-old Mafia don emerged from an Air Brit flight from Fort Lauderdale to Atlantic City, he was swarmed by a half dozen FBI agents and taken into custody on charges that he had conspired with Nicholas "Nick the Crow" Caramandi and Philadelphia City councilman Leland Beloff in the attempted $1 million extortion from Philadelphia land developer Willard Rouse.

Sporting a business suit and a cashmere overcoat, Scarfo had a deep winter tan as he smiled for reporters and photographers documenting his arrival and subsequent arrest.

Scarfo was taken to FBI headquarters in Linwood, New Jersey, for processing, and then held overnight at the Cape May County jail, some 30 miles south of Atlantic City.

Scarfo would then be transferred to a detention center in Philadelphia to await a bail hearing, and less than a week later, Little Nicky was formally denied bail.

His 33-year-old nephew, Philip Leonetti, was now the acting boss of the Philadelphia–Atlantic City mob.

> *When my uncle went to jail, we were in bad shape. It wasn't like when he was in La Tuna and me, Chuckie, Lawrence, and Salvie kept things going. This time around, there was nobody left. Salvie was dead; Chuckie was in a jail cell in Camden; and Lawrence wasn't really around anymore. It was basically me and Faffy, and guys like Joe Punge. We all had cases pending, and we knew we were gonna get locked up; it was only a matter of time.*

For the first two months of 1987, Philip Leonetti attempted to use men like Francis "Faffy" Iannarella in Philadelphia and Pasquale "Patty Specs" Martirano in North Jersey to carry out his uncle's orders—orders that basically consisted of making sure that Scarfo's street tax and tribute money were being collected and sent down to Leonetti in Atlantic City for his uncle's safekeeping.

> *I was meeting a couple times a week with Bobby Simone, and Bobby had introduced me to a lawyer friend of his named Oscar Goodman from Las Vegas. Bobby told me, "Oscar's one of the best lawyers in the country. If you get arrested, I want him sitting next to you."*
>
> *I was going to see my uncle once or twice a week in Philadelphia and I would go and see Faffy when I got done visiting my uncle*

to pick up our money or to hear what was going on in Philadelphia. I was basically going through the motions, doing what my uncle wanted, but my heart wasn't in it anymore, I knew it was only a matter of time before it was lights out.

In early March, Leonetti and Maria boarded a plane and headed to Scarfo's South Florida estate, Casablanca South, for two weeks of rest and relaxation.

It was me and Maria, and we had a ball down there. It was the two of us and Spike. Spike and Maria were both amazing cooks and they would try to outdo one another, but she would always win. We would sit by the pool all day or take the boat out. Those two weeks were like being in heaven, with everything that was going on. I knew the reality of the situation we were in, but I didn't want to face it.

Several weeks later, on April 9, 1987, Philip Leonetti would be forced to face that reality when he was arrested as he drove from Atlantic City to Philadelphia to meet with Bobby Simone.

It was me and Tory Scafidi in the car, and I noticed the whole time we were driving that we were being followed by what seemed like at least five cars. I said to Tory, "I think I'm going to be arrested." We drove over the Ben Franklin Bridge and into Center City and headed towards Bobby's office, which was near Rittenhouse Square. When we got to 19th and Walnut, the cops were everywhere. They came from behind us; they came the wrong way down Walnut and got in front of us; they came from the park; they were everywhere. They grabbed me and Tory and handcuffed us and put us in separate cars. Bobby must have seen all of the commotion and came down from his office and when he came over to the car and I said, "Bobby, what am I being arrested for?" And he said, "The murder of Salvie Testa."

Police records show that Leonetti and Scafidi were arrested at 1:40 p.m. and 15 minutes later, at 1:55 p.m., Francis "Faffy" Iannarella was arrested inside the Scarfo mob's primary clubhouse, a social club at the corner of Camac and Moore in the heart of South Philadelphia, a half block away from Passyunk Avenue and the candy shop where Salvie Testa was executed.

By 6:00 p.m. that night, Joseph "Joe Punge" Pungitore, Salvatore "Wayne" Grande and his brother Joseph—all former members of Salvie Testa's Young Executioners crew and the three principles charged in his murder—were behind bars with Leonetti, Iannarella, and Scafidi.

A separate indictment unsealed the next day charged the already jailed Nicodemo Scarfo and the entire hierarchy of his criminal organization with numerous racketeering offenses, including: the murder of Judge Edwin Helfant in 1978; the murder of Vincent Falcone in 1979; the murder of John Calabrese in 1981; the murder of Frank "Chickie" Narducci Sr. in 1982; the murders of Pat Spirito, Sammy Tamburrino, and Robert Riccobene in 1983; and finally, the murder of Salvatore "Salvie" Testa in 1984.

Several attempted murders and dozens of other crimes were included in the indictment, which was based primarily on the testimony from cooperating witnesses Thomas "Tommy Del" DelGiorno and Nicholas "Nick the Crow" Caramandi, both of whom had defected from the mob in November 1986.

> *We were all in jail and none of us got bail. The only guy that they let out on bail was Joe Punge's brother Anthony. The rest of us were locked up in one of two prisons, either Holmesburg or the Detention Center, both of which were in Philadelphia. I was in Holmesburg with my uncle, Joe Ligambi, Lawrence, Joe Punge, Faffy, and a couple other guys. I think Tory was with us and the Narducci brothers. My uncle was getting ready to go on trial in the Rouse extortion case, and the rest of us were just getting acclimated to being locked up. Prior to that, none of us had ever been locked up for more than a couple of days, except for my uncle. I remember one day out in the yard we were all together and my uncle said, "We're gonna stick together and we're gonna beat this thing."*

A few weeks later, on May 6, 1987, a federal jury convicted Nicodemo "Little Nicky" Scarfo of conspiracy and extortion stemming from his involvement in the attempted extortion of Philadelphia land developer Willard Rouse.

On August 4, 1987, Nicky Scarfo was sentenced to 14 years in federal prison following his conviction in the Rouse case.

The next thing that happened is that me, my uncle, Chuckie, Faffy, Junior Staino, and Charlie White all got hit with an 848 Continuing Criminal Enterprise on the P2P case, which they unsealed when we got locked up. Of all of the cases they tried to bring, this one was the absolute worst. We did a lot of stuff: murder, loan sharking, extortion, you name it. But we weren't drug dealers.

The jury in that case agreed and acquitted Scarfo, Leonetti, Merlino, and Iannarella of all charges. Ralph "Junior" Staino and Charles "Charlie White" Iannece were both fugitives and, at that time, neither had been caught.

When the jury found us not guilty, the courtroom went nuts. During the commotion, my uncle walked over to the jury box and shook hands with one of the female jurors and one of the marshal's came over and grabbed him. My uncle said, "I just wanted to shake their hands, thank God for them. This is the beginning of the end of the lies and those liars." He was talking about Tommy Del and the Crow. The judge was banging his gavel and saying, "Order, order" and the US attorney Barry Gross said something under his breath to my uncle, telling him to "Shut up," and my uncle screamed back, "No, you shut the fuck up!" As they were leading us from the court-room back to jail, my uncle stopped and screamed at the prosecutors, "Who lied? Caramandi and DelGiorno, that's who! Two lyin' no good fuckin' rats—that's all you got!" Then in the direction of the FBI agents in the room, my uncle said, "And you, you stay the fuck away from our women!" You shoulda seen their faces; they looked like they wanted to cry.

Down in the holding cell we were celebrating, hugging and kiss-ing each other on the cheek. It was the first time in almost two years that me and my uncle were together with Chuckie and everything seemed normal between us, like old times. We were all so happy that we beat the case.

When we got back to Holmesburg, the whole place went nuts. They had seen that we won on TV. Guys were banging on their doors and cheering, and when we got back to our cellblock, which was D block, everyone was lined up waiting for us—Lawrence, Joe Punge, Joe Ligambi, Philip and Frankie Narducci. It felt real good to beat the government again.

Philip Leonetti, now 34, had been found not guilty in the 1980 trial for murdering Vincent Falcone the year before, and now in 1987, he was found not guilty in the P2P drug case.

As 1987 came to a close, a reporter from the *Philadelphia Inquirer* who happened to be taking a tour of Holmesburg for a story he was writing about the prison was amazed when he saw Nicky Scarfo exiting his cell on D block.

The reporter, John Woestendiek, wrote the following:

"Wearing a spotless white T-shirt tucked into prison-issued blue pants, his gray hair neatly swooped back from his forehead, inmate 87-00475 walked easily through the open doorway of cell 425 on D block at Holmesburg Prison."

The story goes on to say that Scarfo *"appeared relatively comfortable, at ease among friends in Philadelphia's toughest and most run-down prison"* and quoted prison officials who said that Scarfo was *"courteous and polite to correctional officers and spent a lot of time reading the newspapers, exercising, and working on his legal case, never straying too far from his inmate bodyguards."*

One prison official said, *"The young black kids treat him like he's a god—it's 'Yes, Mr. Scarfo,' 'No, Mr. Scarfo.'"*

> *For the most part, we didn't bother anyone and nobody bothered us. One time I got into an argument with an inmate, a big black guy—they said he was a drug kingpin or something. He had a big mouth on him and he was always breaking somebody's balls, usually the younger, smaller black guys. One day I told him to knock it off and he didn't like being challenged. One thing led to another and we had a little altercation and the guards broke us up before it got serious.*

As a result of the altercation, Leonetti got five days in solitary confinement, locked in an eight-by-ten-foot concrete cell for 24 hours a day, and the prisoner was immediately transferred to another prison amidst internal reports that Leonetti planned to kill the big black guy over the incident.

We never saw him again, and the other kids that I stood up for were so happy that he got transferred that when I came out of the hole after doing the five days they were cheering for me.

Scarfo, Leonetti, and the rest of their gang would sit behind bars as 1987 turned to 1988, awaiting the Salvie Testa murder trial, which was scheduled for April, and for the massive RICO trial, which was set for September.

With all of us locked up, most of what was going on outside—the street tax and the rest of the stuff we were involved in—had all but dried up. My uncle put his cousin Anthony Piccolo, who he made the consigliere right before he went to jail, in charge out on the street. He was now the street boss. It was him and Nicky Jr. who would collect the money and keep things in order. Nicky Jr. would come and see me or my uncle once or twice a week and let us know what was going on and who was paying and who wasn't paying and who was playing games. We'd send messages through him to guys on the street, but our main focus was meeting with the lawyers and fighting the cases.

As the Testa murder trial began in Philadelphia Common Pleas Court, Leonetti felt confident in facing Caramandi and DelGiorno, having just prevailed several months prior in the P2P case.

It was me, my uncle, Chuckie, Faffy, Joe Punge, Tory, Wayne Grande, Joe Grande, and Charlie White that were on trial. Bobby Simone represented my uncle; I had Oscar Goodman; and Chuckie had Ed Jacobs. I'll never forget how Bobby told the jury in his opening statement that, "You will never hear testimony from people more corrupt and disgusting," meaning the Crow and Tommy Del.

Apparently, the jury agreed with Simone, and on May 10, 1988, after deliberating for only six hours, the jury found Scarfo, Leonetti, and the seven others not guilty of murdering Salvie Testa.

A few days after we beat the Testa case I was out in the yard playing basketball and my uncle comes over and motions for me to come over to where he was standing. He says, "I talked to Bobby and he thinks there is a good chance that you can make bail and get out of here." So I said, "Wow, that's great news." And he replies, "If you do, I want you to slit that motherfucker's throat when you get home."

The "motherfucker" that Scarfo was referring to was his wife, the mother of his two youngest sons, Nicky Jr. and Mark.

My uncle's wife had gambled away a lot of money in the casinos, and when my uncle found out about it, he went nuts. He said, "I want you to slit her fuckin' throat," and he put his hand up to this neck to demonstrate that he wanted me to cut her from ear to ear. He said, "Just make sure Nicky Jr. doesn't know it was us." This is how evil he was; he wanted me to kill the mother of his children, which I never would have done in a million years. He hated her, he only called her "that motherfucker"—that's the only way I ever remember him referring to her.

My uncle also wanted me to kill both Joey and Wayne Grande if they made bail, because he heard that they had gotten one of my cousins involved in dealing drugs. My uncle said, "If you find out it's true, both of 'em get this," and he made the sign of the gun.

A few weeks later, Leonetti's application for bail was denied.

You have to understand, I was charged in the Pepe Leva murder and that case got dismissed. I was found not guilty in the Falcone murder, not guilty in the P2P case, and not guilty in the Testa murder. I was four for four. I knew Bobby and the other lawyers had Tommy Del and the Crow's number down pat, and I was very confident going into the RICO case. Then those guys won their RICO in North Jersey and I started thinking, I'm getting the fuck out of here. I thought I had the government on the run.

The guys in North Jersey were 20 mobsters associated with Anthony "Tumac" Accetturo and the New Jersey faction of the Lucchese crime family that he controlled. They had recently been found not guilty of all charges in a massive federal case that had lasted more than 21 months.

I figured if those guys could win, we could win. All of us felt confident going into the RICO case because two different juries had rejected the testimony of DelGiorno and Caramandi. This was it; this was the big one. If I won this, I was home free. My uncle had to do the 14 years on the Rouse case and him, Chuckie, the Narduccis, Faffy, Lawrence, the Milanos, and Joe Ligambi still had to go to trial for the Flowers murder, but I wasn't in that one. So this was it for me.

The stage was set for jury selection on September 10, 1988, in *United States v. Nicodemo D. Scarfo, Philip M. Leonetti, et al.* This was for all the marbles.

The government's team was led by veteran prosecutors Louis Pichini, Arnold Gordon, Joel Friedman, David Fritchey, Albert Wicks, and Joseph Peters, who were armed with a massive indictment that charged Scarfo, Leonetti, and 15 others with participating in 14 murders and attempted murders, and a slew of other RICO predicate offenses, including extortion, loan sharking, bookmaking, and the distribution of P2P.

The indictment charged the hierarchy of the crime family as follows:

- **NICODEMO *"Little Nicky"* SCARFO**, age 59, as being the boss of the crime family.

- **PHILIP *"Crazy Phil"* LEONETTI**, age 35, as being the underboss of the crime family.

- **FRANCIS *"Faffy"* IANNARELLA**, age 41, as being a caporegime/street boss of the crime family.

- **JOSEPH *"Chickie"* CIANCAGLINI**, age 53, as being a caporegime in the crime family.

- **JOSEPH *"Joe Punge"* PUNGITORE**, age 32, as being a solider in the crime family.

- **NICHOLAS *"Nick the Blade"* VIRGILIO**, age 61, as being a solider in the crime family.

- **SALVATORE *"Chuckie"* MERLINO**, age 49, as being the onetime underboss and later a solider in the crime family.

- **LAWRENCE** *"Yogi"* **MERLINO**, age 42, as being a former caporegime and later a solider in the crime family.

- **CHARLES** *"Charlie White"* **IANNECE**, age 53, as being a solider in the crime family.

- **SALVATORE** *"Wayne"* **GRANDE**, age 35, as being a solider in the crime family.

- **JOSEPH** *"Joey"* **GRANDE**, age 28, as being a solider in the crime family.

- **FRANK** *"Frankie"* **NARDUCCI**, age 35, as being a solider in the crime family.

- **PHILIP NARDUCCI**, age 27, as being a soldier in the crime family.

- **SALVATORE** *"Tory"* **SCAFIDI**, age 27, as being a solider in the crime family.

- **EUGENE** *"Gino"* **MILANO**, age 29, as being a solider in the crime family.

- **RALPH** *"Junior"* **STAINO**, age 56, as being a solider in the crime family.

- **ANTHONY** *"Tony"* **PUNGITORE**, age 35, as being a solider in the crime family.

In their opening statement, the government promised to give the jurors a window into the world of *La Cosa Nostra,* focusing on crimes committed between 1976 and 1987, the heyday of Nicodemo "Little Nicky" Scarfo and his nephew Philip "Crazy Phil" Leonetti.

The trial started at the end of September after a few weeks of jury selection and went all the way through October and into November.
Every day was the same routine. They would wake us up around 5:00 a.m. and transport us to court in a bus with tinted windows. We would be handcuffed and shackled on the bus, and they would lead

us into the courthouse to a basement holding cell, where we would get dressed and would be in the courtroom by 9:00 a.m.

The trial was basically Tommy Del and the Crow and a bunch of FBI agents and cops who had followed us for years. They had some audiotapes and a ton of pictures. They even brought Joe Salerno in to testify against us and they had a bunch of bookmakers and drug dealers we had shaken down. The further the trial went, the more it became apparent that we were literally fighting for our lives and that the government was playing for keeps. They wanted us real bad. By the end of October, I think we were all worn down. We'd have some good days here and there, and then we would have some really bad days. The trial was definitely taking its toll on all of us.

What would happen next would bring Philip Leonetti to tears and further demonstrate the evil nature of his uncle, Nicodemo "Little Nicky" Scarfo.

So one day, while the Crow was on the stand, we took our regular afternoon break. We would all go back into a holding pen and there were these little conference rooms where we could meet with the lawyers when they came back. So Bobby comes back and calls me and my uncle into one of the conference rooms and says, "I got some bad news." And you could just tell by looking at Bobby that it was bad—it was written all over his face. Then Bobby says, "Nick, you're gonna wanna sit down for this one." And my uncle said, "What is it, Bob?" And Bobby said, "Mark tried to kill himself this morning. They found him hanging in the bathroom of Scarf, Inc. They flew him from Atlantic City to Philadelphia on a helicopter, and he is in ICU at Hahnemann Hospital. It doesn't look good."

I remember welling up with tears and feeling nauseous, like I was gonna throw up. This kid was 17 years old and was a beautiful kid, well behaved, good looking, always respectful. He was my uncle's youngest son, his baby, and as Bobby's telling us this, Bobby's choked up, I've got tears in my eyes, and my uncle—this no-good evil motherfucker—has absolutely no reaction, no emotion, nothing. He's just standing there and he doesn't say a word.

A few minutes later the judge brings us all back into court and announces that court is in recess for the day. You could see all the lawyers whispering to their clients, telling them what happened, and every one of them had the same reaction: they looked sick about it. Even the judge and the prosecutors, who hated my uncle, looked sick. How could you not be when a 17-year-old kid tries to kill himself? But my uncle, this cocksucker, he never flinched, never batted an eye.

So now we are all going back down to the holding pen in the basement and waiting for the bus to take us back to Holmesburg. No one is saying a word. Every day after court when we're heading back, we'd always be breaking balls. You gotta remember, there was 17 of us and we're all looking at spending the rest of our lives in prison, so we had to do something to lighten the mood. But on this day, no one said nothing. It was dead fucking silence, and then when we all got into the holding pen and sat on the benches waiting for the bus to come, out of nowhere, my uncle went nuts and he exploded on me.

His eyes got real big and he was pointing at me and said, "You know I blame this on you and your mother, the way she would scream and holler at Mark and that vein would come out of her throat. This is your fault. You and that witch sister of mine. You're just like her." And then he mumbled something to himself in Italian.

While this was going on, all the guys we were on trial with were all sitting on the benches that were up against the wall, staring straight at the floor. None of them made eye contact with either one of us and none of them said a word.

Here I am sitting there, absolutely disgusted. Not only was I disgusted over what had happened with Mark, I was also disgusted with myself. I'm 35 years old and I'm sitting in this holding cell, handcuffed and shackled, and I'm looking at spending the rest of my life in jail. I dedicated every waking moment of my adult life to my uncle and La Cosa Nostra, and this no-good, evil motherfucker is going to sit there and blame me for his son trying to kill himself. But the thing with me, the thing that always made me smarter than him, is the fact that no one, including him, ever knew what I was thinking or what I was feeling. I could read him like a book. I always knew what he was going to do before he even thought about doing it. He was predictable. Mentally, he played checkers with me, where I played chess with him.

At that moment, sitting in that cell listening to him blame me for Mark, I don't know if I have ever felt such a combination of raw emotion and such rage, both at the same time. I'm not the kind of guy who's gonna get into a screaming match with anyone, let alone in front of 15 other guys, and let my opponent or adversary know what I was thinking. And at that very moment, he was no longer my uncle, he was no longer my boss. He was my adversary, my enemy.

I made up my mind right there in that split second that my life was going to go one of two ways. Number one, if I won the RICO case, I was going to take Maria, Little Philip, and my mother and we were out of here. No more Atlantic City, no more Philadelphia, no more mob, no more of my uncle, I was done with it all. Number two, if I lost the RICO case, I was going to cooperate with the feds; even if they still gave me 100 years, I didn't care. This was about breaking with my uncle and La Cosa Nostra, it wasn't about jail time. The time didn't matter to me, it never did. If I never saw the light of day, so be it, but I was going to live the rest of my days for me, for Maria, for my son, for my mother, not for my fuckin' uncle and not for his La Cosa Nostra.

As the RICO trial continued, with the unrelenting onslaught from the federal prosecutors and the overwhelming depth of the government's case, Leonetti knew that his chances for an acquittal were slim at best.

On November 19, 1988, after two full days of deliberation, the jury convicted Nicodemo Scarfo, Philip Leonetti, and all 15 codefendants of every charge in the indictment.

In the end, there was too much for us to overcome. All the killings, all the violence, all the treachery—it was almost like we had made it easy for them to convict us. How could they not with everything they heard. I know this sounds crazy, but when they found us guilty, I felt a huge sense of relief. I knew we were finished, and I knew that this life, La Cosa Nostra, was over for me.

Nicky Scarfo Jr., who was running the day-to-day operation of the now decimated crime family with Anthony "Cousin Tony" Piccolo, Scarfo

Sr.'s first cousin, came to visit both Scarfo and Leonetti behind bars a few days after the verdict.

> *Nicky Jr. comes in and he's telling me and my uncle what is going on out in the street. He says, "Nobody's paying; there's no structure anymore; it's every man for himself." He says, "I went and saw Bobby the other day and I told him what was going on," and my uncle says, "What did he say?" And Nicky says, "He said it was over and that you have no shot on appeal." My uncle said, "Nothing is over as long as we're still breathing," and he points to me and him. "You tell that to Bobby and anyone else who thinks it's over. As long as we're around, it ain't ever over." And Nicky Jr. just nodded.*
>
> *I said, "How's Mark doing?" And Nicky Jr. said, "He's still in a coma, but the doctors say he's gonna make it and that maybe we can bring him home at some point." My uncle says, "I can't have him back to Georgia Avenue after what he's done."*
>
> *I got up and left the visit without saying another word. I went back to the cellblock and I picked up the phone and I called the FBI.*

Philip Leonetti—who as a teenager served as a mob messenger taking messages from his imprisoned uncle and the family's boss Angelo Bruno to their soldiers on the street, became a mob associate in his early 20s, a mob killer at 23, a made man at 27, a *caporegime* at 28, an underboss at 33, and an acting boss at 34—had now taken steps, at the age of 35, to do the unthinkable: become an informant and cooperate with the government.

> *When I called the FBI, I get Jim Maher on the phone. He was one of the agents who worked organized crime. I said, "Do you know who this is?" And he said, "No, I don't." And I said, "I thought you were a voice expert." He said, "I am, but I don't know your voice." I said, "This is Philip Leonetti," and there was dead silence on the phone. I said, "Would you like to speak with me?" And Agent Maher said, "Yes, I would, but if we speak now I have to notify your attorney. If we speak after you are sentenced, then no one needs to know."*
>
> *Our sentencing had been scheduled for May, which was still six months away, and I said, "In May, after I get sentenced, I want you to come and see me so that we can talk." And he said, "I absolutely will," and that was the end of the call.*

Leonetti would spend the next six months in Holmesburg with his uncle and the rest of the mob, waiting to get sentenced.

But Nicky Scarfo and several others still had one more case to go, a trial charging them with the murder of Frank "Frankie Flowers" D'Alfonso in 1985.

> *In that case, it was my uncle, Chuckie, Lawrence, Frankie Nar-ducci, Philip Narducci, Faffy, Gino Milano, Nicky Whip, and Joe Ligambi. I wasn't in that case. Now, Joe Ligambi only had a gam-bling charge in the RICO case, so he pled out and got three years, and the Whip took off and they didn't catch him until after the RICO case. They caught him in Las Vegas with Spike, the guy who took care of my uncle's home in Florida.*
>
> *Now, right before the trial started in March of '89, Gino Milano worked out a deal to cooperate and testify against everyone else, including his brother, the Whip.*

On April 5, 1989, after deliberating for just over 90 minutes, the jury found Scarfo and his associates guilty of murdering Frankie Flowers.

> *At this point all I am focused on is lying low and making it to sentencing—which was about a month away—and then sitting down with the FBI. By this time I told Maria what I was going to do, and naturally she supported it, and I had spoken to my mother about it and she said, "Do it. Absolutely do it."*

As Scarfo, Leonetti, and the others counted down the days to their sentencing, the mood was nothing but doom and gloom. Whatever camaraderie had once existed was all but gone and replaced with jeal-ousy and tension.

> *My uncle was still the boss and that's how he continued to con-duct himself. Nicky Jr. was coming a few times a week and letting him know what was going on, and he was meeting with Bobby and some other lawyers about filing an appeal. Most of the other guys were either keeping to themselves or fighting with each other. There was a lot of tension during those final weeks. I remember Junior Staino and Joe Punge got into it, and another time Junior*

got into it with Wayne Grande. I was just laying low, waiting for
my sentencing date.

Over the course of several days in early May 1989, all of the defendants in the RICO case would be sentenced.

Anthony Punge got 30 years; Junior Staino got 33; Frankie Narducci got 35; Wayne Grande got 38; Joe Punge, Charlie White, Philip Narducci, the Blade, Joey Grande, and Tory Scafidi each got 40; Faffy, Ciancaglini, and Chuckie each got 45.

Nicodemo Scarfo would receive a 55-year sentence, which would run consecutive to the 14-year sentence he received for the Rouse extortion, plus whatever sentence would be imposed on him for the Frankie Flowers murder.

Little Nicky was likely to spend the rest of his life behind bars.

Philip Leonetti would receive 45 years, but Crazy Phil proved not to be so crazy after all, and was scheduled to begin negotiations with the FBI for a reduced sentence in exchange for his defection from *La Cosa Nostra* and his anticipated cooperation with the government.

No one had any idea what I was doing, and the FBI wanted to keep it secret until we were all out of Holmesburg and started getting designated in whatever federal prisons we were going to be assigned to. They told me to just sit back and wait, and that's exactly what I did.

One person who didn't sit back and wait was Lawrence Merlino, who had once been one of Philip Leonetti's closest friends in the mob.

In early May, the 42-year-old Merlino reached out to the FBI and struck a deal to cooperate, and then was whisked away by the US Marshals.

My uncle broke Lawrence's balls so bad when we were in Holmesburg, it's almost like he wanted him to cooperate. When my uncle found out about Lawrence, he said to me, "I told you he was no good. I shoulda killed him three years ago."

I just walked away. I know Chuckie took it bad when Lawrence became a cooperator, but Lawrence had been distancing himself from us for the last couple of years, even before my uncle took him and Chuckie down. I always liked Lawrence; me and him were very,

very close. But before we got arrested, Faffy came down to Atlantic City and told me that he heard Lawrence tell someone, "Don't say nothing in front of Philip unless you want him to go back to his uncle with it," which was an absolute lie. That bothered me and I didn't have too much to do with Lawrence after that.

Mob turncoat Tommy DelGiorno would receive a mere five years when he was sentenced in June 1989, and one month later Nick "the Crow" Caramandi would receive eight years.

In late July 1989, Nicky Scarfo, Chuckie Merlino, Faffy Iannarella, Frank Narducci Jr., Philip Narducci, Nicky "Whip" Milano, and Joe Ligambi would all receive consecutive sentences of life imprisonment without parole following their convictions in the Frankie Flowers murder case.

The federal government had finally succeeded in doing to Nicky Scarfo and his gang what they had done to so many during their reign of terror in the late 1970s and throughout the 1980s on the streets of South Philadelphia and Atlantic City: they whacked them out.

It was all over.

ACT THREE

Good-Bye, Good Riddance

THE FEDERAL PRISON SYSTEM IN THE UNITED STATES IS RUN BY THE BUREAU OF PRISONS, A FEDERAL AGENCY MORE COMMONLY REFERRED TO AS THE BOP. ANY DEFENDANT WHO IS CONVICTED OF A FEDERAL CRIME AND SENTENCED TO A TERM OF IMPRISONMENT IS CLASSIFIED AS A HIGH-, MEDIUM-, OR LOW-SECURITY INMATE, AND THEN DESIGNATED BASED UPON THAT CLASSIFICATION TO SERVE THEIR SENTENCE AT A FACILITY THAT THE BOP DEEMS MOST APPROPRIATE.

In late July/early August 1989, we all got transferred out of Holmesburg and moved to the federal prison in Otisville, New York, which is upstate. Me, my uncle, and Chuckie had all been designated as high-security inmates because of our leadership positions in La Cosa Nostra. *At the time, Otisville was a federal transfer center where all inmates going into the federal prison system had to pass through before they got to their designation. It is where you got classified by the BOP. The place was like a big warehouse full of guys who had been sentenced and were on their way to federal prison.*

One of the first guys I bumped into in Otisville was Bobby Manna, who was the Chin's consigliere and helped my uncle become boss. He had just been sentenced to 80 years and was waiting to get classified and shipped out. He said to me, "Your uncle made the right choice in picking you as his underboss," and I thanked him and we talked for a little while.

Bobby was a good guy, a stand-up guy. Being the Chin's consigliere, he had seen it all. What happened was, Bobby and some of the North Jersey Genovese got convicted of racketeering and trying to kill John Gotti and his brother Gene. Bobby told me that Gotti and the Gambinos were trying to move in on the North Jersey gambling–loan-sharking operation that the Genovese took from "Tony Bananas" Caponigro after they killed him.

Me and my uncle weren't on the same cellblock, but I would see him sometimes in the yard or if we had visits on the same day. I'd see some of the other guys—like Faffy, Joe Punge, Philip Narducci, and Chuckie—the same way, but we were all on different cellblocks. Joe Massino, the boss of the Bonnano crime family, was on my block, and he and I became friendly.

Now this whole time I'm in Otisville, I'm calling home and I'm speaking to Maria, to Little Philip, but mostly to my mother, who was communicating with the FBI for me. She would mention things in code about what they were telling her and I knew that in a matter of weeks I would be out of Otisville and shipped off to a Wit Sec prison for those in Witness Protection. Both my mother and grandmother were just like me and my uncle in that they were very good at speaking in code. My mother was telling me what the FBI was telling her, but was saying it in a way that no one would know what she was talking about. As days went by, I began to hear through the grapevine where the other guys had gotten designated and who was going where.

One day, I'm down in the visiting area to see Nicky Jr. This is late August 1989. He was still running the operation on the street for his father, but he was telling me that things weren't good out there. He was telling me that Chuckie's son Joey and Chickie Cian-caglini's son Michael were very aggressively trying to muscle in on what had been our operation in South Philadelphia. He said, "They've got guys who should be paying my father, paying them because they got six or seven guys and I got me and Cousin Tony." I told him, I said, "Nick, why don't you get out of that and go do some-thing else? What do you wanna do—end up in here or get killed?" And he said, "You're right, Philip."

Now, Nicky Jr. is my cousin. We grew up together on Georgia Avenue. I was 12 years older than him, so he looked up to me like a big brother. I looked him dead in his eye and said, "You're going to end up getting killed; leave that life alone," and he just nodded.

I knew sitting there that I would likely never see him again and if he didn't take my advice that he would end up either dead or in jail.

Toward the end of our visit, I asked him how our Mom-Mom was doing and he told me some story about her chasing some reporter off the steps of our apartment building, and we both laughed, and then I asked him about Mark. He just shook his head and said, "He just lays there. It's like he's dead, but he's still alive. . . ." And his voice trailed off. We sat there in silence for a minute or two, both of us thinking about how my uncle, his father, had fucked up our family.

I stood up and hugged him and kissed him, I had my hands on his face and I told him that I loved him and I said, "Nicky, remember what I told you, this life is no good, it's not for you. Go do something else," and he didn't say anything and we hugged and kissed again. I told him, "Tell Mom-Mom I love her," and as I was walking away I remember getting a little teary-eyed knowing I was never going to see him again, and that if he had any problems, I couldn't do anything to help him.

Now Nicky Jr.'s visit was divided between me and my uncle. They brought me down first, and then when my visit was done, they would bring my uncle out. So when I'm done the visit they put me in a cell and I am waiting for someone to strip-search me, and then for an escort to take me back to my cellblock, when all the sudden my uncle comes walking in with his escort. They put him in the cell directly across from me and they have to strip-search him before they let him go out for the visit. Everything in federal prison is regimented like this. Me and him are five feet away from each other.

Now I hadn't seen my uncle in maybe a week or two, and in all likelihood this is the last time I am ever going to see him, and the first thing he says to me is, "Did you handle that thing I asked you to do?"

I knew by his tone that he was annoyed that I hadn't done whatever it was, and I said, "What thing?" and he said, "The thing for Joe Black," and I said, "I looked into it, but I couldn't get an answer one way or the other," which was bullshit. My uncle says, "I'll look into it, and I'll get the answer," and I could tell by his tone that he was worked up about something. Then he says, "I heard you and Bobby were talking," meaning Bobby Manna, so I said, "I bumped into him, so what?" And he said, "You weren't going to tell me," and I said, "You wanna know everybody I bump into in here; there's a thousand guys in here," and then I could hear the guards coming. He says, "Did Nicky Jr. tell ya where I'm goin', where these motherfuckers are sendin' me?" And I shrugged my shoulders and shook my head no. He said, "Marion, Illinois." I said, "Jesus Christ, that place is the worst."

Right then a guard came and yelled, "Scarfo!" and they led my uncle into another room to search him. As they were walking him out, my uncle said, "Fuck Marion, these cocksuckers ain't never gonna break me," and then he starts giving me instructions on what to do when I get to whatever prison I get designated to. He says, "Call Bobby Simone and have him tell Nicky Jr. so he can let me know where you are and who you are with," and with that they open the big steel door and I know that in about 20 seconds, when that door shuts behind him, that I may never see him again or have to hear that fuckin' voice of his barking out orders at me.

As the guard yells "Gate!" the door is electronically going to close and my uncle is still talking. He says, "Did Nicky tell ya what those two fuckin' snake kids are doing downtown?", which was a reference to Joey Merlino and Michael Ciancaglini in South Philadelphia. And with that the door shut and it was quiet. He was gone.

That would be the last time Philip Leonetti would ever see his uncle, Nicodemo Scarfo, as Scarfo would be shipped the next day from the federal transfer center in Otisville to the nation's toughest and highest-security federal prison, the one in Marion, Illinois.

Inmates at Marion typically spend 23 hours a day inside their 8 x 10 concrete cells, and did not eat, exercise, or attend religious services with other inmates. They would get 30 minutes out of their cells to exercise alone in a small fenced-in area that resembled a dog kennel, with high barbed-wire fences that were enclosed on all sides, including the roof.

They would shower alone three times per week and would receive 300 minutes each month in which they could make telephone calls, which were recorded and monitored by the Bureau of Prisons.

The party was over for Little Nicky, who had spent his 58th, 59th, and 60th birthdays birthdays behind bars, and would now spend the rest of his life inside a cage.

A few days after Scarfo's transfer out of Otisville, the US Marshals came for Leonetti.

> They called me down, but I had no idea where I was going. The marshals took me and turned me over to the FBI, to special agents Jim Maher and Gary Langan. They drove me from Otisville to an office somewhere in New Jersey, maybe in the Cherry Hill area, which was outside of Philadelphia. We talked the whole ride down, trying to get to know one another. They seemed like decent guys and all they kept saying was, "If you tell us the truth, we can help you; if you lie to us, there is nothing we can do to help you or your family," and I told them that I understood.
>
> When we got to the office, there were a few more FBI guys and one of the US attorneys. The US attorney told me, "If I find your cooperation to be 100-percent truthful, I will recommend to the judge that he consider giving you a lower sentence. You have to understand, the judge is not bound by my recommendation and that, in fact, even if you do cooperate, you may still have to serve your entire 45-year sentence. Do you understand?" And I said, "Yes, I do."

Philip Leonetti would spend the next several days being debriefed by the same FBI agents and US attorneys who had brought the Scarfo mob to its knees.

> They put me in protective custody in a county jail in South Jersey, either Salem or Gloucester County, under an assumed name, and every morning they would come and pick me up and take me to the same office and they would ask me a series of questions about everything you could imagine about La Cosa Nostra, historical stuff. They asked about Ange, Phil Testa, my uncle, the Riccobenes, Salvie, you name it. They were very, very thorough, and they treated me well. They were always respectful. They knew everything, even stuff from the early '70s when we first got started. All them years we thought we had them outsmarted, they had us down pat.

After a week of intensive debriefings, the FBI agents surprised Leonetti by bringing his mother, Maria, and Little Philip to the office one day.

I hadn't seen them in a few months—this was now late September 1989. Jim Maher and Gary Langan had brought them up, and I was very happy to see them. We had a nice lunch together, and the mood was light, and then Jim Maher told us, "Tomorrow morning, while it's still dark out, two things are going to happen. The first thing is Philip is going to be picked up by the marshals and put on a plane and taken to a federal prison. We won't know which one until he gets there. They are going to put him in a top secret witness security unit and no one will know who he is or where he is, including you guys," and they were talking to my mother, Maria, and Little Philip, who was now 16 years old, and then Gary Langan said, "But don't worry about him; he will be safe."

Then I jumped in and said, "What about my family?" And Jim Maher said, "The other thing that is going to happen tomorrow morning while it is still dark out is we are going to send a moving van down to Georgia Avenue and your family needs to leave there before the sun comes up. They need to bring only what is essential and they cannot say good-bye to anyone or tell anyone that they are leaving. This has to all happen before sunrise tomorrow." I said, "Where are you taking them?" And Jim Maher said, "We can't tell you that," and Gary Langan said, "But don't worry about them; they will be safe."

I said, "Listen, this is very serious and we have to do what they tell us. Nobody can know what we are doing, not even Mom-Mom. We can't take the chance that she says anything to Nicky Jr. or his father. You guys need to stick together, lay low, and only concern yourselves with your safety. Don't worry about me. I can take care of myself wherever they put me."

We all told each other we loved each other, and we said our good-byes. It was very emotional and very scary. We were all taking a very big risk. Once my uncle learned what I was doing, I knew for certain that he would try and kill all of us—me, my mother, Maria, and even my son, Philip. That's how dangerous this situation was, and we all knew the stakes.

The next morning, at approximately 4:00 a.m., a team of heavily armed US Marshals picked up Philip Leonetti from the county jail where he was staying and took him to the Philadelphia International Airport, where they bordered a chartered flight and flew him under an assumed name to El Paso, Texas.

I didn't ask where they were taking me, because I knew they wouldn't tell me. But when we got to El Paso, I knew they were taking me to La Tuna, the same place my uncle had been in 1982 and '83 during the war with the Riccobenes. I remembered flying to El Paso with Bobby Simone on that trip that got cut short when Bobby saw the two guys in our room, and then flying down to pick my uncle up when he got out in January 1984. On one of those trips, Bobby had told me that La Tuna is where Joe Valachi was kept when he became the first member of La Cosa Nostra *to become a government witness in the early '60s. Bobby said, "They even built this cocksucker his own cell. They called it the Valachi Suite."*

Sure enough, when I get to intake in La Tuna, one of the guys processing me says, "You ever heard of Joe Valachi and the Valachi Suite?" And I knew that's where they would be putting me.

As Philip Leonetti was on a plane heading to Texas, his mother, Maria, and Little Philip had quietly loaded their belongings into a moving van with the assistance of a handful of heavily armed FBI agents, under the direct supervision of special agents Jim Maher and Gary Langan. They were then whisked away from the Scarfo compound on Georgia Avenue in Atlantic City and taken to an FBI safe house deep in the Pocono Mountains, almost three hours away.

The operation was successful. The Leonettis were safe and sound. For now.

The End of an Era

Once I got settled at La Tuna, I was placed in the Valachi Suite, which was separate from all the other prisoners, even the other guys who were in Wit Sec. I was all by myself, except for a guard who stayed with me in the suite 24 hours a day, seven days a week.

They had like three or four guys who would rotate in and out, and these guys weren't regular COs (corrections officers)—they were part of a special unit. We'd watch TV together, play cards, but for the most part I kept to myself.

As far as being in prison, they called the place a suite because it was like a little condominium that was connected but separate from the rest of the jail. I had a living room with a TV, a kitchen with a big dining room table, I had a treadmill in there, a nice-size bathroom, and then in the back was a cell where I would sleep at night, but on a regular bed, not the normal cot the other prisoners slept on. During the day, I had access to the roof of the suite, which was like a concrete patio where I could exercise and get some sun. I'd sit up there and read, and let me tell you, that sun was fuckin' hot down there. I could see the Rio Grande from one of the windows in the suite, that's how close to Mexico I was. Up on the roof, it had a big black tarp, so that the other prisoners couldn't see me from their cells or when they were in the yard. They had no idea who was in there, only that it was someone important or significant. Even the guards in the rest of the prison had no idea I was there, because the crew that guarded me had no contact with them and didn't work at La Tuna.

I had been in La Tuna for maybe a week or so, and Jim Maher and Gary Langan flew down to see me. This is late September/early October 1989. They came right to the Valachi Suite, and we all sat together at the dining room table. The first thing Gary Langan said was, "Your family is safe, and they are in a great place." I told him, "Great, I am very happy to hear that," and then Jim Maher said, "We received some information that your uncle found out that you are with us now. I don't know the specifics just yet; we are waiting for the BOP to send us recordings of his phone calls, but we think it came from either Bobby Simone or Nicky Jr." I said, "It makes sense with my family disappearing from Georgia Avenue," and Jim Maher is looking at me like he didn't finish his sentence, and he says, "And from what we know, your uncle isn't too happy."

I said, "Not too happy? My uncle's not happy on Christmas? He's gonna go fuckin' nuts and try and have all of us killed. Me, my mother, my girl, and my son."

Gary Langan said, "I will personally assure you that you and your family will remain safe—that is my guarantee to you, Philip."

I grew to like all of the agents I dealt with, especially Jim Maher, Jim Darcy, Klaus Rhor, and Gary Langan, and found these to be honorable men and 100 percent straight shooters. With these guys, there was no bullshit, especially Gary. Me and him became very close. If they said they were gonna do something, they did it. They always kept their word.

They told me that they were coming back down in a month or so with some agents from New York to do some more debriefings. They said the agents they were coming with were involved in ongoing investigations into John Gotti and the Chin and La Cosa Nostra in New York.

I said, "I'll be here; I ain't going anywhere, except maybe up on the roof," and we all laughed. Jim Maher then told me that Nicky Jr. was having major problems out on the street. He said, "He's getting a lot of resistance in South Philly, and from what we are hearing, New York is moving in up in North Jersey and taking a lot of what you guys had up there. The only place he seems to be keeping under control is Atlantic City."

At that time, it was Nicky Jr., Cousin Anthony, and a few little guys that they were using to try and keep control of the family for my uncle. Patty Specs, who was the capo in charge of North Jersey, had fled to Italy and some of the other capos loyal to my uncle, like Santo Idone, were locked up with their own cases. According to Jim Maher, the only guys on the street with any muscle was the crew that was led by Chuckie's son Joey and Chickie's son Michael.

I told Jim Maher and Gary Langan, "Listen to me when I say this, my uncle's gonna get my cousin killed. Chuckie's son is no fuckin' good and one of those guys downtown is gonna make a move against my cousin and kill him. I told that kid to get out of that life, but he didn't listen. Whatever happens to him, it's because of his father."

Philip Leonetti spent the rest of October 1989 settling into the Valachi Suite in the La Tuna federal prison in Anthony, Texas, while his mother, girlfriend, and 16-year-old son were adjusting to a new life under assumed names in a small, rural Pennsylvania town in the Pocono Mountain region.

Several hundred miles away from them sat Nicodemo "Little Nicky" Scarfo, the 60-year-old, jailed-for-life Mafia don. At the same time he was growing accustomed to spending the rest of his life inside an 8 x 10 concrete cell, Scarfo was also full of rage and vengeance, angered over the stunning betrayal of his sister and his nephew.

Little Nicky would vow revenge from the confines of his cage. The word on the street was that there was a $500,000 bounty that would be paid to anyone who found and killed his sister Nancy, and his nephew Philip Leonetti.

But what was most pressing in the tortured mind of Nicky Scarfo was keeping his son Nicky Jr. safe from a blossoming rival mob faction, and preserving both his power and legacy as the undisputed boss of the Philadelphia–Atlantic City *La Cosa Nostra*, despite being sentenced to spend the rest of his life behind bars.

Nicky Jr., 24, was the only one of Nicky Scarfo's three sons who gravitated toward *La Cosa Nostra*. Scarfo's oldest son, Chris, had legally changed his last name and was working as a legitimate businessman in the Atlantic City area, having very little, if anything, to do with his imprisoned father.

Scarfo's youngest son, Mark, still a teenager, remained in a comatose state following a suicide attempt on November 1, 1988, in the middle of his father's RICO trial.

Nicky Jr., who was not yet a formally made member of *La Cosa Nostra*, was acting as his father's proxy, and as such, was tasked with meeting underlings and carrying out his father's orders, working side by side with his father's cousin, Anthony "Cousin Tony" Piccolo, who had briefly served as Scarfo Sr.'s consigliere and was now his handpicked street boss.

On October 31, 1989, almost a year to the day of his brother Mark's suicide attempt, Nicky Jr. traveled from Atlantic City to Philadelphia in the late afternoon to meet with Bobby Simone to discuss his father's appeal. After meeting with Simone, Scarfo Jr. and a companion headed downtown for a dinner meeting with several associates inside of Dante and Luigi's, one of South Philadelphia's premier Italian restaurants, and one of Nicky Sr.'s favorites.

Inside the restaurant, the young son of a jailed mob solider stopped by Nicky Jr.'s table and said hello. A few minutes later, what appeared to be a trick-or-treater entered the restaurant wearing a black costume with a yellow mask and carrying a bag. This individual did not attract any immediate attention, as it was in fact Halloween night and the neighborhood was crawling with kids out looking for candy.

The trick-or-treater moved quickly into the dining room and headed straight for Nicky Jr.'s table, swiftly removing a Mac 10 machine gun pistol from his candy bag, and started pumping bullets into Scarfo Jr.'s chest and neck, hitting him nine times in the process.

As the gunman fled into the night, he symbolically dropped the Mac 10 outside of the restaurant, a nod perhaps to Al Pacino's character, Michael Corleone, in *The Godfather*.

Scarfo Jr. was bleeding and badly wounded, but he would survive.

His father's plan to run the beleaguered crime family from prison would not.

> *When I heard what happened to my cousin, I immediately believed Chuckie's son and Michael Ciancaglini were behind it. But there was nothing I could do about it. I tried to talk to my cousin in Otisville and warn him, but he didn't listen. Instead, he listened to his father, and it almost got him killed. The whole thing made me sick. I knew my uncle was going absolutely bananas in Marion. When Nicky Jr. got shot, that was it—that was basically Philadelphia telling my uncle to go fuck himself.*

Immediately after being released from the hospital, where he spent nine days following the shooting, Nicky Scarfo Jr. left Philadelphia and sought refuge under the protection of the North Jersey branch of the Bruno–Scarfo *La Cosa Nostra*, staying for a few weeks at a Sheraton Hotel near the Newark airport, and then moving to another Sheraton Hotel in nearby Woodbridge.

Nicky Jr.'s movements were carefully measured, he avoided South Philadelphia at all costs, and he only sporadically visited his mother and grandmother on Georgia Avenue in Atlantic City.

The shooting sent a clear message: the Scarfo Era was over.

But unfortunately for the man Leonetti and Scarfo Sr. both believed was the messenger, there would be little time to rejoice.

In early January 1990, less than two months after the shooting at Dante and Luigi's, Joseph "Skinny Joey" Merlino, the 28-year-old son of former Scarfo underboss Salvatore "Chuckie" Merlino and the man Leonetti believed was involved in the plot to kill Nicky Jr., was sentenced to more than two years in federal prison following a conviction for participating in a 1987 armored car heist that netted the aspiring young mob leader more than $350,000.

Two weeks later, Santo "Big Santo" Idone, one of the last remaining pillars of the crumbling Scarfo organization, was convicted in federal court on racketeering charges, thanks in large part to the testimony of the federal government's newest assassin: Philip "Crazy Phil" Leonetti.

I never took any pleasure in testifying against anyone, but this is what I had to do to get away from La Cosa Nostra *and break free of my uncle. When I testified against Santo, they flew me from El Paso to Philadelphia. They had me with so many armed US Marshals, you woulda thought I was the president. When I was done testifying, they flew me right back.*

Back in the Valachi Suite in La Tuna, Leonetti's marathon debriefing sessions continued.

A couple times a month a different group of agents or US attorneys would come down and ask me questions about La Cosa Nostra—*the structure, the rules, who was who. Santo was the only made guy from our family that I testified against, but they used me against the Luccheses from North Jersey, the Taccetta brothers, Tumac and Tommy Ricciardi; they used me in Pittsburgh, New England, and in New York against four of the five families there.*

In the summer of 1990, Philip Leonetti would figure prominently in the federal government's civil racketeering suit that resulted in a court-ordered takeover of Local 54, the casino union that Leonetti and his uncle, Nicodemo Scarfo, controlled during the early '80s.

Leonetti's testimony formed a basis for the reasoning why several key Local 54 officials, who had once been aligned with the Scarfo mob, were removed from their positions.

Back inside the Valachi Suite in La Tuna, Leonetti would watch helplessly as his prophecy regarding his cousin Nicky Jr. continued to be fulfilled, when on August 21, 1990, Nicky Scarfo Jr. was arrested, along with 30 other North Jersey–based mobsters, and charged with various racketeering offenses.

The case against Nicky Jr. was built in large part on secretly recorded conversations between Scarfo Jr. and a North Jersey mobster named George Fresolone, who was one of the men assigned to protect the young mob scion following his October 1989 shooting.

Unfortunately, for both Scarfo Sr. and Jr., Fresolone was cooperating with the New Jersey State Police and was wired for sound.

> *I told the FBI that my uncle was gonna get my cousin killed or put in jail, and within 10 months of me saying that he gets shot nine times and indicted for racketeering because he's hanging with a guy that we didn't know, and the guy is wearing a wire. I mean, Jesus Christ, the writing was on the wall, but my uncle didn't give a fuck, that's how obsessed he was with the power of being the boss.*

But Little Nicky's days as boss were coming to an end.

In October 1990, less than two months after Nicky Jr. was indicted, Anthony "Cousin Tony" Piccolo, the 68-year-old caretaker street boss of his cousin Nicodemo "Little Nicky" Scarfo's decimated crime family, was summoned to a meeting in North Jersey with Robert "Bobby Cabert" Bisaccia, the capo in charge of the Gambino family's North Jersey operation. Bisaccia informed Piccolo that John Gotti and the Commission had decided to take "Little Nicky" down and replace him as boss of the Philadelphia–Atlantic City *La Cosa Nostra* with John Stanfa, the 50-year-old, Sicilian-born South Philadelphia–based mobster who drove Angelo Bruno home on that fateful night in March of 1980. Bisaccia informed Piccolo that he would be named Stanfa's consigliere.

> *Those are the rules; New York always makes the boss. The Commission. They made Ange the boss; they made Phil Testa the boss; and they made my uncle the boss. So when they call Cousin Tony up and they tell him they are taking my uncle down and making John Stanfa the boss, that's it. My uncle might not like it, I know he didn't like it, but there is absolutely nothing he could do about it. Those are the rules.*
>
> *I think Gotti was pushing Stanfa in large part so that the Philadelphia proxy vote on the Commission would swing back to the Gambinos, like it had under Ange. I think by this time, the Chin had zero interest in my uncle or the Philly mob, especially with us*

losing Local 54 and with Bobby Manna in jail. Not to mention I had heard from one of the agents that when we all got locked up that the Gambinos and the Genovese chopped up most of North Jersey, leaving us, Philadelphia, with practically nothing.

Remember, this is the same territory that the Commission gave to Caponigro in the '70s, when him and Funzi Tieri were fighting over it, and it's the reason why the Chin and his guys set Caponigro up and whacked him out—so they could take over more of North Jersey.

Me and my uncle never really dealt with Stanfa. I think I met him maybe once or twice. I know that he was involved with Caponigro and Sindone when they hit Ange, and I know that he got very lucky that time he came to New York and the Genovese guys thought he was my uncle. Otherwise, he woulda ended up like Caponigro and Freddie Salerno. He disappeared for a while and then got locked up because he wouldn't testify about what happened the night Ange got killed.

The next time I heard anything about him was when me and my uncle went to Staten Island to meet Gotti and Gravano, and I remember Gotti asking my uncle if we would give Stanfa a pass and let him return to Philadelphia when he got out of jail. My uncle said, "I don't have any problems with him as long he comes home and does the right thing and doesn't cause any problems."

With Nicky Scarfo spending the rest of his life behind bars and now formally deposed as boss, Leonetti's federal handlers turned their attention to a new target: the Dapper Don, John Gotti.

In the fall of 1990, I spent a lot of time with the FBI and the US attorneys from the Eastern District of New York who were building a racketeering case against John Gotti and "Sammy the Bull" Gravano. I remember one of the agents from New York saying to me, "You are the highest-ranking member of La Cosa Nostra to ever cooperate; did you know that?" And I told him that I did not. They told me that they wanted to bring the indictment against Gotti by the end of the year and that when the case went to trial, I was going to be one of their main witnesses, based upon all of the things that me and Sammy had done together, different things he had told me, and, most importantly, the meeting me and my uncle attended on

*Staten Island with John and Sammy in 1986 where John laid out
the details on the Castellano hit. They put me in front of a grand
jury, and I testified about both John Gotti and "Sammy the Bull"
Gravano. I wasn't trying to hurt anyone; all I did was tell the truth.
It was all business, nothing personal.*

On December 11, 1990, armed with a RICO indictment that charged
five murders, including the hit on Paul Castellano, a swarm of FBI agents
and New York City police detectives raided the Ravenite Social Club in
Manhattan and arrested John Gotti, his underboss, Salvatore "Sammy
the Bull" Gravano, and his consigliere, Frank "Frankie Loc" Locascio. All
three men would be held without bail while awaiting trial. The indictment
was based, in large part, on intelligence culled during debriefing sessions
with Philip Leonetti in the Valachi Suite and from his top secret testimony
before a New York grand jury.

*By this point, I had been in La Tuna for more than a year. You
gotta remember, even though I was in the Valachi Suite—which
beat bein' in a regular cell—I was all by myself, with the exception
of the guards who watched me and the agents and prosecutors who
came to debrief me. I told Jim Maher and Gary Langan, "You gotta
get me out of here. I'm going stir crazy being in here by myself.
Put me in Wit Sec somewhere, anywhere, but I gotta get outta this
Valachi Suite."*

On the Road Again

*In early 1991, they moved me from La Tuna into the Wit Sec unit
at FCI Phoenix out in Arizona. This place was about 25 miles outside of Phoenix, smack dab in the middle of nowhere, all the way
out in the desert, and was surrounded by what they called the Black
Canyon Mountains. I thought the sun was hot in La Tuna, my God,
that sun in Arizona, some of the guys would cook things right on the
asphalt, that's how hot it was out there.*

In 1991, Philip Leonetti was arguably the most significant federally protected witness in the United States. Now housed with approximately 70 other protected witnesses, Leonetti had to settle into his new home.

I liked it there. I played basketball every day out in the sun. I ran five miles every day on the track. I was in absolute tip-top shape, and the view of the desert and those mountains was amazing. There were a lot of Mexican guys down there, guys from the Mexican Mafia, but everyone kept to themselves and it was easy doing time there.

Now when you're in Wit Sec, they don't use your name, only your initials, but eventually everyone knows who you are and what you are there for. One day, I get done playing basketball and this kid comes up to me and says, "Aren't you Philip Leonetti, Nicky Scarfo's nephew?" And I say, "Who are you?" And he says, "My name is Willard Moran, but everyone calls me Junior." I remember thinking to myself, "Jesus Christ, what a small world." This is the kid they said whacked out John McCullough, the union boss, and I had never met him a day in my life, and here we are, eleven years later in the same unit in a prison in Arizona. He was a good kid. I got to know him, and I grew to like him.

A few months later, I'm walking the track and I see this guy coming towards me, making a beeline for me. Don't forget, I'm still in jail with a bunch of killers, so my antenna is always up. The guy gets closer and I think he could tell I had a defensive posture, and he says, "Philip, don't you recognize me? It's me, Gino Milano."

Now Gino was one of Salvie's top guys—it was him and Joey Punge. Gino was on trial with us in the RICO case, and then he flipped before the Flowers case and he testified in that case against my uncle and everybody, including his own brother, Nicky Whip.

So, me and Gino catch up and he tells me that he was in prison for a while in Minnesota with Lawrence, and he tells me what was going on in there with him. He's telling me about the Flowers trial, bringing me up to speed on a lot of stuff, but never once did either of us mention Salvie. I think he knows it bothered me as much as it bothered him. It was like Salvie and all that stuff was in a different life. It's hard to explain. Both of us were out here doing our time hoping that when we got resentenced, we'd get better deals and we could go home. Don't forget, we were both young. I was 38 at the time, and Gino was 32.

Prosecutors in New York would call Leonetti as a witness in the infamous Windows Case, which featured mobsters from several New York crime families, including Peter Gotti and Venero "Benny Eggs" Mangano, the underboss of the Genovese family who Leonetti played cards with while his uncle met with Vincent "The Chin" Gigante on the day that Scarfo was formally named boss of the Philadelphia–Atlantic City *La Cosa Nostra*.

As Leonetti was growing accustomed to life inside FCI Phoenix, his mother, Maria, and Little Philip decided to leave the Poconos and relocate to a small town near Tampa, Florida.

Now that I was out of La Tuna, I had better communication with my family and I knew that they were doing really good. Maria got a good job, and Little Philip was doing well in school. I learned that my mom was secretly calling my grandmother back in Atlantic City, and that she was doing okay, but that she was having some minor health problems and that my uncle was torturing her from jail, which didn't surprise me. He tortured everybody that came in contact with him. Around this time is when the feds started asking me questions about Bobby Simone.

At 56 years old, Robert "Bobby" Simone was widely regarded as Philadelphia's most prominent criminal defense attorney. His client dossier read like a who's who of the Philadelphia mob elite of the '70s and '80s: Angelo Bruno, Philip Testa, Salvie Testa, Frank "Chickie" Narducci, Frank Sindone, and Joseph "Chickie" Ciancaglini.

But Simone became best known as Nicky Scarfo's attorney of choice following Simone's performance in the Vincent Falcone murder trial, which resulted in an acquittal for Scarfo, Leonetti, and Simone's client at the time, Lawrence Merlino.

I've seen a lot of lawyers throughout the years and, by far, Bobby was the best. He had this way about him that made it tough not like him—unless you were a judge or a prosecutor—and juries fuckin' loved him, especially the women. He kind of looked like Phil Donahue.

My uncle loved Bobby, and so did I, and even though he wasn't formally a part of La Cosa Nostra, *we always treated him like he was one of us, which he was.*

And that was Bobby Simone's problem.

Dogged for years by federal prosecutors on charges ranging from tax evasion to racketeering, Simone found himself in the exact same situation as all of those clients he had represented throughout the years—under indictment and facing years in prison.

I did everything I could not to hurt Bobby in those debriefing sessions, but the deal was if I got caught lying about anything, I was done. So I had to tell the truth. All those years I was in La Cosa Nostra, *I followed the rules. Now when I'm out of the mob and cooperating with the government, I was following their rules.*

As federal prosecutors in Philadelphia built their case against Simone, federal prosecutors in New York scored a major victory: they flipped John Gotti's underboss, Salvatore "Sammy the Bull" Gravano, the No. 2 man in the Gambino crime family, and Leonetti's close friend.

Gravano told the same FBI agents and US attorneys who had debriefed Philip Leonetti that once Leonetti flipped, he knew that it was over. The Bull told them, "I knew what Philip knew, what me and John had told him, especially about the hit on Paul. I knew that with him testifying, we didn't have a chance."

Gravano was whisked out of the Metropolitan Correctional Center in Manhattan and taken to the United States Marine base in Quantico, Virginia, where he was debriefed at length regarding the inner workings of the Gambino crime family and *La Cosa Nostra* in and around New York City.

By the end of 1991, after Gravano had spent several months at Quantico, the feds needed a new place to stash Sammy the Bull—someplace he could relax before being brought back to New York to testify against Gotti.

When I was in FCI Phoenix, you gotta remember, there are only 70 to 75 inmates in our unit. So anytime someone new came, it was a big deal. So one day one of the guards comes up to me and says, "You're never gonna guess who's here," and I said, "Who?" And he said, "Sammy the Bull."

Salvatore "Sammy the Bull" Gravano, who at 46 had followed Philip Leonetti's lead and defected from *La Cosa Nostra*, was now being held in a segregated area less than 50 yards from where Leonetti's cell was located.

For a week, they keep you in isolation to make sure you're not sick or carrying a disease. Once you're medically cleared, they release you into the unit.

A week after arriving at FCI Phoenix, Sammy the Bull was reunited with Crazy Phil, and while Leonetti was helping Gravano get acclimated to life inside the Wit Sec unit at FCI Phoenix, Gravano was updating Leonetti on everything that had been going on in the world of *La Cosa Nostra*.

You have to remember, by this time I had been in jail for almost five years; Sammy had only been locked up for a year. He told me they had made John Stanfa the boss because the siggys in the Gambino family were pushing for him. He told me that the Chin was definitely behind the car bombing that killed Frankie DeCicco, and that there was bad blood between Gotti and the Chin.

Sammy told me that he was there when Frankie DeCicco got blown up, and that when he went to grab Frankie's body, there was nothing there. Sammy said his hand went through him. Sammy used to talk about Frankie DeCicco all the time. He said he was a man's man, a real gangster.

Sammy told me that when John Gotti came to him and Frankie about killing Paul Castellano, Frankie DeCicco said to Sammy, "I got no love lost for Paul, so if this guy," meaning Gotti, "wants to whack, let him whack him. And then if this guy don't work out, me and you will kill him. Fuck John Gotti."

He told me that him and Gotti had had a falling out in the Metropolitan Detention Center in New York over some things Gotti had said about Sammy that the feds had picked up with a listening device, and that Gotti was worried about me being a witness against him. And I said, "I bet he's more worried now about you and not me."

He told me that the feds wanted to use both me and him to help build a case against the Chin.

We caught up on old times and had some laughs and we always worked out together. We walked that track every day. But Sammy still wanted to be Sammy the Bull, and I didn't want to be Crazy Phil anymore—to be honest I never did. It's what my uncle wanted, not me.

On the one hand, it's great to see someone you know, like it was for me with Gino Milano. But on the other hand, mentally I am done with La Cosa Nostra, so seeing Sammy, while it was nice to see someone I had been close with, that part of my life was over and I was really ready to just move on.

As 1992 got underway, Philip Leonetti continued to be debriefed by FBI agents and federal prosecutors, who were now focusing their attention on Vincent "The Chin" Gigante, the boss of the Genovese crime family.

They told me they were going to use me to testify against John Gotti and they wanted to use me against the Chin. They flew me and Sammy from Phoenix to New York in late February/early March for the Gotti trial, and they had us staying in what looked like hotel rooms that were in the basement of the courthouse. This is where the US Marshals would stay when they were traveling. Once Sammy flipped, they really didn't need me in the Gotti case, but I think they brought me as an insurance policy.

On April 2, 1992, the jury convicted the onetime Teflon Don on all charges in the indictment, and Gotti was sentenced to life imprisonment without the possibility of parole.

The 51-year-old chief of the Gambino crime family was immediately shipped out to the maximum-security federal penitentiary in Marion, Illinois, which had been Nicodemo "Little Nicky" Scarfo's home for the past two and a half years.

When I got back to Phoenix, it was early April 1992 and I had been locked up for the last five years. When we got sentenced, we were under the old federal sentencing guidelines, which meant we had to serve two-thirds of our sentence. I got 45 years, so unless I got a reduction, I would have had to do 30, which means I had 25 years to go. Today, the feds make everybody do 85 percent of their sentence.

Around this time, I get a phone call from Jim Maher and Gary Langan, and they say, "Philip, we have to bring you back to Philadelphia to see the judge. He's going to hear your motion for a new sentence."

Philip Leonetti was now 39 years old and everything was riding on his motion for a new sentence. Without it, he would spend at least the next 25 years behind bars and wouldn't be eligible for release until he was 64 years old.

When I started cooperating, there are no promises, no guarantees. You go into it knowing that you could testify against a thousand guys, and no one can make the judge do anything to help you. In other words, everything I had done or everything I would do, it was all meaningless, at least in the sense of helping me personally, unless the judge reduced my sentence.

In early May 1992, just three years after he was sentenced to 45 years in federal prison, Philip Leonetti was back inside the same federal courtroom before the same federal judge asking for a reduction of his sentence.

The room was packed with FBI agents and prosecutors that at one time hated my guts when I was with my uncle and La Cosa Nostra, and were now coming to court to speak on my behalf and tell the judge everything that I had done since I began cooperating.

Before the hearing started I got a chance to catch up with most of them and they treated me with respect, like a human being, not like the monster they had made me out to be three years before in the same courtroom. The government appointed a lawyer to represent me named Frank DeSimone, who I got along with and who was a good guy.

I remember feeling jittery when they said "All rise!" and the judge, whose name was Franklin Van Antwerpen, came out. This was just like waiting for the jury to say guilty or not guilty in every case I had been in. Even though I was nervous, I always felt lucky in court or when I got charged with something. Remember, I had beaten the Pepe Leva murder case, the Falcone murder case, the extortion case with Mike Matthews, who was the mayor of Atlantic City, the P2P case, and the Salvie Testa murder case. My only loss had been the RICO case.

So the US attorneys are talking, the agents were talking, my lawyer talked, and then the judge asked me if I had anything to say. I told him that I decided that I no longer wanted to be associated with my uncle or with La Cosa Nostra, *and that since that day I have done everything in my power to prove to the federal government that I am 100 percent done with that life. I told the judge that I wanted to join my family and raise my son and live a peaceful, law-abiding life. I told him I wanted a shot at going straight and doing the right thing, doing it all over.*

Judge Van Antwerpen called Philip Leonetti "the most significant crime figure who had ever chosen to cooperate" and hailed his cooperation and his transformation as a human being both "extraordinary" and "outstanding."

The judge then reduced Leonetti's sentence from 45 years to a mere six and a half years. With the time he had already done, Philip Leonetti would be a free man in less than four months.

I will never forget that feeling. I felt like I had a shot at a whole new life where I could just be a regular guy and be around regular people. I spent my whole life around vicious and treacherous murderers, and I was just like them. But now I had a chance to start over, to do things right.

Leonetti would return to the Wit Sec unit at FCI Phoenix, but the news of his courtroom victory was not made public.

I never involved myself in other people's business, and I didn't like it when people got involved in mine. When I got back to Arizona, no one knew that I was getting out in a few months, and that's the way I wanted it. I spent that summer doing what I had done the whole time I was there—playing basketball, exercising, hanging with Sammy, and reading books.

*But I gotta tell you: that last stretch, the summer of 1992, it
was the longest four months of my entire life. The anticipation of
getting out of jail and being reunited with my family made it difficult to sleep. I was very antsy.*

Starting Over

ON SEPTEMBER 9, 1992, AT THE AGE OF 39, PHILIP MICHAEL
LEONETTI, THE FORMER UNDERBOSS OF THE PHILADEL-
PHIA–ATLANTIC CITY MOB, WALKED OUT OF THE FCI PHOENIX
FEDERAL PRISON NEAR MESA, ARIZONA, A FREE MAN, AND WAS
IMMEDIATELY GREETED BY HIS ONETIME NEMESIS TURNED FRIEND,
FBI AGENT JIM MAHER.

*Jim Maher flew all the way from Philadelphia to Arizona to
make sure that everything went smooth when I got out. A guy who
was the special agent in charge of the Philadelphia FBI office, who
didn't like me, told Jim Maher not to come and he came anyway,
because that's what type of stand-up guy he was.*

*Jim and I drove from the prison to the airport in Phoenix and
we got on a plane and headed for the Tampa area, where my mother,
Maria, and Little Philip were living. Both of us flew under assumed
names and we had a detour, stopping in Houston, and then board-
ing another plane. I remember it was late, maybe nine or ten
o'clock, when we landed, and it took us maybe another hour or so to
get to the house.*

Shortly before midnight, a small rental car being driven by FBI agent
Jim Maher, with Philip Leonetti in the passenger seat, pulled into the
driveway of a nondescript two-story house in a quiet residential neighborhood about 30 miles outside of Tampa.

Inside the house were Leonetti's mother, Nancy, his longtime girlfriend, Maria, his now 18-year-old son, Philip, and FBI agent Gary Langan.

> *It was very, very emotional. There was a lot of hugging and kissing and crying. It was one of the best feelings in my life. It was like being born again and getting to start my life all over, away from my uncle and* La Cosa Nostra.

As Leonetti spent his first night as a free man, sleeping in what had now become his family's home, the two FBI agents who had befriended him and assisted him in leaving *La Cosa Nostra* stayed in a nearby hotel.

> *The very next morning, I was up early, before anyone in the house. I remember going to the kitchen and making a cup of coffee, and then walking out onto the back porch and just sitting there, looking at the grass and the trees and thinking: there's no walls here; there's no barbed wire; no guards. I'm free.*
>
> *The thought of being free was very surreal to me. I went upstairs and told Maria, "I'm going for a run," and she said, "You have no idea where you are. How are you gonna find your way home?" And I said, "I made it here, didn't I? I'm sure I can find my way back."*

That morning, at approximately 7:30 a.m., Philip Leonetti started out on what had become his daily ritual of running five miles. Only now, instead of running around a track in the recreation yard of a federal prison, surrounded by men like "Sammy the Bull" Gravano, he was running through the streets of the small suburban town where his family had chosen to relocate.

> *When I'm out running, I'm seeing people leaving for work, kids going to school, dogs running around barking, people's sprinklers going on—all basic stuff that most people see every day and take for granted, but not me, not on this day. I must have had the biggest smile on my face, and it was the best run I had ever taken. I was waving at the people in the neighborhood, and no one had any clue who I was or where I had just come from. I could have run 100 miles that day. And the best part was that I did find my way home.*

Back at the Leonetti home, Jim Maher and Gary Langan were treated to a continental breakfast, courtesy of Maria, and the two agents spent several hours sitting on the back porch, talking with Philip.

> *They told me that they knew my mother had been communicating with my grandmother back in Atlantic City, and that if my grandmother, even by accident, knew anything about where we were and it got back to my uncle, that he was going to send somebody down to kill us.*
>
> *Jim Maher said, "You guys have to be extremely careful; you are all in very serious danger if anyone finds out who you are and where you are," and Gary Langan said, "And it's not just your uncle. It's the Gambinos, the Genovese, the Luccheses—it's everyone you testified against. If given the chance, all of them would kill you and your family, and it's going to be like that for the rest of your lives."*
>
> *I told them I knew that going in and I know the situation I have put myself and my family in. It is what it is, but I am going to be careful and do the best I can—that's all I can do.*

For the next several hours, the agents went through the proper protocol of how Philip Leonetti was going to transform into a John Doe, with a new name and a new background.

That night the Leonetti family and the two FBI agents went out for a huge celebratory dinner at one of the Tampa area's top restaurants and they reminisced over the past and waxed philosophical over something that was undoubtedly uncertain for Philip Leonetti: the future.

Leonetti had mastered the rules of *La Cosa Nostra* and life as a federally protected witness in La Tuna and FCI Phoenix. That was easy to him; those skills were innate. He was a survivor. But mastering the rules of living life as someone else, a civilian, would be Philip Leonetti's toughest challenge yet.

> *Those first couple of weeks I was just driving around, learning the area and seeing what was going on down there. Every day was like a new adventure for me. I laid low for the first two months. I was just getting acclimated to the area, my new identity, and life away from La Cosa Nostra. And then they called me back to Philadelphia to testify in the Bobby Simone trial.*

While Leonetti may have been released from jail, he was still required to appear as a witness if called to do so by the federal government.

Testifying against Bobby Simone was the hardest thing I ever had to do. It was easier killing Vincent Falcone and getting sentenced to 45 years, then it was to testify against Bobby. Bobby was always good to me and I considered him a dear friend, but I had to tell the truth and the feds knew what the truth was. The evidence was so overwhelming I couldn't have lied even if I wanted to. There were a lot of times when I was testifying in that case that I had tears in my eyes—that's how difficult that was for me. Any chance I got to try and help Bobby, I did. I wasn't trying to hurt him, and he knew it. There were a lot of questions that were asked of me where my answer was "I don't recall" or "I don't remember"—and trust me, if I had remembered, it wouldn't have been good for Bobby.

When it was over, Bobby Simone was convicted of racketeering and sentenced to four years in federal prison, with a concurrent 15-month sentence in a separate tax case.

Around this time—I think it was the Spring of 1993—we moved from where we were staying and bought a four-bedroom house right outside of Naples, Florida, which was a few hours south of where we had been living. The place was gorgeous and was right on the water. I started a small landscaping company and things were going good for us.

Even though he was done with *La Cosa Nostra*, in the early part of 1993, Philip Leonetti decided it was time to take another oath.

Maria and I got married. She had stuck by me through everything. I remember her telling me, "I'm not going anywhere," and that was after I got the 45 years. I don't know if I would have been able to do what I did without her.

By this point, Little Philip wasn't so little. He was now 19, and was going to a big university in Arizona. He had come out to see me a few times while I was in FCI Phoenix and he told me that he wanted to go to school there. I couldn't have been prouder that he turned out the way he did, considering everything he had to deal with when he was a kid. He had just turned 13 when we got locked up in 1987.

Looking back, I remember his 10th birthday. We had a party for him on Georgia Avenue. We had it inside the Scarf, Inc. office and in the courtyard that separated our two buildings. They didn't have Chuck E. Cheese back then. All of his friends came to the party and I remember being in the Scarf, Inc. office with Lawrence. My uncle, who was home at the time, never came down to the party. That's the kind of guy he was. Always the big shot, always a jerk off. So me and Lawrence are in the office and I look out the window and I see this shadow move back and forth very quickly—you could see it was a person, but it looked like they were wearing a mask and you could tell they were right on the other side of the door. I say to Lawrence, "What the fuck is that?" And he says, "I don't know."

I told him, "Go out the back door and sneak through the alley, and when I open the door, I want you to grab the guy from behind." So Lawrence does what I tell him, and when I know that he is in position, I open the door and Lawrence grabs the guy and the guy is wearing a dinosaur costume. We drag the guy into the Scarf, Inc. office and we are punching and kicking him and trying to get his mask off. I think this is a hit—that someone sent this guy to kill either me or my uncle. So Lawrence gets the mask off and we see that it's a teenager, and the kid is crying and he's scared to death.

I'm trying to help him up, but he's shaking like a leaf and Lawrence is trying to give him cake and soda to calm him down. I tell him, "I'm sorry that this happened, we just didn't know who you were. Please let us give you some money in case we damaged your costume." That kid said, "I don't want your money. I just want to go home," and he runs out the door crying right in front of Little Philip and all of his friends. This is my son's 10th birthday party. Me and Lawrence beat up the dinosaur who someone got to come to the party and entertain the kids because we thought the dinosaur was there to kill us. This is how fucked up our life was. This is what my kid saw on his 10th birthday.

So the fact that he made it into a prestigious university, coming from where he came from, was a fuckin' miracle, I couldn't have been prouder.

Philip Leonetti was a now 40 years old, happily married, running a landscaping company, and putting his son through college.

I felt normal, like everybody else, but I knew there was nothing normal about my life. Normal people hadn't killed people and lived the type of life that I had led, but that was in the past.

While it seemed that Philip Leonetti was living in a dream, it seemed like anyone still associated with what remained of *La Cosa Nostra* in Philadelphia and Atlantic City was living a nightmare.

For starters, reigning mob boss John Stanfa was engaged in a war with a faction that was dubbed the Young Turks, and consisted of Michael "Mikey Chang" Ciancaglini, Joseph "Skinny Joey" Merlino, and a half dozen of their friends, many of whom were the sons, brothers, and nephews of the defendants who were convicted with Nicky Scarfo and Philip Leonetti in the late '80s.

What happened was, Stanfa named one of the Ciancaglini brothers as his underboss. There were three brothers. One of the brothers, John, was in jail and the other two, Joey and Michael, were on the street. Stanfa names Joey Chang his underboss and his brother Mikey Chang is in a group with Joey Merlino who are now opposing Stanfa. These kids were very dangerous and very treacherous. They are the ones who I believe had shot Nicky Jr. in that restaurant.

Now I'm reading what's going on in the papers and I'm hearing things when I'm talking to the agents, and one day I say to Frank DeSimone, who was my lawyer, I said, "Frank, you watch, the one Ciancaglini brother is going to go after the other Ciancaglini brother," and Frank said, "No way, they are brothers." And I said, "Frank, you watch, this is how these siggys are." And, sure enough, I was right. I always felt bad because their father was such a beautiful guy, a real man's man. I felt bad that he had to watch this happen to his sons from prison.

On March 2, 1993, several gunmen burst into the Warfield Breakfast and Luncheonette Express, a small eatery owned by John Stanfa located only feet away from the warehouse that served as Stanfa's headquarters near the corner of Warefield Street and Wharton in the Grays Ferry section of South Philadelphia. Joseph "Joey Chang" Ciancaglini Jr., Stanfa's 33-year-old underboss and the son of imprisoned Scarfo mob capo Joseph "Chickie" Ciancaglini, was exiting the walk-in freezer to begin the prep work for the morning breakfast rush when two gunmen ambushed him and hit him with six bullets at point-blank range.

Ciancaglini would survive, but he would never be the same. The young wise guy lost his eyesight in one eye, had his speech and hearing impaired, and was forced to walk with a cane following the hit.

Stanfa believed that the hit had come from the Young Turk crew headed by Ciancaglini's own brother, Michael "Mikey Chang" Ciancaglini, and Joseph "Skinny Joey" Merlino, so he decided to strike back.

On August 5, 1993, two gunmen shot and killed Michael Ciancaglini and wounded Joey Merlino in South Philadelphia. Three weeks later, on August 31, 1993, a white van pulled up next to a car—containing John Stanfa, his son Joe, and an associate who was driving them—and opened fire, spraying bullets from two portholes in the side of the van into Stanfa's car, wounding Stanfa's son but failing to exact revenge for the death of Michael Ciancaglini.

Two months later, Nicky Scarfo Jr. was sentenced to seven years in state prison following his conviction in the racketeering case he was indicted for in 1990.

While Natale and Merlino masqueraded as self-appointed mob leaders in Philadelphia, Philip Leonetti was thriving in South Florida.

I spent the rest of 1993 and 1994 building up the landscaping business, but that was pretty much it. They brought me back to New Jersey in '93 to testify against the Taccettas from North Jersey, but other than that I had very little contact with the government. I would hear from Jim Maher or Gary Langan once in a while, but for the most part life was good and things were quiet. It looked like all of the chaos from La Cosa Nostra was behind me.

The Diary of a Madman

I N MARCH OF 1994, JOHN STANFA'S SHORT AND UNEVENTFUL TEN-
URE AS THE BOSS OF THE PHILADELPHIA–ATLANTIC CITY *LA COSA
NOSTRA* CAME TO AN ABRUPT END WHEN THE 53-YEAR-OLD SIGGY
DON AND THE ENTIRE HIERARCHY OF HIS ORGANIZATION, INCLUD-
ING HIS CONSIGLIERE, ANTHONY "COUSIN ANTHONY" PICCOLO,
WERE ARRESTED ON MURDER AND RACKETEERING CHARGES AND
HELD WITHOUT BAIL.

Stanfa's 32-year-old archnemesis, "Skinny Joey" Merlino, would align himself and his Young Turk South Philly street crew with Ralph Natale—the onetime union official and former associate of Angelo Bruno—who, at 60, had spent the last 14 years in federal prison and at one time was Merlino's cellmate.

> *When we were having that dispute with Ange over running the union in Atlantic City, Ralph Natale was one of the guys that Ange was pushing instead of us. John McCullough was the other. So after Ange died, we killed John McCullough and we sent word to Ralph Natale that if he ever stepped foot in Atlantic City, we were gonna kill him, and he knew we would have done it. That was the last I heard of him until he got out of jail, and he and Joey Merlino were running the mob. It was a joke; it wasn't La Cosa Nostra. They made themselves the boss and underboss. Ralph Natale wasn't even made, for Christ's sake, so how's he gonna be the boss of a La Cosa Nostra family? There is no fuckin' way it was sanctioned by New York or the Commission. This is how bad things had gotten in Philadelphia; this is what it became.*

Nicky Scarfo was now 65 years old, having spent the last seven years behind bars, the last four-and-a-half years in isolation at the federal prison in Marion, Illinois, with the Dapper Don himself, John Gotti, locked down in a nearby cellblock.

But Little Nicky's situation was about to go from bad to worse, even though that didn't seem possible.

In November 1994, the BOP opened the United States Penitentiary Administrative Maximum Facility in Florence, Colorado. The supermax prison, known as Florence ADX, was nicknamed the Alcatraz of the Rockies and was built to restrictively house the most dangerous prisoners in the US federal prison system.

Among the first to be transferred there was Nicodemo "Little Nicky" Scarfo, the jailed-for-life former boss of the Philadelphia–Atlantic City *La Cosa Nostra*.

Scarfo was one of approximately 400 inmates sent to Florence ADX, where he was housed in an underground concrete cell in conditions that made Marion look like a five-star hotel.

In a series of letters written to his elderly mother between the winter of 1994 and the summer of 1996, Little Nicky's writings offer a unique insight into the workings of his evil mind from behind bars.

In one letter, Scarfo discussed life at Florence ADX and his dissatisfaction with the prison job to which he had been assigned:

"All I get to see here is the sky thru the roof. I can't see nothing else but the sky. I live like a dog in a kennel. . . . They got me on my feet three hours a day in this furniture factory which is an upholstery shop making a lousy 22 cents an hour. I work 15 hours per week and make $13.00 a month."

In another letter Scarfo blasts current mob leader Joey Merlino as a "drunken idiot" and lambastes Merlino and other mobsters for giving interviews to the local newspaper:

"In the newspapers all I read about is drunken idiots and drunken junkie punks. Since when is it OK to give interviews to the newspaper, they sound like crybabies. They are a disgrace like that lyin' rat ex-grandson of yours. I predict this drunken idiot will wind up just like 'Crazy Phil.' These people make me sick."

Later in the same letter, Little Nicky boasts:

"It's better to live one day as a lion, than a thousand days like a lamb. And in the end, the lambs get slaughtered."

Scarfo's remarks are chilling when he says of those who have wronged him:

"I forgive no one and I never forget."

When Scarfo learns that Lawrence Merlino, a onetime loyal ally turned mob informant, may have died, he offers this:

"Is it confirmed that Lawrence died? I hope it's true so then they could bury him in the government's cemetery where all the rats like him get buried. Eventually that's where his punk nephew, the drunken idiot, is gonna end up, right next to my crazy, lyin', rat, ex-nephew."

The sentiments expressed in those letters didn't surprise Philip Leonetti.

> *This is what I lived with every day of my life with this man. Every day it was someone else who wronged him. Everybody was always out to get him. It never stopped.*

And it didn't.

As the letters continued, the jailed don grew more erratic and more agitated about his frustrations regarding his son Nicky Jr., *"the drunken idiot"* Joey Merlino, and his rage and disgust over the betrayal from his sister Nancy and her son Philip, who he belittled as the witch and her crazy son.

"Tell Nicky to stay out of those clubs. He is acting like the idiots, only difference is them idiots mean business, they are not fucking around and Nicky is stupid because he doesn't listen. Tell him to look up the word procrastinate, which means to put off until a later date. Ask him why is he procrastinating with this drunken idiot?"

More than two decades removed from any contact with his uncle, Philip Leonetti knows exactly what Little Nicky is saying in this 1996 letter to his mother.

> *My uncle wants my Mom-Mom to tell Nicky Jr. that he has to kill Joey Merlino and that he wants it done right away. He's also telling her to let Nicky know to be careful because these guys are dangerous, and if they get the chance, they may try to kill him first. So he is telling him to stay out of nightclubs and places he will run into them and not to waste any more time.*

Little Nicky explodes on his 86-year-old mother in a letter dated January 9, 1996, in response to comments she had made to him about still loving her daughter Nancy and her grandson Philip Leonetti:

"I want you to live forever, but I want you to have your senses so you could see what happens to wild animals."

He later added:

"It makes me sick to think that you have love for them animals. I hate lying, thieving rats like that crazy bastard grandson that you still love so much. Maybe you should have went with them, could it be that they didn't want you? That's how much they love you and besides all of that, fuck God, too. If you really do love that witch, you better say all your prayers for her and that crazy son of hers, because I don't need no prayers. Their day will come and I will get my satisfaction."

Unfortunately for the deranged Little Nicky, even his own mother appeared to be growing sick of his antics and never-ending tirades.

> *My mother stayed in touch with my grandmother from the time she left Georgia Avenue. My grandmother knew why we did what we did, and she never gave us any grief about it. When I got out of jail and got settled down in Florida, I was speaking with her several times a week. She tolerated my uncle and all of his craziness because she had to; that was her son and—despite everything he had done to our family, all of the turmoil he had caused—she still loved him.*

During the time Nicky Scarfo was writing these letters from Florence ADX, his nephew Philip Leonetti was making a name for himself, albeit an assumed name, in South Florida.

Lost at Sea

B Y EARLY 1994, PHILIP LEONETTI'S LANDSCAPING COMPANY WAS MAKING MONEY AND HE BEGAN TO BRANCH OUT INTO OTHER RELATED VENTURES, STARTING A SMALL CONSTRUCTION BUSINESS AND INVESTING IN SOME REAL ESTATE ALONG THE COAST AROUND NAPLES.

Before I went to prison, I had a decent amount of my own money put aside. I ended up spending a lot of it on legal fees, but I still had a nice little chunk and it allowed me to get involved with a few different things. The landscaping business had grown a little bit and I started a small construction business; I was doing some contracting work and started investing in some real estate. It was nothing major, but we could take a house that needed some work, do the work and flip the house and make a nice little chunk and then roll the money into a new house and do the same thing.

At that time, I had a nice little office right outside of Naples, and we had a little garage in the back where I kept the trucks and all of the equipment. I was up every day at 5:00 a.m. and I would go for my run, five miles, and I'd come home, get showered and head to the office by 7:00 a.m., ready to start the day. I was always careful, always had my antenna up, always watching my mirrors, and always taking different routes. I would never, ever, let anyone get the jump on me. I was always ready, always on alert.

I had a secretary, Maria was working in the office doing my books, and I had a couple crews of laborers that worked for me doing landscaping and small construction jobs, and eventually I got back into doing concrete like I did at Scarfo, Inc. in the early days. Things were going good. It was me, Maria, and my mother; Little Philip was out West going to college. I was very fortunate that the work was steady, and financially we were very comfortable.

Just like when I was in the mob, I enjoyed the camaraderie of being with my guys, who were all young guys, laborers who went to work every morning to make money to take care of their families. I admired that. I also enjoyed meeting the customers and getting to know them. I think my perspective of being in the mob gave me a unique insight and also the ability to read people and situations that allowed me to succeed in legitimate business just like it did when I was in the street.

While Leonetti had easily made the transition from mob hitman to government witness, he had also easily transitioned himself into virtual anonymity as a suburban small-business owner. The one-time mob underboss was now the boss of his own little empire of businesses, but deep down he wasn't happy.

I was ready for a change. The truth is, as much as I enjoyed what I was doing down in Florida, I knew that I didn't want to be cutting people's grass or pouring concrete for the rest of my life. And while I liked being in Florida, I knew that it wasn't the safest place for me or my family.

As 1994 drew to a close, Leonetti began to plot his next move.

Some of the best times I ever had were when I was behind the wheel of my uncle's boat, The Usual Suspects. *I never felt more at peace or more free than when I was on the water. There was something about it; I was a completely different person when I was on the boat. Toward the end of 1994 I became obsessed with getting a boat and spending time back on the water.*

But getting a boat to take fishing or going out for a leisurely cruise wasn't what Leonetti had in mind.

The 41-year-old ex-hitman was looking for a boat on which he, Maria, and his mother could live as they traveled from port to port looking for a new place to call home.

When I told Maria what I wanted to do, she said, "Now I know why they called you 'Crazy Phil.'" But she was supportive, and so was mother.

By mid-April 1995, Philip Leonetti had sold off all of his real estate holdings in South Florida, sold his landscaping and construction business, and bought a 44-foot motor yacht that would now become his traveling home.

I loved that boat. It was absolutely perfect for what we were doing.

As Leonetti, his wife Maria, and his mother set sail, the former mob underboss couldn't have been happier.

Driving that boat in the ocean, without a care in the world, now that was freedom.

Maria and my mother would sit on the deck of the boat and talk to each other for hours, or they would read or sunbathe and I would drive the boat. It was so peaceful, so relaxing.

Our first stop was Key West, and then we went to Key Largo and Miami. We basically hit all of the coastal towns in Florida. We were just cruising and we were having a ball. Then we hit Hollywood, Fort Lauderdale, and West Palm Beach. We stayed a little while in Fort Lauderdale, where I knew the area from when my uncle had his house there, Casablanca South. I went by the house and I was surprised that it still looked the same as it did back in 1987. Whoever owned it now hadn't done much work to it.

I took my mother and Maria to a fancy Chinese restaurant where me, my uncle, and all the guys used to eat at all the time. We would take five or six cars and have 20, 25 guys come and we'd spend almost $2,000 every time we went. Spike would have us laughing for hours. My uncle would sit at the head of the table and hold court like a king. We would eat and drink for hours in that place.

We spent most of June around Daytona Beach, and by the Fourth of July we made it to Hilton Head. We spent the rest of the summer in Hilton Head, and we absolutely loved it there.

Our next stop was Myrtle Beach, where we stayed for most of September, and then we vacationed for most of October in North Carolina, the Outer Banks. It was beautiful there. They had wild horses running on the beach; I had never seen anything like that. Then we went to Virginia Beach, and we stayed there through New Year's.

We got to Ocean City, Maryland, in early 1996, and we ended up staying for a couple of months.

After more than a year on the ocean, in the late spring of 1996, Leonetti got some unsettling news from back home in Atlantic City.

Around this time we found out that Mom-Mom had had a stroke and wasn't doing good, and my mother was adamant about returning to Atlantic City to take care of her. Before we got the news about Mom-Mom, Atlantic City was the furthest thing from all of our minds, but that phone call changed everything.

Philip Leonetti was now on his way home, behind the wheel of his 44-foot yacht, heading back to New Jersey to visit his ailing grandmother.

My plan was to lay low and sneak back into Atlantic City without anyone knowing I was there.

But sometimes, even the best plans don't work.

Going Home

A few days after we found out about my grandmother's stroke, we got into Cape May and docked at a marina down there, and me and my mother rented a car and we drove up to Atlantic City, which was 40 minutes away. Maria stayed on the boat. This was early May 1996, and I hadn't been in Atlantic City since April of 1987.

I wasn't nervous, but I was anxious. I knew that this was extremely dangerous, but the way I saw it, I had no choice. My grandmother was sick, and I had to do what I had to do.

I drove right to Georgia Avenue and dropped my mother off in front of our buildings, and then I went and parked the car around the corner on Florida Avenue. My mother and I agreed that she would go outside on the back porch, which had been my uncle's porch, and smoke a cigarette 30 minutes after she got there if the coast was clear for me to come inside. I remember that my heart was pounding waiting for her to come outside on that porch. The only person I didn't want to bump into was Nicky Jr. because I knew from talking with my grandmother that he was still involved with my uncle and I didn't want any aggravation from him because I wasn't sure where his head was. I knew he himself wouldn't try anything stupid, but I wasn't sure who he was hanging with and if one of them would try and make a name for themselves if they saw me. I knew that if word got back to my uncle that me and my mother were back on Georgia Avenue, he would have ordered us to be killed on sight, even if we had come back to take care of his mother. He didn't give a fuck.

So 30 minutes later, I'm sitting in the car on Florida Avenue and I'm waiting for my mother to appear on the porch with the cigarette so I can go in. I can go right through the same back alleys we used to use when we were sneaking out of Georgia Avenue when had the bail restrictions during the Falcone case.

Now, Philip Leonetti would use those same back alleys to sneak back into the Scarfo compound on Georgia Avenue to avoid detection.

It was just like the old days, only in reverse.

And Philip Leonetti was no longer the underboss of the Philadelphia–Atlantic City *La Cosa Nostra*. He was a man with a $500,000 bounty on his head.

All the sudden, I see my mother on the porch and, boom, I'm out of the car. I quickly walk through the alleys and hop the little brick wall and no one sees me. I go right up the back steps and me and my mother go into what was my uncle's apartment, but was now where my grandmother lived.

When my grandmother saw me, she started to cry and so did I. It was very emotional. She was lying in her bed, which was where my uncle had his bedroom, and looked me in the eye and said, "Philip, I never thought I was going to see you again." I kissed her and I held her hand and I told her, "We're here, Mom-Mom. We're going to take care of you," and she was crying and squeezing my hand.

My mother and I went into the living room to talk and we agreed that my grandmother was in pretty bad shape, worse than we had expected. My mother said without hesitation, "I'm moving back in here with her; she needs me." My mother was a lot like my uncle in the sense that she was stubborn and, like him, once she said she was doing something, it was done—there was no talking to her. That was the Scarfo in her.

I told her that we would keep the boat in Cape May for the next few months, and I would be close in case she needed me. I told her that I would come up every other day to help out and do whatever she needed me to do. My mother was a tough woman and very street smart, so I wasn't worried about her safety. Nobody, including my uncle, would do something to my mother and leave me alive. If they were going to hurt her, they would have to kill me first. If they didn't and anyone so much as raised their voice to my mother, they know I would have killed them. So I figured the only time she was actually in danger was when I was actually around. Plus, I knew she was going to stay in the house and wouldn't be going out, and I was only 40 minutes away.

That night, Philip Leonetti drove back to Cape May and stayed with Maria on the boat, while his mother stayed on Georgia Avenue with his ailing grandmother.

The next day, I'm up early and I call the house and my mother says, "I saw your cousin last night," meaning Nicky Jr., and I told her I will be right there, and she said, "It wasn't what you think." And I said, "Whatever it was, I'm on my way; I'll see you in an hour." Now my heart is racing because now Nicky Jr. knows that at least my mother is back, and he probably knows that I am not too far away.

For the first time since leaving *La Cosa Nostra* in 1989, Philip Leonetti is back home and he knows that if he is spotted, his life is in danger.

As I'm driving to Atlantic City it occurs to me that I should have a gun in case anyone saw me and decided to try something. I took a shot and I went to a bar in Ducktown that was owned by a kid I used to play basketball with. So I park the car and I walk into the bar, and I am wearing sunglasses and a baseball hat and I see him behind the bar, stocking it. He was getting a delivery because when I was coming in, the delivery guy was going out. It's early in the morning. He sees me and says, "We don't open til' noon," and I go up to the bar and I take my sunglasses off and I say, "But I'm thirsty now." He's getting ready to tell me to get the fuck out of his bar when all the sudden his eyes get real big and he says, "Jesus fuckin' Christ, is that who I think it is?" And he comes around the bar and gives me a big hug and a kiss, and then we have a drink together, a Cutty and water, just like the old days.

Me and Lawrence used to drink in this bar, and so did me and the Blade. It brought back a lot of memories sitting there with him. The guy says, "Do you remember the last time you were in this place?" And we both started laughing and I told him, "I'll never forget it."

It was the late fall of 1986, a couple of months before my uncle got locked up. I was the underboss at this time and I went down to the bar to watch the football games and have a few drinks. It was a Sunday afternoon. I was all by myself. A couple of guys from the neighborhood were there.

I'm sitting there drinking, having a good time, minding my own business and the phone in the bar rings and it was my mother, and she says, "Your uncle needs you back here. He wants you to drive him down to Margate." I finished my drink and I start walking back to Georgia Avenue, and I am steaming and I was a little drunk. I'm thinking to myself: This cocksucker can't leave me alone for a couple of hours. He can't find someone else to drive him to his girlfriend's house. Why is he always breaking my balls?

So as I'm getting close to the office at 28 North Georgia, my uncle is standing outside and he is talking to a guy who worked for Vince Sausto at Scannicchio's. He was a waiter there, a fuckin' two-bit wannabe wise guy that always had something to say. Anytime he saw me or my uncle, he fawned all over us and he would sometimes bring food and liquor to the house for us. So me and my uncle tolerated him.

As I walk up, the guy looks at me and says, "Hey, Philip," and I hear the guy talking about "motherfucking" Vince, calling him "a jerk off" and saying all kinds of things about him. And my uncle is just standing there listening to the guy. I don't say a word to either one of them, but I grab the guy by the throat and I start choking him. This guy is gasping for air and his eyes are real big and his arms are flailing. I got both hands around his fuckin' neck and I'm just squeezing the breath out of this guy. His face is purple and his head looks like it is going to explode. My uncle is goin' nuts. He says, "What are you doin'? You're gonna kill the guy." And after a few more seconds, I let go and I shove the guy to the ground, and he goes down right in the gutter next to his car.

I say to my uncle, "You let this cocksucker (and now I'm kicking this jerk off) come around here and talk about Vince like that? Vince is our friend; Vince is my friend," and I start going in on this guy, kicking him good. If I had a gun on me, I woulda killed this guy. I was in such a fuckin' rage—not so much at the guy or what he said about Vince, but at my uncle. It was the accumulation of everything, all of his bullshit.

I reach into my pocket to take out my car keys; I was going to throw them at my uncle, and I was going to tell him, "Drive yourself to Margate." But I realized I had left my keys at the bar. At this moment, the guy who owns the bar is walking up Georgia Avenue with my keys; he's bringing them to me. He senses that he is coming up on a bit of a situation. He sees the guy down on the street and I guess he senses the tension between me and my uncle. He says, "Philip, why don't you let me drive your uncle to Margate?" And right away my uncle says, "Let's go." It was like he couldn't wait to get away from me, so much so, that he is going to get in a car with a civilian and drive to Margate, which is something my uncle would never do in a million years because he is the boss of La Cosa Nostra, but he knew the guy was from our neighborhood and that the guy was with me, so he went.

They pull away and I go over to the guy in the street and I tell him, "Don't ever come around here again. If I see you on this street, I'll kill ya." And I went upstairs. My uncle never said another word about it, and the guy never came back to Georgia Avenue.

So here I am back in this bar more than 10 years later, and my friend says to me, "What are you doin' back here, trying to get yourself killed?" And I told him about the situation with my grandmother. He says, "Jesus Christ, Philip, I'm sorry to hear that. Is there anything I can do to help?" And I said, "Yeah there is—you got a gun?" And he pulls a small little .38 from underneath the bar and slides it across the bar to me. He says, "I never saw you and you didn't get that from me," and I tuck the gun into my pants and I gave him a hug and a kiss and I thanked him, and as I was leaving he said, "Philip," and I turned around and he said, "Take care of yourself and be careful." And I said, "You, too," and I was out the door.

I parked the car on Florida Avenue, like I had the day before, and I had a bag with some groceries for my grandmother. I put the groceries in a plastic bag and I tore the bottom of the brown grocery bag and I stuck my hand inside the hole of the bag and *had the loaded .38 in my hand. I walked through the alley, hopped the wall, and went up the steps into the apartment and saw my mother. The first thing I said was, "Is Nicky here?" And she said, "No. He has a restaurant down in Ventnor and he is down there." I said, "What happened when he saw you?" And she said, "He was very respectful. He gave me a hug and a kiss and he told me that he figured you'd be coming around with Mom-Mom being sick." I said, "What did he say about me?" And my mother said, "He said if you're around, it's better that you two don't see each other on account of his father."*

Now here I am standing in what was my uncle's apartment on Georgia Avenue in Atlantic City, with a .38 in my pants and I'm thinking to myself, "My name must be 'Crazy Phil,' if after everything I went through, I ended up right here in the same fuckin' place that I started."

The freedom that Philip Leonetti had experienced on the boat was now replaced with the anxiety that he would be spotted and forced to shoot it out with whomever came looking for him, including his cousin Nicky Scarfo Jr.

I said to my mother, "Where is Nicky's restaurant?" And she gave me the address, and then her eyes got real big and she said, "You're not going down there, are you?" And I told her, "I want to get this over with. I'll be back in an hour."

As Philip Leonetti drove the short distance from the Scarfo compound on Georgia Avenue to Nicky Jr.'s new restaurant, Amici's Ristorante, on Atlantic Avenue in Ventnor, he wasn't sure what to expect from his cousin, who was now 32 years old and who had been his uncle's proxy since his father and Philip went to jail in April 1987.

I drove by the place, and it looked like a classy joint. Right away I noticed the law parked right across the street, watching the place. I knew Nicky had been away and I figured maybe he was on parole, so they were watching him like they used to watch us. I drove right by them and went up the side street and parked halfway up the block. They never made me.

There was a side door on the place that had a green door that went into the kitchen, and I could tell there were workers in there prepping food because I could hear them talking when I walked by. They were all talking Spanish. I opened the door and none of them flinched, and I said, "Where's Nick?" And one of them nodded towards the dining room that was through a set of double doors that swung in and out like you see at restaurants. I could see through the window in the door that Nicky was sitting at a table with one of the girls who worked there and he had his back to the kitchen.

I took my sunglasses off and I walked through the doors and Nicky had no idea I was there. I pulled a chair up, and when he saw me he turned white as a fuckin' ghost. I said to the girl at the table, "Dear, can you give us few minutes?" And she left. The first thing I did was give him a hug and a kiss to put him at ease. He put his hands up and said, "Philip, I don't want any trouble; I got enough trouble," and I said, "Nick, I'm not here to cause you any trouble, I'm here because Mom-Mom is sick." I took the gun that I had in the small of my back, the .38, and I put it on the table. I said, "I'm not here to hurt you. Maybe I can help you." And I could see right away he relaxed.

Philip Leonetti had been in New Jersey for less than 48 hours and already he had been to Georgia Avenue twice, got himself a gun, and now he was having a sit-down with his cousin Nicky Scarfo Jr.

I said, "Tell me about your problems," and he said, "I wouldn't know where the fuck to start. I got my mother and Mark that I gotta take care of, then there's Mom-Mom. I'm up to my neck with this fuckin' place, and I got problems with the guys in South Philly breaking my balls and trying to shake me down. It's just me out here; I'm all by myself. Then I got my father with all of his shit, and on top of that, I got those motherfuckers who are parked across the street watching everything I do."

After he laid out all of his problems, Nicky nodded towards the gun on the table and said, "You know what, do me a favor—shoot me in the fuckin' head after all," and we both laughed.

Philip Leonetti quickly recognized that he wasn't going to have any problems with his cousin.

I knew exactly how he felt. He was going through the motions to appease his father, just like I did, and I knew within two minutes of sitting with him that his heart wasn't into La Cosa Nostra, *and he wasn't going to do anything stupid.*

I told him, I said, "Nicky, remember the last time I saw you in Otisville? I told you to leave this life alone; it's no good for you. I told you not to listen to your father, but you ignored me and look what happened. Since that time, you got shot and you went to jail. Now you're sitting here seven years later and you are having problems with the same guys in South Philly, and you got the law parked out in front of this restaurant. That's not gonna end good either way it goes." And he said, "I hear ya, but what am I gonna do, pick up and move? I got my mother and Mark to look after, they are my responsibility. They have no one else. I'm fuckin' stuck here."

I said to him, "What's going on with you and the guys in Philly?" And he said, "It's Joey Merlino and Johnny Ciancaglini. Typical shakedown shit, but I got nothing to give them." I told him, "Nicky, while I'm here, if you need help, you let me know. Whatever I need to do to help you, I will do. You are my blood, do you understand?" And he said, "Yes, I do, Philip," and I hugged him.

What I was saying to him was that if anybody posed a threat to him, that I was here to protect him and that I would do whatever needed to be done, including eliminating the threat.

I started looking at one of the menus and I said, "Nicky, this is a classy joint," and he pointed to one of the items on the menu. It was an Italian dish, but it had an Irish name, and he said, "You wanna hear something funny? My father went fuckin' nuts when he saw that." And I said, "Why, what the fuck does he care what you call it?" And he said, "My father called and said, 'You don't name an Italian dish after a fuckin' Irishman. What's the matter with you, you wanna go out of business?'" And we both started laughing. The thought of my uncle sitting in his jail cell at Florence Supermax going nuts over the name of a fuckin' restaurant dish over a thousand miles away said it all.

*We exchanged some funny stories and I left and I told him
that if he needed to get a hold of me to talk to my mother. I called
my mother on Georgia Avenue and told her everything was fine at
the restaurant. As I'm leaving, Nicky walks me back through the
kitchen and I say to him, "Nick, you should really keep that side
door locked. It's perfect if someone wanted to come in and make
a move on you," and Nicky started laughing. I said, "What's so
funny?" And he said, "My father said the same thing. He made me
take pictures of every square inch of this place and send them to
him, and that is the first thing he said to me."*

*I gave Nicky a hug and a kiss, and I left. Instead of going back to
Georgia Avenue to see my mother and my grandmother, I remember driving back to the boat in Cape May and getting a pounding
headache as I did. All I wanted to do was get back on that boat and
set sail again, and now I was getting mixed up in all this bullshit in
Atlantic City with my cousin.*

Philip Leonetti would stay in Cape May and avoid Atlantic City for the
next week, checking in on his mother and grandmother by phone.

*Me and Maria were living on the boat, which was docked at a
marina. We would go to the beach, we would go shopping, we would
go out to dinner, and I was bouncing around Ocean City, Wildwood,
Rio Grande, Sea Isle City, Stone Harbor, and Avalon, but I wasn't
relaxed like I had been prior to us stopping in New Jersey. I wasn't
happy with the situation that I had put myself in by coming back to
Atlantic City.*

In addition, the FBI had gotten in touch with Leonetti and told him
they wanted him to testify against Vincent "The Chin" Gigante in a RICO
case, and that they were interested in using him as a witness in the upcoming Frankie Flowers retrial, which had been scheduled after Nicky Scarfo
and his codefendants had their convictions reversed in that case.

*One day I call my grandmother's house and my mother
answers and she tells me that my uncle called the house and she had
answered the phone. My mother said, "He cursed at me in Italian
and he hung up." I told my mother, "That's it, we cannot stay here,*

*I will bring Mom-Mom with us, but we cannot stay here anymore—
it's not safe."*

For the next several weeks, leading up to July 4, 1996, Philip Leonetti
was sneaking into Atlantic City three or four times a week and visiting
both his mother and grandmother to try in earnest to get them both to
leave Atlantic City. Leonetti's routine in getting to the Georgia Avenue
compound was always the same.

> *I would park on Texas or Florida Avenue and I would walk
> through the alleys with my hand up under the brown shopping bag
> with the hole cut in it and I was carrying a .38.*
> *Whereas before I was slipping in undetected, now some of
> the old ladies who lived back there and knew me since I was kid
> started seeing me. Some of them would say things in Italian to me
> like, "Fare attenzione," which means, be careful and pay atten-
> tion. I knew that it was only a matter of time before someone was
> going to come looking for me, but I couldn't get my mother and
> grandmother to leave, and there was no way I was going to leave
> them behind.*

The very next day there was someone on Georgia Avenue who was
looking for him. It was the FBI.

Gary Langan, who was Philip's FBI handler and who become one of
his most trusted allies, had gotten word that Philip was back on Georgia
Avenue and went looking for him to find out the truth.

> *One day, I'm inside Mom-Mom's house and there's a knock at
> the door and my mother answers it, and it's Gary Langan. I knew
> he wasn't happy because he was always talking about us being care-
> ful and here we were on Georgia Avenue in my uncle's apartment.
> Gary said, "Philip, we received information that Joey Merlino has
> been sending guys around here looking for you. The word is out
> that you are back. You're putting yourself in a very bad position."
> I said, "Who is he sending, so I know who to look for?" And he said,
> "I'm not joking—you can't stay here; it's not safe."*
> *I knew he was right, but what was I going to do? Right around
> this time my mother got sick with lung cancer and she was going to*

the doctors, and now in addition to checking on my grandmother,
I had to check in on my mother and take her to her appointments.

As the summer of 1996 continued, Ralph Natale and Joey Merlino were running what remained of the Philadelphia–Atlantic City *La Cosa Nostra*.

Nicodemo "Little Nicky" Scarfo, now 67, remained behind bars at Florence Supermax ADX in Colorado, and Philip Leonetti was living on a 44-foot yacht in Cape May, New Jersey, and traveling to Georgia Avenue in Atlantic City on an almost daily basis.

One of the guys who lived in one of my grandmother's apart-
ments and who had always helped me and my uncle by telling us
who was coming around, was still on the front porch of his apart-
ment—all day, every day, smoking a cigarette, and keeping an eye
on the comings and goings of the street. He knew me and my mother
were around.

One day, he sees me in the courtyard between the buildings and
he says, "Philip, all week there's been a car parked up the street with
two guys in it and they ain't cops. I seen one of them real good and
he looked real sloppy, kind of dirty," and I knew right away that he
was talking about a bum who was part of the North Jersey branch
of our family. I never liked him and neither did my uncle, and now
I'm thinking to myself, "This is the guy they are sending down to
kill me."

The next day, when I come to Georgia Avenue, I park in the
same spot, only this time I walk all the way down to Atlantic and
come right up Georgia Avenue for anyone who was looking for me
to see. I wanted him or someone else to jump out and take a shot
at me, because I was ready. I had the .38 in the shopping bag and I
woulda blasted any one of them.

For the next week, Leonetti made his presence on Georgia Avenue known by continuing to walk up and down the street, eating at Angeloni's, which was on the corner, and doing anything he could to attract anyone looking to make a name for themselves.

This is how crazy I was at this point—I wanted one of these
guys to come after me. Put it this way, they knew I was there. If they

really wanted to do something, they would have done it. The fact is, none of them guys wanted any problems with me. They knew I'd kill every last one of them, and I think they knew I was trying to bait them. I never worried about Joey Merlino or any of his guys, because they were always punks to me. They weren't men; they weren't gangsters; they weren't La Cosa Nostra. *I worried about the guys from New York or someone my uncle might send, because I knew I was vulnerable being back in Atlantic City.*

That summer was very, very hectic. Finally, in early September, I convinced my mother and grandmother to leave Atlantic City and I put them both on a plane and flew them down to Hilton Head. Maria and I were going to take the boat from Cape May back down to Hilton Head and start looking for a house.

Leonetti's days on the water were coming to an end.

I saw Nicky Jr. only one more time before I left and I reiterated what I told him about getting out of this life, and his answers were always the same. He came to see me on Georgia Avenue and I told him I was taking Mom-Mom with me. He got a chance to say good-bye to her, which he did. I even saw my uncle's wife, Mimi, and she said to me in her Italian accent, "You a lookin' good," and I just walked right by her without saying a word.

The only unfinished business I had in Atlantic City was going back to the bar in Ducktown and giving my friend his gun back. I told him, "Where I am going, I won't be needing this."

The Back Nine

PHILIP LEONETTI HAD DONE THE UNTHINKABLE: HE SPENT THE SUMMER OF 1996 AT THE JERSEY SHORE AND MANAGED TO SUCCESSFULLY DODGE THE MOB. BY EARLY NOVEMBER, HE AND MARIA HAD MADE IT TO HILTON HEAD, WHERE THEY JOINED HIS MOTHER AND GRANDMOTHER AND QUICKLY FOUND A HOME IN AN UPSCALE, GATED COMMUNITY ON ONE OF HILTON HEAD'S MOST EXCLUSIVE GOLF COURSES.

As everyone was settling in, Nicodemo Little Nicky Scarfo, now 67, was also settling into some new digs—the maximum security federal penitentiary in Leavenworth, Kansas, where he was housed with his successor, John Stanfa, who had received five life sentences following his conviction in the RICO case brought against him.

As 1997 got started, Little Nicky Scarfo, Chuckie Merlino, and several members of the old Scarfo mob were brought back to Philadelphia and housed in the same prison while awaiting their retrial for the 1985 murder of Frank "Frankie Flowers" D'Alfonso.

The FBI had called Leonetti's home in Hilton Head and told Philip they wanted to use him as a witness against his uncle in the retrial.

I knew they were going to use me at the Chin's trial later in the year, but now they wanted me to come back to Philadelphia and testify against my uncle in the Flowers case. I told them, "Absolutely not." When I made my deal, I told them I would never testify against my uncle and I never did. It's not that I was against testifying against him; it's that I never wanted to give him the satisfaction of seeing me testify so he could snicker at me or make some remark. Every time we were on trial and someone would testify against us—whether it was Joe Salerno, Tommy Del, or whoever it was—my uncle would say, "Look at this cocksucker, look at this rat," and the feds knew this, they

knew that I would never put myself in that situation, to be in the
same room with him.

Now, they were trying to break that deal. They already had
Lawrence, Tommy Del, Nicky the Crow, and Gino Milano as wit-
nesses, so I don't know why they needed me. I told Jim Maher, "Tell
them if they force me to come, I ain't gonna help their case," and
that was the last I heard about it.

In the spring of 1997, Little Nicky Scarfo was reunited with several
members of his gang, when he and his codefendants—including Salvatore
"Chuckie" Merlino, Francis "Faffy" Iannarella, Frank Narducci, Philip
Narducci, and Joe Ligambi—were housed together at Philadelphia's newest prison, the Curran Fromhold Correctional Facility (CFCF), which was
situated off of I-95 in North Philadelphia.

One of the agents told me that all of the guys looked like they
had aged 20 years since the last time they were in Philadelphia,
except for my uncle. They didn't use me as a witness and they didn't
use Lawrence—just Tommy Del, the Crow, and Gino Milano. And
this time around, my uncle and the rest of them beat the case.

The acquittal in the D'Alfonso retrial meant little to Nicky Scarfo,
as he was still serving consecutive 14- and 55-year sentences. But to his
codefendants, the not guilty verdict meant that they would one day walk
out of federal prison, albeit in another twelve or 15 years, depending upon
their sentences.

The only defendant to immediately benefit from the acquittal was
57-year-old Joe Ligambi, the alleged triggerman in the D'Alfonso murder
who had received only three-and-a-half years in the RICO case. Ligambi
was immediately released from jail.

The dynamic inside the courtroom was unique in that the defendants
were separated from the courtroom gallery by thick, bulletproof glass and
many of those in the audience were members of Skinny Joey Merlino's
crew, including Merlino himself.

Merlino was there to support his father, who sat directly in front of
Scarfo during the trial. The two men, lifelong friends turned bitter ene-
mies, seemed to exchange pleasantries from time to time, with the elder
Merlino making jokes with Scarfo as Tommy DelGiorno testified.

On several occasions, Little Nicky reportedly turned around and fixed an icey stare on Joey Merlino, the man he belittled as "the drunken punk" in those prison letters, and the man many believed was responsible for shooting his son in 1989.

Merlino, no longer a kid, was now the 35-year-old underboss of the mob under new boss Ralph Natale. Known as the Prince of Passyunk Avenue, he had become a cocksure celebrity gangster who was the toast of the town. Joey stared right back at Little Nicky.

With the D'Alfonso trial behind him, Scarfo was transferred to the maximum security United States Penitentiary in Atlanta, which was also home to his former underboss Salvatore "Chuckie" Merlino. The two men would live on the same cellblock, but on different tiers, and work together in the prison dining hall. According to sources, they did not socialize with one another.

It is believed that while Merlino immersed himself in illicit activities inside prison like gambling on sporting events and running card games in which items from the prison commissary served as money, Scarfo, the regal mob don, thought such activities were beneath him, and spent most of his time in his cell reading or walking the track with an inmate that he felt was more suited to a man of his character, Vittorio "Vic" Amuso, the imprisoned boss of New York's Lucchese family.

Scarfo reportedly convinced Amuso to formally initiate his son, Nicky Jr., into the Lucchese crime family, and very quickly the younger Scarfo was placed under Amuso's protection, which meant rival mobsters like Chuckie Merlino's son were prohibited from harming him, and would draw the wrath of the powerful Lucchese family if they did.

The FBI believes that Scarfo and Amuso were planning on using Nicky Jr. to expand the Luccheses' existing North Jersey operation into South Jersey, namely Atlantic City, with the hope that one day the younger Scarfo, with the backing of the Lucchese crime family, would regain control of the Philadelphia–Atlantic City mob, and run it under the Lucchese umbrella.

My uncle was obsessed with La Cosa Nostra *and being the boss, so I have no doubt he spent all of his time in jail trying to regain control of the mob using Nicky Jr.—and finding and killing me and my mother.*

That summer, I went to New York, and me and Sammy the Bull both testified against the Chin. The whole time I was testi-

fying, the Chin was sitting in a wheelchair, slumped over, and he looked disheveled. I'd catch him mumbling to himself, but every once in while I'd catch a look in his eye and I knew his whole act was bullshit. He wasn't insane crazy, this guy was crazy like a fuckin' fox. He was the last true Cosa Nostra boss, the last of the dons. After him, it wasn't the same.

Sammy told me a story about a sit-down that him and John Gotti had with the Chin where Gotti told the Chin that he was making his son John Jr. and inducting him into the Gambino crime family. Sammy told me the Chin said, "Geez, I'm sorry to hear that," with the implication that no father who loved their children would want them involved in this life. When Sammy told me this story, I immediately thought of what my uncle had done with me and what he was doing with Nicky Jr. and I shook my head and said to myself, the Chin wasn't the crazy one, it was my uncle and Gotti who were.

Me and Sammy got a chance to catch up, and he told me he was living in Arizona and invited me to come and see him. Little Philip was actually living about 20 minutes from where Sammy and his family had settled, but as much as I liked Sammy, I wasn't interested in going to Arizona to hang out with him. I was very happy with my new life and being away from everyone and anyone that had any connection to La Cosa Nostra.

Like Scarfo, Amuso, and Gotti before him, the 69-year-old Gigante was convicted of violating the RICO statute and shipped off to spend the rest of his days in a maximum-security federal prison.

Things couldn't have been better for me at that time. I was living in Hilton Head, and I had started up a small contracting business just like I did in Florida. The difference this time was that I was doing a lot less of the grind work. I put together a nice little crew, and they did most of the work. This was my routine for the rest of 1997 and 1998: stay low-key, go to work, relax, enjoy life, and keep makin' money.

Looking Back, Moving Forward

P HILIP LEONETTI WAS NOW 46 YEARS OLD AND A DECADE REMOVED FROM HIS LIFE IN *LA COSA NOSTRA*.

But instead of looking forward, Leonetti found himself looking back.

In early 1999, I had heard from one of the agents that Lawrence was out of jail and that he was sick with cancer and that Saul Kane was in a prison hospital in Kentucky and he wasn't doing well. I knew the Blade had had a heart attack and died back in 1995 in a prison hospital in Missouri.

I started thinking a lot about the old days in Atlantic City, before my uncle was the boss, and all the fun I had had with guys like the Blade, Lawrence, and Saul Kane. And now these guys were dying. It made me sad. At this time, my mother was very sick and getting sicker with the lung cancer, and my grandmother wasn't doing great either. I knew it was only a matter of time with my mother. Little Philip, who was now 25 and had just graduated from graduate school, came to stay with us in Hilton Head. As my mother got sicker, we all spent that time being together as a family. It was me, my mother, my grandmother, Maria, and Little Philip. We had been through a lot together, but we toughed it out and we stuck together through thick and thin.

Philip's mother, Annunziata (Nancy) Scarfo Leonetti, would pass away on April 23, 1999, after courageously battling lung cancer. She was 68 years old.

I took it very hard, but we knew that it was coming. I had her body flown back to New Jersey and we buried her in the family plot, which was in Pleasantville, just outside of Atlantic City. We all flew back for the services and it was very low-key and quiet. Gary Langan came, and he and I caught up, but after we had the services, we all flew back to Hilton Head.

By the summer of 1999, what was left of the Philadelphia–Atlantic City mob was crumbling. Ralph Natale and Joey Merlino were jailed and facing racketeering charges, as were most of their top associates. And the worst news yet was that Natale, the reputed boss, was cooperating with the government.

According to the FBI, former Scarfo mob solider Joe Ligambi, recently released from prison following his acquittal in the Frankie Flowers retrial, would soon be named acting boss of the Philadelphia–Atlantic City mob.

Joe's a good guy and was one of the best bookmakers in the history of South Philadelphia. He knew every single college team and he knew all of the players; he was like an encyclopedia. I always got along with Joe and I liked him, so did my uncle. Joe and my uncle shared a cell together when we were all at Holmesburg.

As 1999 came to a close, Philip Leonetti was now setting his sights on looking ahead, instead of looking back.

The New Millennium

PHILIP LEONETTI SPENT THE NEXT SEVERAL YEARS LIVING ANONYMOUSLY AND WORKING IN HILTON HEAD.

My grandmother died in 2003, and I flew her back to New Jersey and buried her in the family plot with my mother and my grandfather. And again I saw Gary Langan. By this time, both Lawrence and Saul Kane had died in prison, and so did John Gotti. Joey Merlino had gotten 14 years in his racketeering case and now Nicky Jr. was back in jail doing a 33-month sentence on gambling and loan-sharking charges. I read in the news that Joe Ligambi was now officially the acting boss and my uncle was still in Atlanta with Vic Amuso trying to regain control of the mob and figuring out a way to kill me.

Once my grandmother died, I told Maria that I wanted to get out of Hilton Head, and she agreed, so we sold our place there and I sold my contracting business. I had actually grown tired of being on the East Coast and I was ready for a change of scenery. Little Philip was back in Arizona, so we headed west and spent the next few months relaxing and trying to figure out what we were going to do with the next chapter of our lives.

In early 2004, Philip Leonetti was 51 years old and living in a spacious condominium not too far from where Little Philip, now 30, was living in an area just outside of Scottsdale, Arizona.

Since the day I got out of jail in 1992, I was living primarily in South Florida or Hilton Head or traveling the East Coast on the boat. After a while I got antsy, and both Maria and I wanted to settle down somewhere and make a home where we could stay for the rest of our lives.

When we were in Arizona, Little Philip and I flew into Las Vegas a couple of times, and I really liked it because it reminded me of Atlantic City. I liked the action. On one of the trips, we stayed at the Bellagio, and right away, I fell in love with Vegas, but I knew we couldn't stay there.

Eventually, Maria and I headed a little further west and like we did on the boat back in 1995, we went up the coast looking for a nice quiet place to settle down.

By June 2005, Philip Leonetti and Maria were living comfortably on the West Coast, a short distance from the Pacific Ocean, in a beautiful, secluded home.

The first time we saw the place, I told Maria, "This is it, this is home," and she agreed. After all these years of moving around, we were finally able to settle down.

For the next four years, life for the Leonettis was peaceful and quiet and rather uneventful.

And then in the fall of 2009, the FBI called.

Again.

Que Sera, Sera

ALMOST 17 YEARS TO THE DAY THAT HE HAD BEEN RELEASED FROM PRISON, PHILIP LEONETTI RECEIVED A CALL FROM ONE OF HIS FORMER FBI HANDLERS, WHO WAS NOW RETIRED FROM THE BUREAU.

The phone rang, and he said, "Philip, I got a call from one of the agents in Philadelphia on the Organized Crime Task Force, and he has reason to believe that your identity and location have been compromised and that you and your family are in imminent danger."

I remember getting a pit in my stomach because he sounded concerned, and he wasn't an alarmist type of guy. I said, "Jesus Christ, where did this come from?" And he said, "We are still trying to piece it together and get confirmation. I am going to have the agent in Philadelphia call you and debrief you." And then we hung up.

Now I'm sitting there thinking to myself, "I've been out of jail for 17 years and out of La Cosa Nostra for 20 years and, all of the sudden, out of the blue, I get this call that me and my family are in danger?" It wasn't adding up to me.

Later that night, I got a call from the agent in Philadelphia and he was very firm with me on the phone. He said, "Philip, we have reason to believe that an attorney who has done work for several La Cosa Nostra members may know your name and current location, and if he does, you and your family are in danger and need to move." I said, "With all due respect, I'm going to need a little more information than that before I consider moving myself and my family. We are established out here; we have a great life." And the agent said, "That's all the information I have at this time," and I thanked him for the call.

Now my mind is racing with all of the what-if scenarios, because in all of the years that I had been away from La Cosa

Nostra, I had never gotten a call like this from the FBI. When I was in Atlantic City during the summer of 1996, I knew that I was putting myself in danger, but I had no choice. My grandmother was sick. But now 13 years later when I'm living 2,500 miles away and now I'm in danger? The whole thing had me confused.

Leonetti learned that the attorney the FBI believed may know his new name and location was a 35-year-old, well-respected, Atlantic City–based criminal defense attorney named James Leonard Jr.

The first person I called was another retired FBI agent who was now running a security consulting firm and working as a private investigator. He knew all of the players in Atlantic City and had already heard the news when I called him. He said to me, "Philip, I met this kid a couple of times and, from what I can tell, he's straight paper. I can't see him doing anything to cause you or your family any problems if this is true, which we still don't know for certain, one way or the other." I spoke to another agent, and he agreed.

But the agent in Philadelphia was telling me that this lawyer had talked several times on the phone with my uncle, and that when my cousin Nicky got out of jail in 2005, my uncle sent him to see the lawyer so that they could form a relationship. He also told me that the lawyer had worked with Joey Merlino and had gone to visit him several times in prison.

The story I had gotten was that a friend of Little Philip's knew a friend of a friend of the lawyer's and had told him that he knew where we were living and what our names were. The story was that the information was then passed on to the lawyer, and the theory was IF he knew my name and location, that he could have told my uncle, my cousin, Joey Merlino, or one of his other mob clients, and that we could all be in danger as a result.

This was a very serious concern for me if it were true. But nothing was concrete, nothing was solid regarding whether the lawyer actually knew my identity and where I was living—and if he did, whether he had told anyone about it.

As 2009 turned into 2010, Philip Leonetti was still in the dark about whether this threat was real or just perceived.

The agent that I was talking to was just doing his job and his job is to always err on the side of caution, to look out for us. So his philosophy was, "Why take a chance?" The problem was, we were well established where we were living. The last thing I wanted to do was pick up and move again, especially if we didn't have to.

So I decided that I was going to go back to Atlantic City and see the lawyer myself and find out what the real story was, to try and get a read on him before I made a decision about whether or not to move again. I told Maria what was going on and she was scared, but she agreed that we needed to know for sure one way or the other.

I decided not to tell anyone in the FBI that I was coming back to Atlantic City, because I wasn't sure how things were going to go and I knew how they would react.

In early February 2010, Philip Leonetti boarded a commercial flight and flew into Philadelphia with one thing on his mind: to find attorney James Leonard Jr. and get some answers.

I hadn't been in Philadelphia since I testified in Bobby Simone's trial in 1992. There was a lot of things that I missed about South Philadelphia, but I wasn't there to go sightseeing. I rented a car at the airport and drove over the Walt Whitman Bridge and got on the Atlantic City Expressway and headed straight to Atlantic City, which was an hour away from Philadelphia. After all of these years I was still banned from going into any of the Atlantic City casinos, so I checked into a non-casino hotel and got freshened up.

I had arranged for someone I know, who also knew the lawyer, to schedule a meeting for the two of them at a restaurant in Atlantic City called the Knife and Fork Inn. They were going to meet for drinks at 6:00 p.m., and my plan was to get to the Knife and Fork around 5:00, have some dinner upstairs, and have my friend call the lawyer and tell him that he was running late. Once I knew the lawyer was at the bar, I would come downstairs and talk to him. My friend called me at 6:00 on the dot and said, "He's there," and I paid for my dinner and walked downstairs to the bar, which was on the first floor.

I knew what the lawyer looked like and I spotted him at the far end of the bar with his back to Pacific Avenue, doing something on his phone, maybe texting or e-mailing. He was by himself. I got about 10 feet away when he looked up at me and immediately recognized me, and I could tell from the look on his face that he was startled. I put my hands up to indicate that I was approaching him in a nonthreatening manner and I said to him, "Relax, I just want to talk to you," and I sat down on the stool next to him, which was angled so we were basically looking at one another. I said, "You obviously know who I am; do you know why I am here?" And he said, "I'm guessin' it's not for the tuna tartare," which made me smile and broke the ice a little bit. I said to him, "I've heard a lot of things about you," and he replied, "I've heard a few things about you, too, but I don't believe everything I hear." And I said, "That's good. But what I'm hearing concerns not only me, but my family as well."

At this point, the bartender came over and I ordered myself a drink, and the lawyer said, "I'll have what he's having," and the bartender brought us each a glass of Cutty Sark and a glass of water. I reached into my wallet and took out money and put it on the bar, and when I did, I said, "I want to show you something," and I took out a picture and I handed it to him. As he was looking at it, I said, "Do you know who that is in the picture?" And he shook his head no, and I said, "James, that's my wife, my son, and my grandson," and this time he shook his head up and down, like he understood what I was saying. I said, "I was told by the FBI," and I pointed to the picture, "that they might have a problem and that's why I am here." He handed me the picture back and looked me in the eye and said, "I don't know what the FBI told you, but I will tell you this: I don't know and don't want to know what your name is or where you live— that's none of my business and none of my concern."

My whole life, whether it was in La Cosa Nostra, or when I was dealing with the government, or when I was in prison, or when I got out, one thing about me was I was always good at reading people right away. My uncle was always good at this, too. I had just met this kid and in less than five minutes I knew he was telling me the truth, he wasn't fuckin' around. He seemed exactly as the agent described him—straight paper—and while I startled him by suddenly appearing, he didn't seem scared or intimidated, which told me that he had nothing to hide and was telling the truth.

I finished my drink and I said to him, "James, it was a pleasure meeting you, maybe I'll see you around," and he said, "I sure hope not," and we both laughed. I shook his hand as I stood up to go. He said, "For a guy walking around with a $500,000 bounty on his head, you seem extremely relaxed," and I said, "Que sera, sera," and he look confused because he didn't know what it meant, and I said, "Look it up on your phone," and I walked away and that was it.

Que sera, sera means, "whatever will be, will be." It's an old song from an Alfred Hitchcock movie, which is basically how I see my life when I think back on everything. Both in the sense of resembling a Hitchcock movie and that line—"Que sera, sera, whatever will be, will be"—pretty much sums up my philosophy. If someone comes after me or wants to try and find me so they can kill me, there is nothing I can do about it except be ready and do whatever I need to do to make sure that doesn't happen and I get them first. So going to see this lawyer was both my wanting to assess and see if the threat truly existed, and if it did, to let him know: I can find you just as easy as you might be able to find me.

Now that I was satisfied that neither myself nor my family was in any imminent danger, I went back to the hotel in Atlantic City and checked out and decided to drive to Philadelphia and stay there because my flight back home was early the next morning. On the way back I stopped at the Saloon, which is a restaurant and bar in South Philadelphia, and I had a drink. I used to go there all the time with my uncle, or with Salvie, or with Chuckie when my uncle was in jail. I sat right at the bar, and no one recognized me. I ordered a Cutty and water and sat there and enjoyed a nice quiet drink all by myself.

I had just left Atlantic City, and here I was in South Philadelphia, but at this point in my life, I couldn't wait to get home. I checked into a hotel out by the airport and by 7:00 a.m. the next day I was in the air and headed west.

I landed a few hours later and I drove straight home. My black Lab, Bubba, was waiting at the door for me, and I told Maria about my meeting with the lawyer and that everything was fine, and I could tell that she was relieved, and so was I.

Life went back to normal, well, our normal. I was always careful with everything I did, even when I was with my uncle. I always *watched my mirrors and took different routes wherever I went—in case someone was following me, whether it was the law or someone else. I'd get to places early. I'd always have my antenna up and be ready at all times for whatever was out there. Nobody was ever going to get the jump on me.*

In March 2010, almost a month after his trip to Atlantic City and his impromptu sit-down with attorney James Leonard Jr., Philip Leonetti turned 57 years old.

Leonetti immediately settled back into what had become his daily routine.

Every morning, I am up at 5:00 a.m. and sit outside on our back patio, which has the most amazing view, and I watch the sun come up. It is so peaceful out there at that time of day. I drink a cup of coffee with Maria, and I go on my iPad and I read the morning news.

Around 6:30 a.m. or so, I head to the gym and I run five miles and do my workout, and then I sit in the sauna or the steam room for 15 or 20 minutes, just relaxing. I take a shower and then I head home around 8:00 or so, and on most days I'm at work by 9:00.

As I got older, I got away from the contracting business, and I got myself involved in a totally different field. I work outside, and my new career keeps me fit. I love what I'm doing. Physically I feel like I'm 35 years old. Maria and I have a nice group of friends, but nobody we know, know who we really are. They don't know us as Philip and Maria, and they have no idea where we come from.

This is my life now, and I've never been happier.

EPILOGUE

January 2012, Atlantic City, New Jersey

THE BEGINNING OF THE END TO PHILIP LEONETTI'S STORY TAKES PLACE PRECISELY WHERE IT ALL BEGAN—ON GEORGIA AVENUE IN ATLANTIC CITY.

On a cold, blustery day, we traveled with Philip back to the two buildings that encompass the former Scarfo compound at 26–28 North Georgia Avenue.

Joining us were a photographer, who memorialized the day with a series of photographs—one of which is included in this book—and an armed, off-duty Atlantic City police officer who was friendly with Leonetti.

This is it, this is where we lived.

Philip Leonetti was showing us the former Scarf, Inc. office that doubled as the mob's headquarters on the ground floor of 28 North Georgia Avenue. Taking us into the area that separates the two buildings, he pointed to a second-floor apartment in the building at 26 North Georgia Avenue.

That's where my uncle lived.

He pointed to a ground-floor apartment below his uncle's.

That's where my grandmother lived.

He showed us the apartment where his mother lived—directly behind the office at 28 North Georgia Avenue—and the third-floor apartment where Lawrence Merlino used to live.

That window right there that sticks out, that was Lawrence's dining room.

Philip gave us a walking tour of the back alleys that were used when he and his uncle had to sneak away from Georgia Avenue in the 1970s and '80s while they were on bail restrictions or to avoid the constant surveillance they were under, and he showed us how he used the same alleys to sneak back into the compound during the summer of 1996, when his grandmother was sick.

Being back here brings back a lot of memories, some good, but more bad than good.

Philip pointed to a small alley that headed west toward Arctic Avenue.

This is where my uncle wanted me to kill the Blade. The Blade lived right around the corner, not even a block from here.

Leonetti walked us up Georgia Avenue toward Arctic and into the dining room of Angeloni's, the neighborhood Italian restaurant where he and his uncle held court.

This was our table, right here. Me, my uncle, Chuckie, Lawrence, the Blade, Saul Kane, Salvie, Bobby Simone—this is where we always sat. We lived in this place. The whole mob would be in here. My God, it seems like a lifetime ago, and looking back, it was. I was just a kid when we got started, and I was only 34 when we went to jail. God willing, I'll be 59 next month.

Nicholas "Nick the Blade" Virgilio died at the age of 67 in March 1995 in the Federal Medical Center in Springfield, Missouri, which was a prison hospital, suffering a fatal heart attack almost eight years into his 40-year sentence.

New York mob boss John Gotti would die in the same facility of throat cancer in June 2002 at the age of 62, and his nemesis Vincent "The Chin" Gigante, the man Leonetti called "the last of the dons," died in the same hospital in 2005 at the age of 77 after suffering from chronic heart disease, the same illness that took the life of Leonetti's old pal Saul Kane, who died in 2000 at the age of 65 in a prison hospital outside of Lexington, Kentucky.

Saul Kane was one of the best guys I ever knew. He was my very dear friend, and he and I had a lot of fun together. Saul knew how to make me laugh, which, if you knew me in the '80s, wasn't an easy thing to do. One day when I was in FCI Phoenix, I got a letter from Saul who was in another prison doing his 95-year sentence. I have no idea how he found me or how he got me the letter, but that was Saul. I wrote him back and we exchanged a couple of letters back and forth. Even being locked up all those years and knowing he was never getting out, Saul still had his sense of humor. When he died he listed me as his nephew in his obituary and referred to me as Philip "Flip" Kane. In the letters he wrote me he also called me "Flip," which was a play on my first name and the fact that I went with the government and flipped. I miss Saul.

Some of the other guys I miss are guys like Vince Sausto, Spike, and Teddy Khoury, all of whom have since died. You couldn't find a more entertaining group then these guys. They weren't mob guys, but they were always around. I stayed close to both Vince and Teddy and was able to reconnect with both of them when I got out of jail and I spent time with them both. Vince had a house not too far from where I was living in Florida and that summer of 1996 when I was back in Atlantic City, I had quite a few dinners and a lot of laughs with Teddy. The last I heard of Spike was that he left Florida and moved to Las Vegas and wound up back in Florida and ended up dying down there.

The Blade always reminded me of Dr. Jekyll and Mr. Hyde. One second he was the nicest guy in the world, and the next second he'd be drunk and he would turn into a stone-cold, heartless killer. I always liked the Blade, and he was always good to me, even when he was drunk. When I think of the Blade, I think back to what he did when those guys were robbing Bidda-Beep at the card game, how he protected him from those guys—which is what this thing is supposed to be about: honor and respect—or how superstitious he was when we saw that black cat on the night Ange died and how happy he was after he killed Judge Helfant. He said to me, "Philip, this guy was a crook and I'm not a crook," and he mimicked Richard Nixon's voice. This was a few hours after he killed him. He thought it was funny, and so did I. But that was the Blade.

Lawrence died of cancer in 2001. He was 55. The last I heard he was living out west somewhere and he got sick, and then he died. He had only been out of prison for a couple of years before he got sick. He died of cancer. I always liked Lawrence. We were always very close. We would go out drinking together or go out to dinner. Lawrence loved to have a good time. When I think of Lawrence, I think of his eyebrow catching on fire when I shot Vince Falcone and of Lawrence tackling that kid in the dinosaur suit at Little Philip's 10th birthday party. I got a chance to talk to him one time on the telephone when I was in FCI Phoenix and he was in FCI Sandstone in Minnesota, and I knew that he was bitter with the way things turned out, with the way my uncle treated him and his brother towards the end, and I don't blame him. Chuckie and Lawrence were always loyal to my uncle, but the way my uncle was towards the end, loyalty meant absolutely nothing. Look at the thing with Salvie.

Salvie was one of the most loyal guys and one of the sharpest guys that my uncle had in our family. He and I were very close and very much alike—both being raised in La Cosa Nostra—*me with my uncle and him with his father. My best memories with Salvie were playing racquetball with him, or when he and his girlfriend took me and Maria out to a Broadway show when my uncle was in La Tuna. To this day, every time I go to see a show with Maria, I think of Salvie and I smile.*

When Phil Testa got killed, Salvie went out and avenged his father's death, like a man, killing Chickie Narducci and Rocco Marinucci to honor his father's memory. Salvie knew all the rules and all the moves and eventually my uncle became jealous of him, paranoid that one day he would turn on him, which would have never happened. Salvie looked at my uncle like he was his own father and Salvie was 100 percent loyal to my uncle and 100 percent committed to La Cosa Nostra. *He would have never gone against my uncle, not in a million years. Neither would Chuckie.*

Chuckie's been in jail since 1986. He was 46 years old when he got locked up and today he is almost 73. If he lives long enough, he is supposed to get out in 2016 when he is 77 years old. He's rotting in a federal prison down in Texas. Chuckie was always a great guy and a lot of fun to be around. Other than me, there was no one who knew my uncle as well as Chuckie did. Chuckie could read my uncle like a book. I know that he was very disappointed when Lawrence went bad, but, in a way, I think he always knew that Lawrence wasn't as committed to La Cosa Nostra as he was. When I think of Chuckie, I think back to all of the fun we had when I would go see him in Philadelphia when my uncle was in Yardville. He and I would go to the Saloon. When I went in there for a drink after I saw the attorney James Leonard in Atlantic City in 2010, I had a drink for Chuckie. I hope when he gets out of jail, he has his health and enjoys his grandchildren.

Bobby Simone died in 2007; he was 73 years old. Bobby lived hard, played hard, and worked hard. He was the best attorney I ever saw, and I saw them all. Testifying against him in 1992 was the hardest thing I've ever done in my life. Me and my uncle loved Bobby and I know he felt the same way about us. I know Bobby wrote a book towards the end of his life and—from what I can tell in reading those letters my uncle wrote to my grandmother—I know my uncle wasn't happy that he wrote the book. But you know what, my uncle wasn't happy about anything. Bobby should be remembered as the best criminal defense attorney to ever step foot inside a Philadelphia courtroom.

Faffy's still in jail and so is Ciancaglini. Faffy's 64 years old and will be 68 when he gets out, and Chickie is 77 and will be 80 when he gets out. Faffy was a good guy, a good solider. Towards the end, Faffy was the street boss in South Philadelphia. My uncle always liked him and so did I. He and I were cellmates together for a little while in Holmesburg, and he used to tell me stories about when he was in Vietnam. Faffy had a lot of balls.

Ciancaglini was a gentleman, but also a real gangster. I remember after Tommy Del flipped, Ciancaglini told me and my uncle in jail that he felt responsible for bringing him around because Tommy was part of Ciancaglini's crew. My uncle said, "Chick, it's not your fault," and Ciancaglini said, "Nick, I could go to the government and tell them I want to cooperate, but that I want to see Tommy first, and when they bring him in I will give him a hug and hold him tight, and then I will jump out the window with him and he'll be dead." My uncle looked at him and said, "But you'd die, too," and Ciancaglini said, "Nick, after what this guy did to us, so be it." I know that Chickie had to be devastated after what happened with his sons in the early '90s—them on opposite sides trying to kill each other when Stanfa was the boss, with one of them dying and the other one becoming disabled.

All the other guys we went to jail with are out. Joe Punge is living down in South Florida, and so is Tory Scafidi.

I know that the Pungitores are doing well and that their father, the Blonde Babe, set them up in businesses and in real estate. The Babe was always a moneymaker, and all three of his sons were gentlemen, just like he was. I read in one of the Philly papers that the Babe just died. Joe Punge and I were close because we both had a strong relationship with Salvie, and I know that after Salvie died, Joe Punge seemed less interested in La Cosa Nostra. I mean, Christ, I was 31 when Salvie got killed and him and Salvie were both 27 and 28. We were all just kids. I think Joe Punge will be successful in whatever he does, and it won't have anything to do with the mob.

Tory Scafidi was always a good kid and he was with me when I got arrested in April of '87 outside Rittenhouse Square, and he had my back in Holmesburg when I got into that fight with the drug kingpin. Tory was a tough kid. I hope he stays down in Florida and leaves Philadelphia and La Cosa Nostra behind. He's gotta be 51 or 52 years old by now and he got locked up when he was 26. His younger brother, Tommy Horsehead, ended up cooperating with the government in the '90s and testified against Joey Merlino.

Everybody else is out and back in South Philadelphia. Junior Staino is 80, and Charlie White is 77. Junior is a character, always breaking balls and starting some kind of trouble. I remember at least two fights he started in jail, one with Wayne Grande and another with Joe Punge, and he had almost 30 years on each one of those guys, but Junior always had something fresh to say. Charlie White and I were cellmates for a while in Otisville, and Charlie was always a good guy and I liked him. I remember one time he was telling me that his family was having money problems and I had Nicky Jr. give his son $10,000. My uncle went nuts when he found I had told Nicky to give him the money; he said, "What's the matter with you, are you nuts giving this guy $10,000?" and I said, "The guy just stood up for our family and got 40 years," and my uncle said, "I don't give a fuck what he did." That's an example of how loyal my uncle was to the guys in our family. He didn't give a fuck about nobody but himself.

Frankie Narducci is only a couple of months younger than me, so he is 59 and his brother Philip is 50. I think Frankie Narducci was pretty much along for the ride, but his brother Philip was a gangster, and just as shrewd as his father was.

One time after my uncle become the boss, the Chin sent word through Bobby Manna that he wanted my uncle to send two shooters to New York to whack some guy out. My uncle said to me, "I want you to be one of them," and he asked me who I wanted to use as the second shooter, and I told him, "Philip Narducci." This was after Salvie had died, and both me and my uncle thought Philip Narducci was very capable. The hit got called off. My advice to whoever is running what's left of that organization in Philadelphia is to stay out of Philip's way.

Joey Grande is 52 now. His father was a made guy under Ange and, like the Narduccis, he knows the rules of La Cosa Nostra and all of the moves, but he's a troublemaker. I remember him coming to me one time and whispering stuff to me in front of Joe Punge, to make it look like we were talking about him, which we weren't. Joe Punge picked right up on it and said to me afterwards, "I got a hard-on for this kid. You have no idea all the bullshit him and his brother are doing." I heard that his brother Wayne went bad in the '90s and ended up getting involved in a drug deal while he was in prison, and then cooperated against one of my cousins. Wayne was married to my cousin Rita.

After we beat the Salvie Testa murder and it looked like we were going to make bail, my uncle told me that if I got out, he wanted me to kill three people: his wife Mimi, and then the two Grande brothers, Joey and Wayne. We never made bail, but even if we did I wasn't going to kill any of them. First of all, as much as I couldn't stand my uncle's wife, there was no fuckin' chance I would ever kill a woman ever, and I wasn't going to kill the Grandes because, by this point, I was done taking orders from my uncle. I know from reading those letters he was sending to my grandmother that him and Joey Grande stayed in touch during the '90s, and my grandmother used to tell me that Joey Grande would call her and write her letters from time to time.

I recently read in one of the papers that Gino Milano is going to be a witness in an upcoming mob trial in Philadelphia. Gino is now

53 and, the last I heard, he was living somewhere in the Midwest and working as a car salesman and was living in the Witness Protection Program. His brother Nicky Whip is 51 and may be living at the Jersey Shore. From what I heard, he has nothing to do with La Cosa Nostra and may be working in construction.

My old friend Sammy the Bull is back in jail, rotting away in the same Florence ADX that my uncle once called "a dog kennel" in those letters to my grandmother. Sammy got involved in drugs when he got of jail and got locked up out in Arizona back in 2000. He eventually got sentenced to 19 years and could be out a few years from now when he is in his early 70s, if he stays healthy. I recently read that he is sick and I wish nothing but the best for him with his health, but I am disappointed to hear that Sammy got involved with drugs and wound up back in jail. Sammy was very loyal to La Cosa Nostra, like I was, but just like me, he lost faith in his boss. He told me that one of his biggest regrets was not killing John Gotti so that Frankie DeCicco could be the boss instead. "We fucked up on that one, Bo," is what he would say. Sammy used to call everyone "Bo." I get a kick out of seeing his daughter Karen on the TV show Mob Wives.

My father died in 1983, and my mother and my grandmother are both dead and they are buried in the family plot with my grandfather at a cemetery just outside of Atlantic City. Ironically, two plots down stands the mausoleum of Felix "Skinny Razor" DiTullio, my uncle's first mob mentor. I don't know if he and my uncle bought the plots together when Skinny Razor was alive, so they could be buried next to one another, but it wouldn't surprise me. Those two were very close.

My cousin Chris is still in Atlantic City, running a successful business and doing well for himself, having the smarts to change his last name and distance himself from his father.

Tommy Del and Nicky Crow are out there somewhere, most likely in the Witness Protection Program. I never liked either one of them and one of my uncle's biggest mistakes was making those guys and keeping them around. Tommy Del wasn't even 100-percent Italian, for Christ's sake. He and the Crow were always no good.

I stay in touch with the FBI agents who helped me and became my friends, guys like Gary Langan, Jim Maher, Jim Darcy, and Klaus Rohr. These guys are the real men of honor.

And how about all the guys that got whacked? And for what? Ange, Johnny Keys, Phil Testa, Sindone, Frank Monte—those types of individuals aren't around anymore. They are like dinosaurs; they don't exist. The Chickie Narduccis, the Caponigros. Nowadays, you got a bunch of kids who grew up on the street corner watching guys like Chuckie making moves, guys like Salvie, guys like Ciancaglini, but they didn't grow up in this thing, *they don't know* La Cosa Nostra. *To them those words don't mean nothing. They didn't grow up like I grew up, or how Joe Punge grew up, or how Salvie grew up, or how the Narducci brothers grew up. To them* this life *is like the characters they see in* Goodfellas *or* The Sopranos. *But it's not.*

THE LAST WORD

June 2012, Somewhere Near Las Vegas

A S THE HOT SUN SCORCHES THE NEVADA DESERT, 59-YEAR-OLD PHILIP "CRAZY PHIL" LEONETTI IS SIPPING A HALF-ICED TEA, HALF-LEMONADE CONCOCTION KNOWN AS AN ARNOLD PALMER, OR AN ARNIE, AS LEONETTI CALLS IT. WE ARE SEATED WITH LEONETTI AT A CAFÉ 30 MINUTES AWAY FROM THE LAS VEGAS STRIP WHERE THE FORMER MOB UNDERBOSS AND ONETIME MAFIA PRINCE APPEARS TOTALLY AT EASE WEARING A BLACK BASEBALL HAT AND A FORM-FITTING BLACK DRESS SHIRT.

While Leonetti decided that living in Vegas wasn't necessarily a good idea, it doesn't stop him from frequenting Sin City whenever he gets the chance.

I love it here. I come for a couple of days here and there, maybe six different times a year. It's very easy to blend in out here.

Making sure no one is listening, Leonetti leans in to discuss new developments in the Philadelphia–Atlantic City *La Cosa Nostra* that have recently made the papers.

I hate to say it, because I happen to like the guy, but I think Joe Ligambi is gonna get convicted. How the fuck is he gonna beat those tapes, the ones the guy made who killed himself? But if anybody can do something with those tapes, it's Joe's lawyer Ed Jacobs. He took over where Bobby Simone left off.

Leonetti is making reference to the secretly recorded tapes that a wire-wearing North Jersey mob informant named Nicholas "Nicky Skins" Stefanelli made following a 2010 drug arrest that also reportedly ensnared his son. Stefanelli, a made member of the Gambino crime family, agreed to wear a wire and record conversations with other *mafiosi,* so that his son could avoid being charged in the drug case.

Stefanelli was one of the Gambino family's top operatives in North Jersey, and, as such, had a strong relationship with Joseph "Scoops" Licata, the *caporegime* in charge of the Bruno–Scarfo crime family's North Jersey operation. This relationship allowed Stefanelli to move freely in the Philadelphia–Atlantic City underworld and get close to reputed acting mob boss Joe Ligambi—close enough that Stefanelli would record both Ligambi and Licata talking about mob initiation ceremonies, mob history, current mob feuds, and at least one unsolved mob murder.

Ligambi and Licata are now in the Philadelphia Federal Detention Center together, awaiting trial on racketeering charges based, in part, on the tapes that Stefanelli made. Both men, now in their 70s, were initiated into *La Cosa Nostra* by then-boss Nicodemo "Little Nicky" Scarfo during the Philly mob's heyday in the mid-1980s and are considered old school by the younger mobsters in the family.

Joe Ligambi got out of jail after my uncle and the rest of those guys won the Frankie Flowers retrial in 1997, and the word on the street was that he became the acting boss after Joey Merlino went to jail in 1999. Joe is 72 years old and is now back in jail facing a new RICO indictment. Joe was always a gentleman. He was part of Chuckie's crew, and both me and my uncle liked him. Joe and my uncle were cellmates for a while when we were in Holmesburg. I hope Joe does okay with his trial, because I'd hate to see him spend the rest of his life in jail.

Unfortunately, neither Ligambi nor Licata will have the opportunity to confront their betrayer, Nicholas "Nicky Skins" Stefanelli, at trial, as the 69-year-old, hapless mob rat killed himself in a North Jersey hotel room in February 2012, two days after he killed the man he blamed for his 2010 drug arrest.

I believe Joey Merlino is gonna get pinched. A lot of people have a hard-on for this kid, including the FBI, the US attorneys office, and my uncle. Chuckie's son is now living in South Florida after getting out of jail in 2011. He did 12 years on a racketeering case.

I never liked this kid. If Chuckie wasn't his father's son he woulda been dead 25 years ago. I would have killed him myself, but my uncle wouldn't allow it because of Chuckie. That summer of 1996, when I went back to Atlantic City to see my grandmother, there was a hairdresser who was friendly with Joey Merlino and he sent her to Georgia Avenue to see my grandmother. The woman was friendly with my grandmother as well. She told my mother and my grandmother that Joey sent her over there to find out if I was there. When I found out about it, I told the woman, "Tell him I'm here and that I'd love to see him; tell him to stop by and say hello anytime he wants." She told me later that when she delivered the message to him, he laughed and called me a "rat motherfucker." But guess what—he knew I was there and he didn't come.

My cousin Nicky Jr. is also back in jail again, in the same jail as Joe Ligambi, awaiting trial in two separate racketeering cases, one involving the Lucchese crime family in North Jersey, and the other involving a white-collar fraud case out of Camden. If he is convicted in either trial, he is likely going to spend the rest of his life behind bars. Nicky's got a young wife, two young children, and both his mother and his brother Mark, who is still in a coma after almost 24 years, living in his house. From what I have been told, a group of nurses come by the house and help my uncle's wife take care of Mark. I don't know how that family will survive if Nicky gets convicted. They are barely surviving now.

My cousin's not a gangster and he never was. The only thing he is guilty of being is a loyal son to my uncle. My uncle got him involved with trying to keep control of La Cosa Nostra after we went to jail and almost got Nicky killed. After that, my uncle got him involved with some half-ass wise guys in North Jersey who turned out to be rats, and he got Nicky sent to prison. Then my uncle got Nicky involved with Vic Amuso and the Luccheses and got him sent to jail again, and now he's got not one, but two indictments. My uncle was even an unindicted coconspirator in the fraud case. That's the kind of father my uncle is. My cousin owes my uncle absolutely nothing. I would love to see him cooperate with the government and make a life for himself, not for his father, but for himself and his family, his wife and kids.

That sums up virtually what everyone I know or have known that is relevant to my story or to the Philadelphia–Atlantic City La Cosa Nostra, *with the exception of one person.*

That person is my uncle, Nick Scarfo.

Several times during the mid-'80s, I came very close to actually killing my uncle. I had planned on doing it a couple of times on the way back from Philadelphia, when we would stop and get off of the Atlantic City Expressway out near Hammonton, so we could get out of the car and talk about a sensitive subject to avoid what my uncle thought were the bugs or listening devices that the law had planted in his car. He would motion for me to get off of an exit ramp and I would drive and find a dark stretch of road, usually in a wooded area or out near a farm, and we would get out of the car and walk maybe 100 feet, or so, and have whatever conversation he wanted to have. So many times we would be standing there and I'd be listening to him talk and I would start thinking about just blasting him right there and shutting him up once and for all. Just emptying the gun into him and leaving him there in the woods for some farmer or some hunter to find.

It started after he had killed Salvie, and after he told me that he wanted me to kill the Blade, Chuckie, and Lawrence. At this point, there was no more honor, no more respect, and no more loyalty. La Cosa Nostra, this thing of ours, *became* this thing of his, *and it was all about his unquenchable thirst for power, for greed, for vengeance, and for ego. I no longer swore my allegiance to my uncle, a man who I gave the first 35 years of my life to.*

I thought about sneaking into his apartment and shooting him while he slept, using a pillow to muffle the sound so that I wouldn't wake up my grandmother in the apartment downstairs.

Many times when he and I would be on our boat, The Usual Suspects, *down in Florida, I would catch myself daydreaming about throwing him overboard and leaving him in the middle of the ocean to drown.*

This is how much I grew to hate this man.

When we went to jail in 1987, I knew that it was over between me and him, no matter what happened. If somehow I was acquitted, I was planning on taking Maria, my mother, and Little Philip, and leaving Atlantic City, my uncle, and La Cosa Nostra. *If I lost* the trial and I got sentenced to spend the rest of my life in prison, I knew that I would be away from my uncle in jail.

So either way you look at it, it was over.

If we hadn't gotten locked up when we did, I would have eventually killed him, and I promise you there wouldn't have been too many people sad to see him go.

My decision to cooperate with the government wasn't like Nicky Crow's or Tommy Del's, or even Sammy the Bull's. I wasn't out to save myself. I had already gotten 45 years. It was over for me. My decision to cooperate was to send a message to one person, my uncle, that I was absolutely disgusted by him and that I was no longer going to live my life for him and that I wanted absolutely nothing to do with him for the rest of my days on this earth, wherever they were spent. This decision was made by me in that holding cell on November 1, 1988, the day my cousin Mark tried to kill himself and his evil, no-good father didn't shed a single tear for him. That was it for me; that was my breaking point.

So am I a rat? Let me ask you this: if you're a kid and you find out there's no Santa Claus when you are nine years old, are you going to still believe in Santa Claus when you're 10, 11, or 12? Of course not. You'd stop believing and that would be the end of it.

I believed in La Cosa Nostra, this thing of ours. It was something I was taught from the time I was a little boy. It's how I was raised. Honor, respect, loyalty—these were the values instilled in me by my uncle from the time I was eight years old and I drove in that pickup truck with him—as his decoy after he killed Reds Caruso—and listened to him tell me how he killed the guy, how he stabbed him with the ice pick, and what the guy's final words were. I was eight years old and this was my life. I was 23 when I killed Louie DeMarco, and 26 when I killed Vincent Falcone. I got made when I was 27, and I became a caporegime at 28. I did it all for my uncle and La Cosa Nostra, this thing of ours. I was what you would call a true believer up until I was 33 years old and I became the underboss in 1986, and I stopped believing because the principles I had believed in—the honor, respect, and loyalty—were gone, if they ever truly existed.

We killed Salvie, our most loyal captain. How's that for loyalty? We shot Joe Salerno's father and killed two guys in front of

their mothers, and my uncle wanted me to slit his wife's throat.
Where's the honor in that?

Other than that, what is his legacy? His oldest son disowned
him and changed his name. His middle son almost got killed and is
now in jail because he listens to his father and his father has never
given him good advice. And his youngest son tried to kill himself
and is still in a coma 24 years later. He even wanted his own wife
dead. New York took him down as boss and, in the end, his sister
and even his own mother abandoned him, choosing to leave Atlan-
tic City and coming to live with me, the person he hates more than
anyone on the planet.

When I think of my uncle now, I no longer have a desire to see
him dead. It's not because I found God or anything like that, it's just
that I have a different perspective now. I actually hope he lives to be
120 years old and finds his way into the Guinness Book of World
Records, *rotting in that cage he calls his home, knowing every day*
what an absolute failure of a human being he was—as a father, as
a husband, as a son, as a brother, as an uncle, as a friend, as a mob
boss, and most importantly, as a man.

Fuck my uncle.

Nicodemo "Little Nicky" Scarfo is now 83 years old and remains imprisoned at the United States Penitentiary in Atlanta, with a projected release date of January 4, 2033, when he will be several months shy of his 104th birthday.

In a letter dated October 7, 1995, Scarfo wrote to his mother, Catherine, about rumors that his nephew Philip Leonetti was going to write a book:

"It's depressing to me to hear that the witch's crazy son is writing a book
and is going to add more embarrassment to this family, like he hasn't done
enough to disgrace himself already. It will be another book that will be a flop,
like the rest of them lying, stupid books. Who the hell even buys books like
that? . . . His day will come. . . . I have to live with these thoughts day in and
day out, night in and night out, added to my sorrow and it's not easy. But I'm
the kind of man that can accept anything I have to in this life, no matter how
bad it is or how bad it hurts."

At the time of publication of this book, Philip Leonetti is several months shy of his 60th birthday and spends his days enjoying the sunshine in the West Coast seaside community he now calls home.

My days end almost the same way they begin: out on my patio. I have a Cutty and water, or a nice glass of bourbon, and I light a fire and I sit there under a blanket with Maria by my side and Bubba at my feet, just taking it all in. The way the lights in the distance illuminate the skyline is breathtaking.

It reminds me that the action is always close by, but I am content living in the shadows, watching things from afar.

DEDICATIONS / ACKNOWLEDGMENTS

PHILIP LEONETTI: *This book is dedicated to my Uncle Nick. From the time I was 8 years old, you taught me how to identify the people in our life that had no honor and how to deal with them. As I grew older, I realized that everything I had learned, applied to you. You were an excellent teacher. Only in our case the student proved to be much smarter.*

Cent'anni.

This book is also dedicated to the memories of my mother Nancy Leonetti and my grandmother Catherine Scarfo.

SCOTT BURNSTEIN: *This has been my dream project since I became an author and I want to thank first and foremost, Philip, for allowing me the honor of working with him, my co-author Chris for all of his hard work, my agent Frank Weimann for always having faith in my talent and my mentor George Anastasia, for being such a great teacher.*

This book is dedicated to my grandfather, Donnie B, a true goodfella in every way possible!

CHRISTOPHER GRAZIANO: *I want to thank my entire family and all of my friends and colleagues for all of their love, support and guidance.*

To Scott Burnstein, Frank Weimann, Greg Jones, Julie Ford, Chris Navratil, Jennifer Kasius, Frances Soo Ping Chow, Seta Zink, Craig Herman and everyone at Running Press for making this happen.

To Ann, you would have enjoyed this.

And finally to Philip and the entire Leonetti family, thank you for your trust and your everlasting friendship.

INDEX